The Woman Shall Conquer

To the Immaculate Heart of Mary in thanksgiving

The Woman Shall Conquer

by
Don Sharkey

Prow Books / Franciscan Marytown Press
1600 W. Park Avenue
Libertyville, IL 60048

"I will put enmities between thee and the woman, and thy seed and her seed: she shall crush thy head, and thou shalt lie in wait for her heel."
—Genesis 3:15

Imprimatur:
Rev. Msgr. John R. Torney
Administrator's Delegate
Diocese of Metuchen
November 5, 1986

ISBN 0-911988-71-8

Copyright © 1954, 1973, and 1976 by Donald Sharkey

This fourth printing by AMI Press, Box 976, Washington, NJ 07882 through special arrangement with Prow Books, Libertyville, Ill.

Printed in the United States of America

Contents

Bringing the Story Up to Date............... ix

BACKGROUND

1. Mary Needs Our Help...................... 3
2. When the World Turned Against Its Mother *(1513-1830)*................................ 6

MARY'S MESSAGE TO US

3. Our Lady's First Message to the Modern World *Paris, 1830)*............................. 15
4. Our Lady of Victories *(Paris, 1836)*.......... 22
5. The Badge of the Immaculate Heart *(Blangy, 1840)* 24
6. The Manuscript Found in a Chest *(True Devotion, 1842)*........................... 29
7. The Madonna in Tears *(La Salette, 1846)*..... 34
8. The Immaculate Conception *(Rome, 1854)*.... 41
9. The Lady of the Grotto *(Lourdes, 1858)*...... 45
10. Our Lady Hears Her Children *(Pontmain, 1871)* 57
11. "I Choose the Little Ones and the Weak" *(Pellevoisin, 1876)*........................ 64
12. The Picture from the Secondhand Store *(Pompeii, 1875-1876)*..................... 72
13. Our Lady in Ireland *(Knock, 1879)*.......... 77
14. Other Manifestations of Our Lady *(1841-1906)*. 85
15. "France Will Suffer" *(World War I, 1914-1918)* 94
16. "Men Must Offend Our Lord No More" (Fatima, 1917)........................... 99

vii

17. "The Little Saint" *(Jacinta Marto, 1908-1920)* ... 113
18. The Heart Encircled with Thorns *(Revelations to Lucia, 1925-1929)* ... 119
19. "I Will Convert Sinners" *(Beauraing, 1932-1933)* ... 122
20. Virgin of the Poor *(Banneux, 1933)* ... 131
21. The Unknown Light *(World War II, 1939-1945)* ... 137
22. The Light of the Atom *(Hiroshima, 1945)* ... 148
23. The Doves of Peace *(Portugal, 1946)* ... 154
24. Our Lady Returns to England *(Walsingham, 1945; Stockport, 1947; Aylesford, 1951)* ... 165
25. The Assumption *(Rome, 1950)* ... 174
26. The Pope of Our Lady *(Rome, 1954)* ... 179

MARY'S ROLE IN OUR WORLD

27. God's Mother Is Our Mother ... 187
28. All Graces Come through Mary ... 191
29. Mary Is Our Queen ... 193

HOW WE CAN HASTEN MARY'S COMING VICTORY

30. Total Consecration to Mary ... 199
31. "Say the Rosary Every Day" ... 205
32. "Sacrifice Yourself for Sinners" ... 208
33. Mary's Immaculate Heart ... 213
34. Mary Wants Us as Her Apostles ... 216
Appendix: Land of Our Lady ... 224
Postscript: Excerpt from *Dear Bishop!* ... 240
Author's Sources ... 250
Index ... 258

Bringing the Story Up to Date

The publisher has graciously invited me to write an introduction for this new printing of *The Woman Shall Conquer*. I am happy to have an opportunity to re-assess the book and to note some important developments that have taken place since the last printing.

"This book," I said in my original introduction, "is an attempt to tell the story of the Blessed Virgin in the modern world." I added that I was not a theologian and was writing as a reporter. That applies to this introduction as well as to the book itself.

Much of the emphasis in the book is on apparitions and other manifestations of Mary that have taken place since 1830. As I go over the book today, I am satisfied that the facts about these apparitions and manifestations are up-to-date and as complete as the limited space permits. The Weeping Madonna of Sicily, 1953, is included, and as far as I have been able to ascertain no "manifestation" since then has received ecclesiastical approbation.

Although there is little I would change today in the presentation of facts, there are some personal interpretations I would change. An example is my treatment of the "Protestant Revolt" in Chapter II. I would be less harsh with the leaders of the Reformation. In these post-Vatican II days, we recognize that Catholics have not always been correct in their attitudes and behavior and that Protestants have certainly not always been wrong. And we should credit everyone with good intentions. We should also note

ix

that by no means all of the Reformation leaders opposed devotion to Mary. It was mostly the "second generation" of Protestant leaders who turned against Marian devotion.

A number of Protestants today think that Protestants should take a greater interest in Mary because she is the Mother of Jesus. It is one of the strange developments of these strange times that while many Catholics seem to be taking less interest in Mary, at least some Protestants are taking a greater interest in her.

The Woman Shall Conquer was written at a time when interest in Mary among Catholics was great. Books about Mary poured from the presses. Many magazines were devoted entirely to Mary. Several libraries contained nothing but material about Mary. Crowds flocked to novenas in honor of Mary under her various titles. Clubs, societies, and legions dedicated themselves to Mary.

I was convinced that this trend would not only continue but would increase in momentum. I was convinced that we were on the verge of a great "Age of Mary." This conviction is shown in the book.

Events have not worked out as I had anticipated. Almost overnight, it seemed, the great interest in Mary stopped. People stopped buying books about Mary, stopped buying rosaries, stopped going to novenas. One Marian magazine after another ceased publication. Today, few people visit Marian libraries. There seems to have been a complete about-face.

Explanations for this vary, and no explanation seems entirely satisfactory. Perhaps it is part of a Divine plan. Perhaps there was too much emphasis on Mary's powers, privileges, and titles—and not enough on her humility, faith, and perfect submission to the will of God, virtues which we should contemplate and imitate.

There may also have been a danger that devotion to Mary was developing into a separate entity—something apart from the rest of the Church. If so, two actions of Vatican II helped offset this trend. On October 29, 1963, by the close vote of 1,114 to 1,074 the Council decided that the schema on Mary should be included in the schema on the Church instead of being a separate document. Then, later, the Council declared that greater emphasis should be put on Mary's place in the liturgy of the Church. Thus, Marian devotion was tied directly to the Church, and was not a thing apart.

Perhaps devotion to Mary has not really decreased but has taken different, better, and less obvious forms. Perhaps we are still on the verge of the Age of Mary that was foreseen by saints and mystics of the past. But it will be different from the one many of us had anticipated. We may be sure that Our Lord will not permit his Mother to be neglected.

Chapter XXXI of this book is about the Rosary, and Our Lady of Fatima is quoted as saying, "Say the Rosary every day." But the Rosary has fallen into disfavor with many Catholics.

Does the Council's emphasis on Mary in the liturgy mean that we should not say the Rosary? No. The Council also said of itself: "It charges that practices and exercises of devotion toward her be treasured as recommended by the teaching authority of the Church in the course of centuries...." This would most certainly include the Rosary.

Pope John XXIII, who called the Council, said the entire 15 decades of the Rosary every day for the last several years of his life. In the *Journal of a Soul* he said: "It has come to be an exercise of continuous meditation and of tranquil daily contemplation which keeps my spirit open to the vast fields of magistry and my ministry as chief pastor of the Church and universal Father of Souls."

Pope Paul VI sent a message and a blessing to the million people attending Father Patrick Peyton's Family Rosary Crusade in Barcelona, Spain. His nuncio, Archbishop Roberi, told the throng that the Rosary "is like a summary of the Gospel, a breviary thereof, available to everyone, an intuitive teaching that goes to the depth of the soul." In his peace encyclical of September 15, 1966, Pope Paul devoted nearly half the text to urging the faithful to recite the Rosary during October to Our Lady, Queen of Peace.

As I have noted, the principal emphasis in this book is on apparitions and other manifestations of Mary. Most major Marian shrines are based on such manifestations. What about shrines then? They are in disfavor with some people who consider pilgrimages outmoded. It is interesting to note, however that more pilgrims than ever before are visiting the shrines of Fatima and Lourdes. This is no doubt true of other shrines also. The two recent Popes have also shown great interest in shrines. After he became Pope, one of the first actions of John XXIII was to visit four famous shrines of Mary in Italy.

On November 21, 1964, Pope Paul VI recalled to the Fathers of Vatican II that Pius XII had consecrated the world to the Immaculate Heart of Mary. He then said he planned to send a mission to Fatima with a Golden Rose. He thus revived a papal custom of long ago. The rose was presented on May 13, 1965. In the accompanying message Pope Paul said, "In this manner we intend to entrust to the care of the Heavenly Mother the entire human family with its problems and worries, with its lawful aspirations and ardent hopes."

Two years later—on Saturday May 13, 1967 Pope Paul himself visited Fatima. This was the 50th anniversary of the first Fatima apparition and the 25th anniversary of the consecration of the world to the Immaculate Heart. At a time when interest in Mary seemed to be declining, this visit put Fatima on the first page of almost every newspaper in the free world. The principal purpose of the visit, the Holy Father said, was to pray for peace, both in the Church and in the world.

On the last day of the third session of Vatican II, a Mass in St. Peter's was concelebrated by Pope Paul and the twenty-four Council Fathers whose dioceses contain the principal shrines of Mary. It is plain that Mary's shrines are important to the Popes and to millions of pilgrims. Mary is venerated at these shrines not only by Catholics but also by Protestants, and even by Jews and Moslems.

There was a widespread impression that the Second Vatican Council had voted to "downgrade" Mary. This was due to the decision, already noted, that the schema on Mary should not be a separate document but should be included in the schema on the Church. However, the Fathers who were on the majority side in the vote had no intention of downgrading Mary.

The treatment on Mary is Chapter 8 of the *Constitution on the Church*, the key document of the Council. The full title of the chapter is, "The Blessed Virgin, Mother of God, in the Mystery of Christ and the Church." The chapter contains about 3,500 words. It is the longest statement on Mary ever issued by a general council. In addition to this entire chapter, Mary is mentioned in 11 of the Council's 16 documents. This is not "downgrading."

When Pope John XXIII announced that he was going to call the Council he said that we must above all "trust in the intercession of the Immaculate Mother of Jesus and our Mother" for its success. He set the opening date as October 11, 1962, and he selected this date because it was the feast of the Divine Maternity of Mary. On the opening day, Pope John reminded the Fathers that the Council was being opened under the auspices of the Virgin Mother of God. In their first message to the world the Council Fathers declared themselves "united in prayer with Mary Mother of Jesus." Pope John noted with satisfaction that the first session ended on December 8, the Feast of the Immaculate Conception.

Pope John XXIII died on June 3, 1963. Pope Paul VI said the Council would be continued. On September 29 the second session opened. In his opening address Pope Paul said, "Here certainly the Virgin Mother of Christ is helping us from Heaven." He concluded his address by begging her to assist the Council with her "powerful motherly aid." Later, he commemorated the first anniversary of the opening of the Council with a Mass in the Basilica of St. Mary Major. In the homily the Pope prayed to Mary to inspire and guide the Council Fathers, all Christians separated from Rome, and all mankind.

During the second session the Council Fathers voted that greater emphasis should be put on the role of the

Blessed Virgin in the Church's liturgical cycle. (See Chapter V, *Constitution on the Sacred Liturgy*.)

The chapter on Mary was not completed at the end of the second session, and Pope Paul mentioned it in his closing address. He hoped the chapter would contain an "unanimous and loving acknowledgement of the place, privileged above all others, which the Mother of God occupies in the Holy Church—in the Church which is the principal subject matter of the present council. After Christ her place in the Church is the most exalted, and also the one closest to us."

The third session was opened on September 14, 1964. Pope Paul VI asked the Fathers to have trust in the help of Mary Most Holy.

The debate on the chapter about Mary lasted two days in the third session. The document says of itself that "It does not intend to give a complete doctrine on Mary, nor does it wish to decide those questions which the work of theologians has not yet fully clarified."

In this book I devoted one chapter to Mary as Mediatrix of All Graces, noting that this was not yet an article of Faith. The Council's Chapter 8 mentions the title "Mediatrix" and carefully adds that the title "neither takes away anything from nor adds anything to the dignity and efficacy of Christ the one mediator."

November 21, 1964, the feast of the Presentation of Mary in the Temple, is a day that stands out in the story of Mary in the modern world. It was the day the third session of the Councl ended and also the day the Council adopted the *Constitution on the Church*, which contains the chapter about Mary. As I have already noted, the day began with a Mass in St. Peter's which was concelebrated by Pope Paul and the twenty-four Council Fathers whose dioceses contained the world's major Marian shrines.

That afternoon the session was closed with ceremonies at the Basilica of St. Mary Major. At these ceremonies Pope Paul VI proclaimed Mary to be the Mother of the Church, "that is to say of all people of God of the faithful as well as of the pastors, who call her the most loving

Mother. And we wish that the Mother of God should be still more honored and invoked by the entire Christian people by this most sweet title." The announcement was twice interrupted by applause. (Chapter XXVII of this book is about Mary as Mother.)

Pope Paul followed this announcement with a long address, devoted entirely to Mary. It was in the course of this address that he announced he was sending the Golden Rose to Fatima. The address contained this statement: "Knowledge of the true Church doctrine on Mary will always be a key to the exact understanding of the mystery of Christ and of the Church." At the conclusion of the address, the Pope was given a standing ovation by the Council Fathers.

The fourth and last session opened on September 14, 1965 and was scheduled to end on December 8, the Feast of the Immaculate Conception. Toward the end of this session Pope Paul directed every parish and religious community to hold a triduum of solemn prayer to end on the Feast of the Immaculate Conception, so that the Catholic world would be united in prayer at the conclusion of the Council. During the Mass which concluded the Council, the Pope blessed the cornerstone for a new church to be built in Rome commemorating the Council and dedicated to Mary Mother of the Church.

It is true, then, that there have been some changes since *The Woman Shall Conquer* first appeared. But nothing has happened to change the essential character of Mary's message to the modern world. That message is as important today as it was when this book first appeared.

Background

1

Mary Needs Our Help

ON APRIL 16, 1917, Nikolai Lenin and Leon Trotsky arrived in Petrograd, Russia, to lay plans for the Communist Revolution. Seven months later, on November 7, the Communists took over the government of Russia. This they regarded as but the first step in their sweeping program of world conquest. "First Russia, and then the world," was the motto of the godless, religion-hating Communists.

Between these two dates the Mother of God made her six appearances at Fatima, in Portugal. At one end of Europe the forces of evil were triumphing. At the other end our Lady was rallying the forces of good for a crusade of prayer and penance.

Never were words clearer than those spoken by our Lady at Fatima: "If my requests are granted, Russia will be converted and there will be peace. Otherwise, Russia will spread her errors throughout the world, provoking wars and persecutions of the Church. Many will be martyred; the Holy Father will have much to suffer; several nations will be destroyed."

It is as simple as that. All we need do is heed the requests of our Lady, and there will be peace. The solution to the problem of war or peace is in our hands. Our day-to-day actions are more important than all the deliberations of the United Nations.

But, so far, not enough of us have carried out our Lady's request, and we are reaping the terrible results. Communists are active in every country. ". . . Russia will spread her errors throughout the world. . . ."

In the 1930's, the Communists gained control of Spain and were overthrown only by a terrible civil war. They have since caused wars in Finland, China, Korea, Indo-China, and many other places. ". . . provoking wars. . . ."

Since the beginning of World War II, Russia has seized one country after another. Each new seizure has been followed by a bitter campaign against the Church. ". . . and persecutions of the Church. . . ."

Catholics have been imprisoned and put to death for their religion. . . . "Many will be martyred. . . ."

Pope Pius wept when he learned of the sentence the Communists had given Cardinal Mindszenty. ". . . the Holy Father will have much to suffer. . . ."

The tiny countries of Estonia, Latvia, and Lithuania have been swallowed up and completely digested. Large segments of their populations have been moved out, and Russians have moved in. The countries are not even shown on the newer maps. ". . . several nations will be destroyed. . . ."

All of this could have been prevented if more people had heeded our Lady's warning.

Today the battle between the forces of good and the forces of evil is more intense than ever before. Every country in the world is threatened in some way by atheistic Communism. Judging by surface appearances, all the victories seem to be going to the forces of evil. But the battle is not as one-sided as it seems. Devotion to the Blessed Virgin is increasing steadily throughout the world. More and more people are quietly enrolling in the crusade of prayer and sacrifice. Their deeds are not so spectacular as those of the Communists, but the results will be greater.

We know who will win the battle. The result is written in advance. The Blessed Virgin never loses in her battle against Satan. Did not God promise that she would crush the serpent with her heel? Our Lady herself **said at Fatima,** "In the end my Immaculate Heart will triumph; the Holy Father will consecrate Russia to me, it will be converted,

Mary Needs Our Help

and a certain period of peace will be granted to the world." Saints and mystics tell us that a glorious age is coming in which the Blessed Virgin will be recognized by men as their Queen. This will be the Age of Mary.

But Mary's victory might be delayed by the sins that are being committed throughout the world. A delay might mean more Communist victories, more cruel persecutions, more wars with millions of deaths. The title of this book must not lead anyone into a feeling of false complacency, a feeling that we can relax, that Mary will take care of everything. The victory is certain, but the time depends on us.

"Mother of God," says Thomas Merton in *The Seven Storey Mountain,* "how often have you not come down to us, speaking to us in our mountains, and groves and hills, and telling us what was to come upon us, and we have not heard you. How long shall we continue to be dead to your voice, and run our heads into the jaws of the hell that abhors us?"

For Fatima was not the first of our Lady's messages to the modern world, nor has it been her last. Since 1830, she has appeared numerous times, pleading with us to pray and do penance, warning us of disasters that were to come if her pleas went unheeded. She has appeared as a merciful Mother, too, announcing to her children that their prayers have been heard. On at least one occasion, she has appeared as a Queen to reward her children for duties well performed.

It seems certain that our Lady has made more appearances on earth in the past century and a half than in any similar period in all history. She never appears on this earth unless she has some very good reason for doing so. She has some very important things to say to us, her children.

These appearances fit together like chapters in a story. Fatima and Lourdes are the best known of these chapters, but they are by no means the whole story. It is necessary to read them all in order to know Mary's complete message to the modern world.

Nothing is more important than for us to become acquainted with Mary's message and to act upon it. She is trying to save the world, and she is pleading for our help. By doing what she says, we can have peace in the world; by acting upon her message, we can greatly hasten the coming victory of the Blessed Virgin Mary.

2

When the World Turned Against Its Mother
1513-1830

IT IS difficult to imagine a person who would turn against his own mother—the mother who had brought him into the world, cared for him, taught him his first words, helped him take his first steps, nursed him through his sicknesses, shared his trials and his triumphs. Even hardened criminals usually have a soft spot in their hearts for their mothers.

Yes, it is hard to imagine. And yet, four centuries ago, a large part of the world turned against its spiritual Mother.

Devotion to Mary reached a peak in the Middle Ages. Henry Adams tells us that the palaces of earthly queens were hovels compared with the palaces—churches and cathedrals—of the heavenly Queen. In the 100 years between 1170 and 1270, the French built 80 cathedrals and nearly 500 large churches of the cathedral class. In today's currency, these would have cost several billion dollars. Nearly every great church of the Middle Ages belonged to Mary. If it was not dedicated to her outright, it contained a Lady Chapel.

When the Cathedral of Chartres was built, theologians,

artists, nobles, and common people worked together in honor of the Virgin. They harnessed themselves to wagons and dragged huge blocks of stone and giant tree trunks. Noble ladies helped peasant women mix mortar. All worked in silence and prayed as they worked. No one who thought himself to be in mortal sin dared volunteer. People of that time thought of the Blessed Mother in connection with everything they did. They would not venture upon the simplest undertaking without invoking her aid.

That was a joyous time, because our Lady had her proper place in the scheme of things. The world echoed with the songs of St. Francis and the troubadours. True, there were wars then and bickerings and jealousies—man will never achieve a heaven on earth—but the *spirit* of the times was one of joyousness, as is inevitable when man achieves union with God through our Lady.

"Some Catholic historians have conceded to the adverse critics of the Middle Ages that the people of those times were more brutal than the modern man," says Ed Willock in *Integrity*. "I think that is conceding too much. . . . At least in the Middle Ages, great caution was taken to safeguard the noncombatant women and children. Ours is the brutality of Hiroshima, where a comparatively well-dressed man, deliberately and with little need for courage, pressed a button which brought screaming death around the ears of grandmothers and babes in arms."

It was in the sixteenth century, at the time of the Protestant Revolt, that millions of people turned away from their heavenly Mother. That revolt was one of the most tragic events of history. The world is still suffering from it. Earlier heresies had kept the Sacrifice of the Mass and the sacraments, the principal source of grace. But the Protestant Revolt resulted in a complete break. It set up a new form of Christianity in which each man was free to start his own church, and hundreds did.

The leaders of the Protestant Revolt, in their hatred for everything Catholic, struck especially at our Lord in the Blessed Sacrament and at devotion to the Blessed Virgin.

These, ironically, are the very things we need most in our struggle for salvation.

The reason the early Protestants gave for neglecting Mary was a strange one. "We are Christians," they said in effect, "and as such we owe our allegiance to Christ. If we honor Mary, we are taking away some of the honor due to Christ."

As if you could honor a Son by ignoring His Mother! And Christ was the perfect Son, because He was perfect God and perfect Man.

Jesus had chosen Mary from all eternity to be His Mother. He could have come into the world in any number of ways, but He chose to come through her. He wanted to be carried in her womb for nine months, to be nursed by her, to be brought up and cared for by her, to be subject to her. When He created the angels, He thought of her. When He created the world, He thought of her. When our first parents lost heaven for us, He knew that He would redeem us through her. He preserved her, alone of all creatures, from the stain of original sin, that her body might be a worthy tabernacle for Him.

And the leaders of the Protestant Revolt thought to please Him by neglecting her!

After the sixteenth century, millions of people were raised with little or no knowledge of the Mother of God. Religion became gloomy, foreboding. Without Mary's motherly influence, men became calculating, self-seeking. They thought only of themselves and devoted their lives to gaining power and money.

Our Lady was neglected even by large numbers of Catholics. Her statues were still in the churches, and Catholics continued to pray to her, but she did not play the prominent part in their lives that she should have. The world had truly turned from its Mother.

It is Mary's function to lead us ever closer to God. When she was forgotten, the next step could have been foretold. Thousands of persons turned against God Himself.

The revolt against God was led largely by the so-called intellectuals of France, particularly of Paris. In their classrooms, from the lecture platforms and in books, newspapers, and magazines, these men repeated the same refrain: "Look at the progress man has made in science and in other fields. We are on the verge of solving all our problems. A great new era is dawning for mankind. We no longer need a God."

These ideas were widely accepted first by the upper classes, then by the middle classes. Soon they began seeping down to the ordinary workmen and the peasants. France, which had once been so staunchly Catholic, "the eldest daughter of the Church," now had thousands of freethinkers, agnostics, and even atheists. The leaders of the French Revolution were **so anti-Catholic that they drove priests and sisters from the** country or put them to death. The great cathedral of our Lady in Paris was converted into a temple to the goddess of reason. The Revolution eventually collapsed as a political force, but its antireligious spirit lived on.

From France, the revolt against God spread throughout the world, like a great insidious cancer. Catholic and Protestant countries alike were affected by it and are still suffering from its effects. It became unfashionable to talk about God. The only things that mattered were the things of this world. The nineteenth century was the century of materialism. No great cathedrals were built in the nineteenth century, because man had lost his convictions and had only opinions. Cathedrals are not built on opinions, but only on deep convictions.

For a brief time the God haters seemed to suffer a setback. When Napoleon Bonaparte became First Consul of France he said he intended to restore the Church.

Paris was agog. The city that had witnessed the Reign of Terror, the triumph of "Reason" over "superstition," was to see a return of the Church. Mass was to be celebrated in the churches that had so recently been plundered and defiled.

Napoleon made himself Emperor of France and extended his rule over much of Europe. As was inevitable with a dictator who sought to bend all institutions to his will, he eventually came into conflict with the Church. Religion suffered in all the lands he dominated.

"What does the Pope mean by the threat of excommunication?" Napoleon scoffed in 1807. "Does he think the world has gone back a thousand years? Does he think the arms will fall from my soldiers' hands?"

In the war between God and man, Napoleon had chosen the side of man. In 1809, he imprisoned the frail and elderly Pope Pius VII. Three years later Napoleon marched against Russia. Cold, hunger and disease almost wiped out his army. He actually watched the guns falling from the stiffening hands of his soldiers.

The Napoleonic era ended in 1815. All over Europe there was a period in which various political groups struggled for power. There was revolution and reaction. Through it all, the enemies of religion seemed to make steady progress.

Meanwhile another great change was taking place in the Western World. The invention of the steam engine was altering the habits of centuries. Formerly, men had worked at their trades in their own homes or in small shops. They took great pride in their work and had the feeling of contentment and the satisfaction that go with such pride. They were close to their families, even when they were working. They had sufficient food and clothing, and leisure time in which to worship God and take part in innocent amusements.

Then factories appeared as ugly blotches on the green countryside, poisoning the air with their heavy black smoke. The small craftsman was ruined. He could not hope to compete with the factory and its great machines. He and his family were forced to move to a city and work for the factory that had put him out of business. Every morning the factory bell rang, summoning men, women and children to work. They labored 12 to 15 hours a day at wages averaging less than a dollar a day. They worked, went home and slept, and then trudged off to work again. They lived like animals in disease-infested slums. They took no pride in their work; often they did not know exactly what they were doing. There was little time for recreation or for going to church.

There is, of course, nothing wrong with factories in themselves. The machine age was sure to come, bringing its inevitable changes. If it had come in a spiritual age, however, its effects would have been softened. The factory owners would have recognized their workmen as being created in the image and likeness of God. They would have had some concern for their spiritual and temporal welfare. But the Industrial Revolution came in the age of materialism when the only concern of many was acquiring power and wealth. The best way to do that, the owners reasoned, was to work their employees as long as possible and pay them as little as possible.

Many of the workers, in their great distress, were ready to follow such false prophets as Karl Marx, who was to come along in the middle of the nineteenth century. His solution was an uprising of the workers, class warfare.

When our Blessed Mother looked down at the world of 1830, she saw a world that had revolted against her, against the Church, against God Himself. There were some exceptions. The people of Ireland, for example, and the Belgians, and the people in the region around Lourdes had clung to their faith despite all persecutions. There were good people in every country. But religion was everywhere on the defensive. Thousands who considered themselves Catholics were affected by this spirit of irreligion. They attended Mass on Sunday and received the sacraments on rare occasions, but they scarcely thought of God as they went about their daily work.

As a loving Mother, Mary had never ceased to pray for her children and to try to lead them back to God. In 1830, she made the first of a series of dramatic moves to win the modern world back to Christ.

It is interesting to note that she began the campaign in the heart of the enemy's territory—in Paris.

Mary's Message to Us

3

Our Lady's First Message to the Modern World

PARIS, 1830

"COME TO THE CHAPEL. The Holy Virgin is waiting for you." Zoé Catherine Labouré, a postulant in the Daughters of Charity, awoke to see a child about four or five years old standing at the side of her bed. He was enveloped in a golden light. She later said that she believed him to be her guardian angel.

This happened in the mother house of the Daughters of Charity in Paris. The date was July 18, 1830, the eve of the feast of St. Vincent de Paul, founder of the community.

Catherine sat up, astonished and a little troubled. "How can I get up and cross the dormitory without waking my companions?" she asked.

"Be at ease," the child replied. "It is half past eleven and everyone is asleep. I will come with you."

Catherine followed the child to the chapel, which, to her surprise, was lit up, "as if for Midnight Mass." He led her to the altar rail, and she knelt down. "Here is the Holy Virgin," he announced.

Almost at once, a sound like the rustling of silk caused her to look up. A Lady of incomparable beauty appeared at the foot of the altar. She stepped forward and sat on the chair normally reserved for the Director of the seminary. She was dressed in an ivory robe and blue mantle. A white veil fell over her shoulders.

Catherine rushed forward and threw herself to her knees. She rested her clasped hands on the knees of the Blessed Virgin. It was "the sweetest joy of my life," she said later, "a delight beyond expression."

"My child," the Blessed Mother said, "God wishes you to undertake a mission. For it, you will have much to suffer, but you will overcome that by recalling that you do so for the Glory of God. . . ."

Much of what our Lady said was for Catherine's ears alone and has never been revealed. The words which we do know began Mary's message to the modern world, a message which was climaxed at Fatima and which has not yet been concluded.

"The times are evil," our Lady said. "Terrible things are about to happen in France. The throne will be destroyed and the whole world will be convulsed by terrible calamities.

"But come to the foot of the altar. Here great graces will be poured out upon all who ask them with confidence and fervor. They will be bestowed upon the great and upon the small."

Our Lady made some declarations about the community to which Catherine belonged, adding, "I love it very much.

"But grave troubles are coming. There will be great danger. Do not fear. God and Saint Vincent will protect the community. I myself shall be with you. . . .

"At one moment, when the danger is acute, everyone will believe all to be lost. You will recall my visit and the protection of God. . . .

"There will be victims in other communities. There will be victims among the clergy of Paris. The Archbishop will die. . . . The cross will be trampled on. . . . Blood will run in the streets. . . . The world will be plunged into sadness. . . ."

Catherine understood that some of the events described would take place soon. The others would take place in about forty years, or about 1870.

Our Lady's last words to Catherine on this visit were: "My eyes are ever upon you. I shall grant you many graces.

Our Lady's First Message

Special graces will be given to all who ask them, but people must pray."

When our Lady had disappeared, "like a cloud that had evaporated," the child led Catherine back to her dormitory. The clock was striking two as she got back into bed.

Catherine was not allowed to tell anyone of her experience, except her confessor, Father Aladel. The priest was inclined to dismiss the story as the product of an overwrought imagination.

Father Aladel was surprised a few days later when a Revolution broke out in Paris, but Catherine was not surprised. Our Lady had foretold it. Many were killed. Bands of men and boys broke into churches. Crucifixes were profaned. Convents were pillaged. Priests were ill-treated, and the Archbishop was forced to go into hiding. The mother house in the Rue du Bac shook with gunfire and was surrounded by an angry mob. It did seem that all was lost, but, true to our Lady's promise, the buildings remained unharmed.

Our Lady's second visit to Catherine took place on November 27, 1830, four months after the first one. This time Mary appeared over the high altar in the convent chapel. Her head was covered with a soft white veil. She was standing on a globe. In her hands she held a smaller globe with a tiny cross at the top. She held it out as if offering it to God. Rays of light streamed down to the larger globe from some of the gems in her fingers.

Lowering her eyes, our Lady said to Catherine: "This ball you see is the world. I am praying for it and for everyone in the world. The rays are the graces which I give to those who ask for them. But there are no rays from some of these stones, for many people do not receive graces because they do not ask for them."

The vision changed. An oval frame formed around our Lady. The small globe disappeared, and our Lady dropped her hands to her sides. She became brighter and lovelier as she did so. Around the oval frame appeared in gold the words: "O Mary conceived without sin, pray for us who have recourse to thee."

A voice said to Catherine: "Have a medal made according to this picture. All those who wear it when it is blessed will receive many graces, especially if they wear it suspended from their necks."

Suddenly the entire picture seemed to turn. On the reverse Catherine saw the letter M surmounted by a cross with a crossbar beneath it. Below were two hearts. That of our Lord was encircled by a crown of thorns while that of our Lady was pierced by a sword. Enclosing the entire picture were twelve stars within a golden frame.

In December, the Blessed Virgin appeared for the third time and repeated her request for the medal.

Catherine again transmitted the request to her spiritual adviser, Father Aladel, but the priest did not know what to do. He did not wish to be in the position of disobeying an order from heaven, but he said to Catherine: "I do not have the authority to have such a medal struck. Besides, it is to say 'O Mary conceived without sin,' and the Immaculate Conception is not a dogma of the Church." (In 1830, this doctrine had not yet been promulgated. That was to come twenty-four years later.)

Father Aladel investigated Catherine's story very carefully, and he prayed for divine guidance. Then he consulted the Archbishop of Paris. The medals were struck and distributed in Paris two years after our Lady had made her request. By this time, Catherine had receive the habit of the Daughters of Charity, and had taken the name Sister Catherine.

Sister Catherine was so humble that she did not tell anyone that the Blessed Mother had appeared to her. Not more than two or three persons knew to whom our Lady had given her request for the medal. Even the other Sisters in her convent did not know. Sister Catherine carried her secret to the grave.

During the War of the Commune in 1871, many of the events foretold by our Lady in the first apparition came true. Blood ran in the streets. Many priests were killed. Msgr. Duboy, Archbishop of Paris, was brutally murdered. The insurrectionists were strongly influenced by the teachings of Karl Marx, and so they can be considered the forerunners of today's Communists.

During this revolution many wounded soldiers were brought to the hospital of the Daughters of Charity. Sister Catherine was acting as portress at the time. She passed among the soldiers and gave one of the new medals to each. Most of them, in keeping with the spirit of the times, had no religion at all. Yet, they eagerly accepted the medals.

Other soldiers, who were not wounded, flocked to the hospital to receive the medal.

"But you poor fellows have no faith or religion," Sister Catherine said to them. "What good will the medals do you?"

"True, Sister, we have very little faith, but we believe in that medal. It has protected others; it will also protect us. Should we be under fire, it will help us die like brave men."

The favors and graces that flowed to wearers of the medal were so many that it became known as the Miraculous Medal. It has continued to be called by that name, although the official name is Medal of the Immaculate Conception.

One of the most famous examples of our Lady's granting spiritual favors to the wearers of the Miraculous Medal occurred less than ten years after it had been struck.

Alphonse Rathisbonne was a French Jew who had no religion. When his brother Theodore became a Catholic and then a priest, Alphonse was filled with aversion. He was a typical intellectual of the nineteenth century, a worshiper of humanity, who sneered at anything spiritual.

In November, 1841, Alphonse found himself in Rome although his itinerary had not called for a stop in the Eternal City. There he met Baron de Bussiere. The Baron urgently requested him to wear the Miraculous Medal and to recite daily the prayer of St. Bernard, the *Memorare*. Alphonse did so in the spirit of accepting a dare and without the slightest bit of faith.

On January 20, 1842, Monsieur de Bussiere saw Alphonse walking along the street and invited him into his carriage.

They stopped at S. Andrea delle Fratee because the Baron wished to see a priest there. In order to kill time, Alphonse entered the church.

He was not very much interested and was walking around rather listlessly. Suddenly the church seemed to be plunged into darkness and all the light concentrated on one chapel. Very much startled, he saw there our Blessed Mother bathed in glorious light, her face radiant. He advanced toward her. She motioned with her right hand for him to kneel. As he knelt, he realized at last the sad state of his soul. He perceived that mankind had been redeemed through the Blood of Christ, and he was seized with a great longing to be taken into the Church of Christ. The Blessed Virgin spoke not a word, but these things came to him as he knelt before her.

The next day Alphonse was baptized by Cardinal Patrizi, vicar of Pope Gregory XVI. The Holy Father, as Bishop of Rome, ordered an official inquiry, and after four months the authenticity of the miracle was recognized.

Alphonse Maria Rathisbonne, as he was named after his baptism, devoted the remainder of his life to winning over his fellow Jews to Christ.

Sister Catherine also revealed to her confessor, Father Aladel, that our Lady wished a confraternity of young girls to be established. It was to be called the Confraternity of the Children of Mary, and its badge was to be the Miraculous Medal. Today the organization has thousands upon thousands of members. Girls take pride in wearing the blue medal-ribbon and the image of their model and protector.

It might be thought that once the medal had been struck and the Confraternity established Sister Catherine would be happy. But our Lady had foretold that she would have much to suffer.

During the latter years of her life, she suffered from asthma. She was subject to coughing spells, and she had severe pains in her knees. On every feast of the Blessed Virgin, she became ill or suffered in some manner.

Greater than her physical suffering was her mental anguish.

Our Lady's First Message

She was sure that our Lady wished a statue representing the first part of the second apparition. It was then that she had stood on a globe and held a smaller globe in her hand. Sister talked the matter over with Father Aladel. He was sympathetic but moved slowly in the matter. Some preliminary drawings were made, but Father Aladel died before work on the statue could begin.

Sister had to begin all over again with her new spiritual director, Father Chinchon. He, too, proceeded very slowly. In 1876, he was moved to another post, and the statue still had not been made. Sister Catherine was miserable. She was 70 years old and knew she did not have much longer to live. She could not go into the matter with a third spiritual director! She decided to go to the superioress. Sobbingly she told her story.

The superioress protested that such a statue might do harm to the statue already known as Our Lady of the Miraculous Medal.

"No, no, my Sister, this statue does not concern the Medal. This statue has been the torment and the martyrdom of my life. I should not like to appear before the Blessed Virgin before the design has been accomplished."

The superioress gave her consent. The preliminary drawings were found among Father Aladel's papers. A model of the statue was made. Sister Catherine trembled with joy when she saw it, but her joy was tinged with disappointment: "Oh, but our Lady was much more beautiful than that!"

The statue was made as beautiful as human hands could make it and placed above the high altar where our Lady had appeared. Sister Catherine's last duty had been fulfilled. She knew she was to die in 1876, and she breathed her last on December 31 of that year. Today she lies in state under the statue of the Virgin Most Powerful, the statue that had been the "torment" of her life.

Sister Catherine was canonized on July 27, 1947.

4

Our Lady of Victories

PARIS, 1836

CATHERINE LABOURÉ's pastor in 1830 was Father Charles du Friche des Gennettes. Father des Gennettes' parish included the area in which the mother house of the Daughters of Charity was located. Father probably did not know Sister Catherine because the community had its own spiritual adviser, Father Aladel. He was very familiar, however, with the story of our Lady's appearances in the convent chapel and with the Miraculous Medal.

In 1832, Father des Gennettes was transferred to the Church of Our Lady of Victories. This church had been built in 1629 by King Louis XIII in thanksgiving for favors granted him by the Blessed Virgin. The parishioners, for a century and a half, were known for their devotion to the Blessed Virgin.

With the French Revolution, the church fell upon evil days. All sorts of outrages were performed in it by the revolutionaries. Afterward it was used by a schismatic sect, and after that it became a stock exchange. In 1809, it was restored to its original purpose, but there were few parishioners left.

Father des Gennettes found that scarcely anyone came to Mass or received the sacraments. Being a very apostolic man, he tried in every way he could think of to bring the people back to their faith. He met with nothing but indifference. At length, Father became discouraged. Perhaps another

Our Lady of Victories

priest might be able to do better, he thought. He decided it was his duty to resign as a failure.

On Sunday, December 3, 1836, Father des Gennettes began to say Mass in an almost empty church. He was seized by a frightful distraction, the conviction that he must resign. He could scarcely keep his mind on the Mass. When he reached the Canon, he cried out in distress.

At that moment he heard a calm distinct voice say very solemnly: "Consecrate your parish to the Most Holy and Immaculate Heart of Mary."

After Mass, Father wondered whether he had really heard these words. He convinced himself that it had been his imagination and knelt to say his thanksgiving. Again he heard the words: "Consecrate your parish to the Most Holy and Immaculate Heart of Mary."

He could doubt no longer. Taking up a pen, he composed the rules for a confraternity of our Lady. The Bishop approved the rules that same week.

The following Sunday, Father told the ten people at Mass about his project. He said there would be Vespers of Our Lady that evening and that he would then give the full details of the Confraternity.

When Father des Gennettes entered the church that evening, he found it full for the first time in years. More than 400 people were there. The parish continued to flourish from then on. People began to come to Our Lady of Victories from other parts of Paris, and then from all France, and soon the fame of the shrine was world wide. Today, about 90,000 thank offerings for cures line the walls.

In 1838, Pope Gregory XVI made the Confraternity the Archconfraternity of the Holy and Immaculate Heart of Mary for the Conversion of Sinners. There are affiliated societies throughout the world.

In March, 1855, an octave of thanksgiving was held at the shrine for the proclamation of the dogma of the Immaculate Conception. At the end of the octave, the statue of the Immaculate Heart was seen to move. This happened again. Pope Pius IX took this as a sign of approval for his act, and ordered the statue to be crowned, June 1, 1856.

St. Teresa of the Child Jesus visited the shrine on November 4, 1887. "Having arrived in Paris," she wrote, "Papa took us to see the sights. For me there was only one—Our Lady of Victories. What I felt in her sanctuary, I cannot say. The graces she granted me resembled those of my First Communion. I was filled with peace and joy. It was there that my Mother, the Virgin Mary, told me distinctly that it was indeed she who cured me. With what fervor did I beg her always to keep me and to bring about my dream, to enfold me ever beneath the shadow of the cloak of her Virginity. I besought her again to keep all occasions of sin away from me."

The Miraculous Medal, which our Lady gave us in 1830, shows the Sacred Heart of Jesus with the Immaculate Heart of Mary. The devotion of our Lady of Victories, which originated six years later, is primarily a devotion to the Immaculate Heart. That this was more than a coincidence was demonstrated by our Lady's next appearance in 1840.

5

The Badge of The Immaculate Heart

BLANGY, 1840

OUR LADY'S CAMPAIGN to win our modern world for Christ had just begun. Her next major series of apparitions began just ten years after those of the Miraculous Medal.

On January 18, 1840, she appeared to young Sister Justine

Bisqueyburu who was kneeling at prayer in the novitiate of the Daughters of Charity in Paris. Our Lady was clothed in a long white robe over which hung a bright blue mantle. Her hair fell loosely over her shoulders. In her hands she held her heart from the top of which issued brilliant rays. Her beauty was so dazzling that Sister could scarcely keep from crying out.

The same apparition was repeated four or five times during her novitiate, on the principal feasts of the Blessed Virgin. These appearances seemed to be for the purpose of increasing in Sister devotion to Mary Immaculate and of preparing her for what was to follow.

After receiving her habit, Sister Bisqueyburu was sent to Blangy to teach school. Shortly after her arrival there, she had another vision. This was on September 8, 1840, the feast of the Nativity of the Blessed Virgin. In her right hand our Lady held her heart surrounded by flames, and in her left a sort of scapular. It was a single piece of green cloth suspended from a string of the same color. On one side was a picture of the Blessed Virgin as she had shown herself in the preceding apparitions. On the other side was "a heart all ablaze with rays more dazzling than the sun and transparent as crystal." The heart was pierced with a sword. It was surmounted by a cross and surrounded by an oval inscription. The inscription read: "Immaculate Heart of Mary, pray for us now and at the hour of our death."

An interior voice told Sister that copies of this new scapular should be made as soon as possible and distributed with confidence. It would contribute to the conversion of those who had no faith and, above all, procure for them a happy death.

When the apparition was over, Sister Bisqueyburu could not believe that such a thing had happened to her. She feared it was a delusion. A whole month passed before she wrote a timid note to her superior, Sister Buchepot. She implored Sister to keep the communication a secret. "However," she added, "if you believe it to be necessary to speak of it to Father Aladel, I shall do so."

It had been to Father Aladel that Catherine Labouré, another member of the Daughters of Charity, had confided the secret of the Miraculous Medal ten years earlier. The request for that medal has caused him great anguish. Perhaps he just could not believe that such a thing could happen to a man twice within his lifetime. Or perhaps he could not get the Archbishop's consent to have the scapular made. At any rate, our Lady's instructions were not carried out. On August 15, 1841, and again on September 13, our Lady appeared to Sister Bisqueyburu and complained of the delay.

At length, an engraver was entrusted with making the necessary plates. Again there was a delay. In May, 1842, Sister wrote a letter in which she reported a new vision: "It seemed to me that I heard a voice which told me that she was not pleased because they delayed so long in making the scapulars."

Finally some scapulars were made, but not in large quantities. They were given out by way of experiment and not with great confidence. The results were not very satisfactory.

The Blessed Virgin repeatedly showed her displeasure during the year 1846. "It is absolutely necessary," Sister wrote her superior in July of that year, "that Father Aladel attend to the scapular and that he should disseminate it and do so with great confidence. Heretofore, I am sure, he did not attach great importance to it. He was very wrong. True, I do not deserve to be believed, for I am only a poor girl in every respect. May I entreat him to do this, not for my sake, but I ask him in the name of Mary to do it for those poor souls who die without knowing the true religion; yes, if it be given with confidence, there will be a great number of conversions. . . .

"Answer me, I beg of you as soon as possible; we cannot lose any time."

Father Aladel was convinced by this time, but one difficulty remained. What were the conditions necessary to make the wearing of the scapular effective? He instructed Sister to ask our Lady about this.

On September 8, 1846, our Lady again appeared to Sister

The Badge of The Immaculate Heart

Bisqueyburu. This time her hands were filled with rays of varying lengths. With great reluctance, Sister carried out Father's instructions.

The Blessed Virgin replied that since the scapular is not the badge of a confraternity but simply a double image on a piece of cloth and suspended from a cord, no formal imposition is required. It is enough for it to be blessed by a priest. It can be worn, or it can be placed in the clothing, on the bed, or simply in the room with the person. The only prayer is the one on the scapular: "Immaculate Heart of Mary, pray for us now and at the hour of our death." This should be repeated daily, if not by the one wearing it, by the one giving it. The scapular may be distributed everywhere. Although wonderful graces are attached to it, they are given in proportion to the confidence with which it is given. This was signified by the rays in our Lady's hands during this last apparition.

When these conditions were complied with, many conversions resulted. The first one of which there is any record took place even before our Lady had revealed the conditions for the use of the scapular. A Mr. Copin was bookkeeper for Mr. Letaille, the man who made the plates for the Green Scapular. Mr. Copin had been raised in the antireligious atmosphere so common in France. His employer, a fervent Catholic, held long discussions with him about religion. Mr. Copin saw insuperable obstacles in the way of his becoming a Catholic. He became very ill, and Mr. Letaille had Father Aladel and several Daughters of Charity call on him. He received them courteously, but he said he felt as if he were surrounded by a wall of darkness.

On September 19, 1842, one of the Daughters of Charity sent Mr. Letaille a Green Scapular and asked him to induce the patient to wear it. "If needs be," she said, "be insistent. Bring the Heart of Mary near that unhappy heart, so that her power may break its lock, and that grace may, as soon as possible, penetrate into that soul. All our Sisters are going to join in prayer for him."

Mr. Copin accepted the scapular but thought little of it.

Meanwhile, he seemed no nearer to conversion than he had ever been.

About seven o'clock in the evening of September 30, he was eating with his family. Suddenly, he rose from the table, went into the bedroom and fell on his knees before a statue of the Blessed Virgin. He held the Green Scapular in his hand, kissed it respectfully and shed many tears. He called the scapular the "medium" through which his conversion had come about.

Soon after that he went to confession, and then he made his first, and last, Communion. He was strong enough to go to church to receive Communion, but he became weaker after that. At the end of October, he died, murmuring: "Ah, how glad I am! How glad I am!"

This first known conversion that is attributed to the Green Scapular is typical of many that have occurred since and that are still occurring. "The wonders wrought through the use of the Green Scapular really baffle description," says a Sister of Charity of Emmitsburg, Maryland. Emmitsburg is the center of the Green Scapular devotion in the United States.

Strictly speaking, the Green Scapular is not a scapular at all, since it is not the habit of a religious order. It is really a medal in cloth form. Many authorities feel that it should be called the Badge of the Immaculate Heart of Mary. It seems too late to change the name now, however.

For one hundred years, the scapular had to be made by hand by the Sisters of Charity. When Pope Pius XII dedicated the world to the Immaculate Heart in 1942, the Sisters at Emmitsburg felt that they should obtain permission to manufacture it so that it could be distributed in greater numbers. After they were authorized to do this, it took a long time to find a manufacturer who could turn out the badge as it should be. One difficulty after another was encountered in its production. Now, at last, it is being turned out in large quantities. So it is only in recent years that the scapular has come into widespread use.

Three times within ten years—at Rue du Bac, at Our Lady of Victories, and at Blangy—our Lady stressed devotion to her Immaculate Heart. At Fatima, in 1917, our Lady said that God wishes to establish in the world devotion to the Immaculate Heart of Mary. In 1942, as a result of Fatima, Pope Pius XII dedicated the world to the Immaculate Heart. A few years later he established the feast of the Immaculate Heart, August 22. After that the Green Scapular, Badge of the Immaculate Heart, was widely distributed for the first time.

Our age can truly be called the age of the Immaculate Heart.

6

The Manuscript Found in a Chest
TRUE DEVOTION, 1842

In 1842, a priest was looking through an old chest in a house in Saint Laurent-sur-Sevre, in France. The priest was a member of the Fathers of the Company of Mary, today commonly called the Montfort Fathers, and the house belonged to the community.

At the bottom of the chest, the priest found a stack of old handwritten pages, yellow with age. The priest took the sheets to his superiors. There were many consultations, many readings, much comparing of handwriting. Finally it was announced that these were two manuscripts which had undoubtedly been written by Father Louis Marie de Montfort, the founder of the community.

The Bishop of Lucon authorized the publication of the work, *True Devotion to the Blessed Virgin Mary*. It has since gone through 130 editions and has played a tremendous part in increasing devotion to the Blessed Mother. The other manuscript, *The Secret of Mary*, is a summary of *True Devotion*.

Louis Marie de Montfort was born in a little town in Brittany in 1673, the eldest of seventeen children. He was ordained a priest in 1700. Most of his priestly career was devoted to preaching against the heresy of Jansenism which had taken a strong hold in France. In his preaching he constantly taught devotion to the Blessed Virgin Mary. He stressed the fact that she is the Mediator between God and man. In 1716, worn out by his constant labor, he was struck by a fatal illness. Just before he died, he cried out: "You attack me in vain; I stand between Jesus and Mary. I have finished my course. I shall sin no more."

For a long time after his death, De Montfort was almost forgotten. Then, about a century later, discussion of his virtues began. In 1853, Rome decreed his writings to be exempt from all error that could be a bar to his canonization. He was beatified in 1888 and canonized on July 20, 1947.

Sometime between his ordination in 1700 and his death in 1716, De Montfort wrote *True Devotion to the Blessed Virgin Mary* and *The Secret of Mary*. As he wrote he said, "If I thought that my poor blood could help to carry the truths that I write in my dear Mother's honor to the hearts of men, I would use it instead of ink to form the letters."

But he foretold that the little book would not come to light for a long time. He said that the devil would "envelop it in the silence of a coffer, in order that it might not appear." He went on to prophesy that eventually it would appear and that it would be successful. We have seen that these prophecies were fully realized. The manuscript was lost for 126 years, but the book is now widely circulated.

Although St. Louis Marie lived and died long before the

period covered by this book, he belongs in any study of the Blessed Mother in the modern world.

The True Devotion preached by St. Louis Marie was total consecration to the Blessed Virgin. We give her all our earthly possessions, all our thoughts, words, and deeds. Mary exists only to honor God and to serve Him, so when we offer these things to Mary we really offer them to God through Mary. St. Louis Marie says that we should make ourselves slaves of Mary. He calls his devotion "the slavery of Jesus in Mary."

The devotion did not originate with St. Louis Marie, but to him must go most of the credit for making it widely known and widely practiced. The devotion will be discussed more fully in a later chapter.

For the present, we shall confine ourselves to that section of *True Devotion* which concerns the role of the Blessed Virgin in the modern world. In writing this section, the saint-author seems to have been inspired from heaven, because he looks into the future and tells what is going to happen. Many of the events that are taking place in the world today are more understandable when considered in the light of De Montfort's words.

"God wishes that His Holy Mother should be at the present time more known, more loved and more honored than she has ever been," St. Louis Marie tells us.

This statement helps explain the many manifestations of the Blessed Virgin in the last century and a half and the great increase in devotion to her. The manuscript of *True Devotion* was found in 1842. In the twelve years preceding its finding, there had been manifestations of the Blessed Mother at the convent of the Daughters of Charity in Paris, at Blangy, and at the shrine of Our Lady of Victories in Paris. Four years later, our Lady was to appear to children at La Salette. Twelve years later the dogma of Mary's Immaculate Conception was to be defined. Three years after that our Lady was to appear to Bernadette of Lourdes. And this was only the beginning! Truly, it would seem that God wants his mother more known, more loved, and more honored than ever before.

Why does God wish this?

"It was through Mary that the salvation of the world was begun and it is through Mary that it must be consummated. Mary hardly appeared at all in the first coming of Jesus Christ. But in the second coming . . . Mary has to be made known and revealed by the Holy Ghost, in order that through her, Jesus Christ may be known, loved and served. . . ."

It was through Mary that our Lord came into the world the first time. It is through her that He will come back to the world. In order to accomplish this, Mary herself must become better known and better loved.

St. Louis Marie then elaborates on why God "wishes to reveal and make known the masterpiece of His hands in these latter times:

"It is by her that the souls who are to shine forth especially in sanctity have to find Our Lord. He who shall find Mary shall find life, that is Jesus Christ, who is the Way, the Truth and the Life. But no one can find Mary who does not seek her; and no one can seek her who does not know her. . . . It is necessary, then, for the greater knowledge and glory of the Most Holy Trinity, that Mary should be more than ever known."

That is a further possible explanation for the many apparitions of the Blessed Virgin that have been taking place since 1830.

St. Louis Marie continues: "Mary must shine forth more than ever in mercy, in might, and in grace in these latter times." In mercy, he says, to bring back the strayed sinner. In might, against the enemies of God who shall rise in terrible revolt against Him. In grace, to sustain the soldiers and servants of Christ who shall battle in His service.

He concludes the list of reasons with the following words which seem to have special bearing on the present world situation:

"And lastly Mary must be terrible to the devil and his crew, as an army ranged in battle, principally in these latter times, because the devil, knowing he has but little time, and now less than ever, to destroy souls, will every day redouble his efforts and his combats. He will presently raise up cruel persecutions, and will put terrible snares before the faithful servants and true children of Mary, whom it gives him more trouble to conquer than it does to conquer others."

One has but to think of the events of the past two centuries and of conditions in our modern world to realize that the devil has indeed been raising up cruel persecutions of the Church and that they have been increasing in intensity. St. Louis Marie tells us that these last and cruel persecutions "shall go on increasing daily till the reign of Antichrist."

With such a powerful enemy ranged against us, the situation would be hopeless if we did not have an even more powerful friend and protector. After the fall of our first parents God said to the serpent: "I will put enmities between thee and the woman and thy seed and her seed: she shall crush thy head, and thou shalt lie in wait for her heel."

On this point St. Louis Marie says: "God has formed . . . but one enmity, but it is an irreconcilable one, which shall endure and grow even to the end. It is between Mary, his worthy Mother, and the devil—between the children and servants of the Blessed Virgin, and the children and tools of Lucifer." God has given His Mother such power over the devil, De Montfort tells us, that Satan "fears her not only more than all the angels and men, but in a sense more than God Himself. Not that the anger, the hatred and the power of God are not infinitely greater than those of the Blessed Virgin, for the perfections of Mary are limited but Satan, being proud, suffers infinitely more from being beaten and punished by a little handmaid of God, and her humility humbles him more than the divine power."

The devils, we are told, fear one of Mary's sighs for a soul, "more than the prayers of all the saints, and one of her threats against them more than all other torments."

The battle between the devil and our Blessed Mother has been going on for centuries. It is a battle for souls. The devil is trying to lure all of us into the lowest depths of hell. Mary is trying to lead us to heaven. Today, according to De Montfort, the devil is more active than ever before because he has little time left. As a consequence the Blessed Virgin is making herself better known to us, so that we might resist the devil and enroll on her side. The battle seems to be approaching a great climax.

The saint's words about Mary's power over the devil are consoling ones for these trying days. Satan may rage and roar at us. He may persecute us openly or subtly, but he cannot harm us so long as we stay by Mary's side.

7

The Madonna in Tears
LA SALETTE, 1846

MARY tried to help the world in 1832, in 1836 and in 1840. But the world paid little heed.

Some souls were led back to God through the Miraculous Medal, the Archconfraternity of the Immaculate Heart and the Green Scapular. Some miracles of grace were worked, as in the case of Alphonse Rathisbonne. But the world as a whole ignored Mary's message. Millions continued to pursue their goals of wealth, power and pleasure.

Men of science made new discoveries, and each such discovery seemed to thrust God farther into the background. Books attacking religion were coming off the presses in great numbers. The ranks of freethinkers, agnostics and atheists were swelling every day.

Any ordinary creature would have been tempted to leave the world to the fate it so richly deserved. But not Mary!

The Madonna in Tears

She appeared on the earth again to make a new plea to mankind.

The persons whom she selected as her messengers this time were eleven-year-old Maximin Giraud and fifteen-year-old Melanie Mathieu. The children were tending cows on the slope of Mount Gargas which rises above the village of La Salette in southeastern France. The day Mary chose for her appearance was September 19, 1846, the eve of the feast of Our Lady of Seven Sorrows.

The first thing the children saw was a globe of dazzling light. While they gazed in wonderment, the globe opened and they saw a woman seated on some stones which surrounded the bed of a spring. The spring was dry at the time. The Lady's elbows rested on her knees, her face was buried in her hands, and she was weeping.

The children were afraid. Melanie had been holding a stick, but she let it fall.

"Keep your stick," said Maximin. "If it does anything, I'll give it a good clout."

The Lady rose, crossed her arms, and in the sweetest of tones said: "Come near, my children; do not be afraid. I am here to tell you important news."

The children crossed a little stream and walked toward her. She stood between them. Her face was beautiful, though her eyes were filled with tears. She wore white shoes encircled by roses. Her apron was golden and descended to the bottom of her full white robe. Her arms were concealed within broad straight sleeves which reached beyond her finger tips. A white cape bordered with roses was over her shoulders. She wore a thin chain upon which hung a crucifix. Her headdress was white, and above it was a royal diadem wreathed with roses of many hues. Her beauty was so radiant, so dazzling, that the children could scarcely look at her. Nothing that they saw afterward could begin to compare with her beauty, they said later.

The Lady spoke again in a voice sweeter than the sweetest of melodies. Tears fell from her eyes as she spoke.

"If my people will not submit," she said, "I shall be forced to let go the hand of my Son. It is so strong, so heavy, that I can no longer withhold it."

"How long a time do I suffer for you!" the Lady continued. "If I would not have my Son abandon you, I am compelled to pray to Him without ceasing. And, as to you, you take no heed of it.

"However much you pray, however much you do, you will never recompense the pains I have taken for you."

Maximin did not understand any of this, and Melanie understood it only slightly, but the words were engraved on their minds.

The words deserve very close study. They form the essential part of Mary's message to the modern world.

The Lady continued. She named the desecration of the Sabbath and the taking of her Son's name in vain as two of the sins which made the hand of her Son so heavy.

"If the harvest is spoiled, it is your fault. I gave you warning last year in the potatoes, but you did not heed it. On the contrary, when you found the potatoes spoiled you swore, you took the name of my Son in vain. They will continue to decay, so that by Christmas there will be none left."

Here Mary made clear the fact that many of the calamities befalling the world are the result of sin. At La Salette, she foretold a failure of the potato crop if people did not reform. At Fatima, in 1917, she was to foretell even worse things that would befall the world if people did not change their lives and do penance for their sins. In retrospect, La Salette seems a forerunner of Fatima.

The Lady, up to this time, had been speaking in the noble French of the cultured classes. Melanie did not know the meaning of the word for potatoes. She turned to Maximin to ask what *pommes de terre* meant.

"Ah, my children," the Lady said, "you do not understand. I will say it in a different way."

Then she proceeded to speak in the patois of the district.

"If you have wheat, it is no good to sow it; all that you sow the insects will eat. What comes up will fall into dust when you thrash it.

The Madonna in Tears

"There will come a great famine. Before the famine comes, the children under seven years of age will be seized with trembling and will die in the hands of those who hold them; and others will do penance by the famine.

"The walnuts will become worm-eaten; the grapes will rot."

The Lady then spoke separately to each of the children. Neither knew what she told the other.

The Lady made it clear that the terrible things she had prophesied would happen only if people persisted in their sins.

"If they are converted, the stones and the rocks will be changed into heaps of wheat, and potatoes will be self-sown."

Becoming more personal, she asked, "Do you say your prayers well, my children?"

"Not very well, Madame," they admitted.

"You must say them well, morning and evening. When you cannot do better say at least an Our Father and a Hail Mary. When you have time, say more."

Once again she complained of the few people who attended Mass on Sunday.

When it was time to say good-by, the Lady spoke pure French once more.

"Well, my children," she said, "you will make this known to all the people."

She crossed the little stream saying again, "Well, my children, you will make this known to all the people."

Moving along the tips of the grass, she ascended the mountain for a short distance, then rose about a yard from the ground and remained in that position for a moment. She lifted her gaze toward heaven and then lowered it to the earth. Then she disappeared, but the light remained for another moment.

Maximin had no idea who the Lady was. He had heard of sorceresses, and he thought that she might be one. When she spoke of the heavy arm of her Son, he thought she meant her son had been beating her.

Melanie was not much better informed than Maximin, but she was older and more reflective. As the Lady disappeared the girl said, "Maybe she is a great saint."

This was a new idea to Maximin. "If we had known she was a great saint, we would have asked her to take us with her," he said.

"Oh, I wish she were still here," exclaimed Melanie.

Maximin reached out to catch some of the light, but it was gone.

Both children were rather slow of mind. Melanie was not judged by the Sister to have sufficient knowledge to receive Holy Communion until she was seventeen, and Maximin was unable to remember the Our Father until he was fifteen. Yet when questioned about the apparition, they gave complete information. When they were questioned separately, their stories agreed in all details.

People began flocking to La Salette. The spring where our Lady had appeared flowed again, and marvelous cures were worked through the application of its waters.

The calamities foretold by our Lady took place. The potato famine had already begun in 1845. In 1846 this famine became so severe in Ireland, that Queen Victoria had to appeal to Parliament for special funds. The wheat shortage was so severe in Europe that more than a million people died. A grape disease decimated the vineyards all over France. Babies died trembling in their mothers' arms, as our Lady had foretold.

In 1848, the horrors of the "February Revolution," the "March Revolution," and then the "June Days" shook Paris. This was the same year that saw the beginning of Communism in France.

The punishments would probably have been worse except for the fact that many people heeded the message of La Salette. They began attending church in large numbers. Cursing and swearing became less common. The shops were closed on Sunday, and people stopped doing unnecessary work on that day.

The Bishop ordered a thorough investigation of the appari-

The Madonna in Tears

tion and the cures. After examining all the testimony and evidence, he satisfied himself that the appearance had been authentic. He founded the Missionaries of Our Lady of La Salette to carry out her command: "You will make this known to all the people."

Pope Pius IX approved the devotion of La Salette. His successor, Leo XIII, built a great basilica on the mountain.

Five years after the apparition, Pope Pius IX said he would like to know the secrets. The children agreed to write them provided they would be placed in sealed envelopes and delivered directly to the Pontiff. Maximin wrote his four or five paragraphs quickly. Melanie took longer. While she was writing, she asked the meaning of the word "infallibility" and the spelling of "antichrist."

The secrets were taken to Rome by two priests of the Grenoble diocese, Father Rousselot and Father Gerin. On July 18, 1851, the two priests were received in audience by Pope Pius IX. The Holy Father, seated at his desk, arose and gave them his ring to kiss. He took the sealed letters from their hands, opened them, and began to read that of Maximin. He smiled.

"Here," he said, "is all the candor and simplicity of a child."

The priests concluded that Maximin had been entrusted with a message of mercy and consolation.

Then, that he might read more easily, he went over to a window and opened the shutter. He began to read Melanie's letter. No smile now. This secret seemed to be longer and different in import. As he read, the Pope pressed his lips more tightly together and puffed out his cheeks.

"Calamities threaten France," he said. "But she is not the only guilty nation. Germany, Italy, and all Europe are guilty and deserve punishment. I have less to fear from open impiety than from indifference and human respect. It is not without reason that the Church is called militant, and here," touching his breast, "you see her leader."

That is all that is known of the secrets except that years

later the Pope said: "Do you wish to know the secret? This is it: Unless you do penance, you shall all perish."

The two priests went out from the audience deeply moved. The next day they visited Cardinal Fornari of the papal household. The Cardinal was familiar with the story of La Salette. He said: "I am terrified at these prodigies, we have everything that is needed in our religion for the conversion of sinners, and when heaven employs such means, the evil must be very great."

The greater part of what is known about the secrets of La Salette has been fulfilled.

France, Germany, Italy, and all Europe have suffered from war, famine, and desolation. They must have suffered not once but many times since 1846.

The dogma of papal infallibility—the word that puzzled Melanie—was pronounced in 1870.

Many people believe there is a connection between Communism and antichrist. If so, it is interesting to note that the apparition of La Salette took place less than two years before Karl Marx published his *Communist Manifesto*.

The Holy Father's statement, "I have less to fear from open impiety than from indifference and human respect," is a perfect description of our times. This indifference is found both outside and inside the church. In their annual message a few years ago, the Bishops of the United States said: "The Church has less to fear from her open enemies than from the indifference of so many Catholics."

"And so it was," says Father James P. O'Reilly, M.S., in *The Story of La Salette*, "after perusing a few humble pages written by two ignorant shepherds, Pius IX made the memorable statement which obviously was a logical consequence of their letters: "It is not without reason that the Church is called militant, and here you see her leader." Against what enemies, especially, was this leader to fight during the longest papal reign in history? Against indifference and free-thinking, scepticism with regard to religion and the timid human respect of many Catholics.

"Was it not remarkable that the Pope found all that implied in a few pages drawn up by two unlettered peasants?"

At La Salette, our Lady addressed herself to the peasants of the region and talked of such common things as walnuts and grapes. Yet, the message was not meant for the peasants alone. The forceful language that opened the eyes of the country folks could not fail to astound others as well. The implication was perfectly clear that all France suffered from the moral diseases of decadence and degeneracy. And beyond France lay the whole Christian world which had been infected also by the irreligion of the times.

The keynote of our Lady's message lay in the words: "If my people will not submit." Thus she summed up the great evil of the times, human pride. Her message was for all times and all places, but particularly was it meant to show how false was the idea that man no longer needed God.

In 1946, the centenary of La Salette was observed. Pope Pius XII called it a centenary "of that blessed afternoon, the 19th of September, 1846, when the Madonna in Tears came to adjure her children to enter resolutely the path of conversion to her Divine Son, and of reparation for so many sins that offend the August and Eternal Majesty."

8

The Immaculate Conception

AN AWED SILENCE fell over the throng that had gathered in St. Peter's for this history-making ceremony. The tall stately Pope Pius IX had just celebrated Mass at the great main altar. Now he was stepping forward to read his proclamation. Tears of joy glistened in his eyes. In a voice loud and clear but ringing with emotion, he read: "We declare, affirm and define that the doctrine which states that the Blessed Virgin Mary was preserved and exempted from all stain of original sin from the first instant of her conception in view of the merits of Jesus Christ, the Saviour of all mankind, is a doctrine revealed of God and which, for this reason, all Christians are bound to believe firmly and with confidence. . . ."

As he reached the end, his voice broke and tears ran unchecked down his cheeks.

Forty·thousand voices sang the hymn *Te Deum Laudamus.* The dome of Michelangelo resounded with the triumphant notes. The bells of Rome's churches rang joyously. That night, Rome was ablaze with light.

This happened on December 8, 1854.

For centuries, millions of Catholics had believed that the Mother of God had been conceived without the stain of original sin; anything else would have been unthinkable. But the Holy Ghost had reserved the solemn definition for modern times. Our Lady had told Venerable Dominic of Jesus and Mary, a Carmelite who had lived at the time of St. Louis Marie de Montfort, that the promulgation was "saved for the latter days of the Church." This was part of the divine plan, foretold by St. Louis Marie, to make our Lady more known, more loved and more honored in our time than she had ever been before. The Blessed Mother herself had paved the way for the proclamation in 1830 when, to Catherine Labouré, she called herself "Mary conceived without sin."

The doctrine was an especially appropriate one for the nineteenth century. The great heresy of the day—which has persisted into our own time—was man's elevating himself to equality with God. The Immaculate Conception reminds us that only Mary, of all human creatures, was conceived without the stain of original sin. All the rest of us came into the world with this mark on our souls. As a result of this sin, we are weak and inclined toward evil. Only God's help

The Immaculate Conception

will keep us on the road to salvation. We are absolutely dependent on God.

As the Blessed Virgin was intensifying her campaign, so was the devil. This very city of Rome, which was outdoing itself to honor the great Mother of God, had, just six years before, been the scene of the wildest disorders. They had been directed principally at Pope Pius IX, Christ's vicar on earth.

In those days the Pope, besides being head of the Universal Church, was a king. He ruled a country known as the Papal States, and Rome was its capital. In the city there were many "liberals" who opposed the rule of the Pontiff on the pretense that they were in favor of a democracy. Actually, they hated the Church, and they knew no better way of fighting it than by attacking its visible head.

Riot followed riot. The revolutionaries managed to get control of the civic guard, so the Pope was powerless to stop the riots. Events reached a climax in November, 1848. On the 15th, a group of conspirators stabbed to death the Pope's Prime Minister, Count Pellegrino Rossi. The mob celebrated the murder by carrying the bloody knife triumphantly through the streets. It was even carried to the home of the widow who was alone with her daughter.

Later that night, the mob marched to the Papal Palace. Shots were fired, and some found their mark. Several people were wounded. Monsignor Palma, the Pope's secretary, was shot dead.

On November 24, 1848, the Pope was forced to flee from Rome. The city was left in the hands of the "liberals," the men who were "to usher in a new era for mankind, the glorious era of a redemption far different from that announced by Christ."

It was different all right—horribly different. Under the "Roman Republic," freedom of the press and freedom of speech were rigidly suppressed. Taxes were increased. All bank deposits, all gold, silver and jewelry were confiscated, as was all the property belonging to the Church. People were thrown into jail without a trial. The Minister of Finance requisitioned all hospitals, orphan asylums and other charitable institutions. The inmates were turned into the streets.

In 1830, our Lady had struck in the heart of the enemy's territory—Paris. Now, eighteen years later, the devil had struck at the city which was the capital of Christ's Church—Rome. As things are usually judged in this world, the devil seemed to have the better of it. Mary had appeared in the quiet of the night to a humble little postulant in a convent chapel. So far as anyone could tell at the time, she had had no effect at all on the city or the world. The enemies of religion, on the other hand, were in complete control of Rome. The Holy Eucharist was defiled in public ceremonies.

But this control did not last long. Louis Napoleon, nephew of Napoleon Bonaparte, had become head of the French government. He decided to help Pius IX, who was in exile at Gaeta. A French army marched against Rome, and the "republic" fell on June 30, 1849. The Pope returned to the city on April 12, 1850.

His return did not mean the end of his troubles. He was kept in power only by Louis Napoleon, who was ready to sacrifice him the moment he could gain thereby. Rome was still filled with "liberals" who were ready to repeat their revolution of 1848. King Victor Emmanuel of Piedmont and his crafty premier, Cavour, were campaigning for a united Italy with Rome as its capital. Most people were sure that eventually they would be successful. In addition to the troubles in Rome, there was scarcely a country in the world where the rights of the Church were not being infringed upon. Switzerland, Russia and Prussia were especially violent in their persecutions.

With the Church beset on all sides, there were many who freely predicted that its days were numbered. It was not possible, these people said, for any institution to withstand so many attacks coming from so many quarters at the same time. From a strictly material viewpoint, these people were right. But they forgot Christ's promise that He would remain with His Church always and that the gates of hell should not prevail against her. They forgot—or did not know—that "Mary must be terrible to the devil and his crew, as an army ranged in battle, principally in these latter times."

In the midst of all her troubles, the Church had one of her most glorious moments, when Pius IX proclaimed the doctrine of the Immaculate Conception.

Less than four years after the proclamation, Pope Pius IX was to learn with joy that our Lady had appeared at Lourdes and had put what seemed to be the seal of approval on his action by saying, "I am the Immaculate Conception."

9

The Lady of the Grotto
LOURDES, 1858

THE NINETEENTH-CENTURY revolt against God was led by some of the most brillant men the world had ever known. God had given them their wonderful minds that they might better serve Him. Instead, they turned against Him. He permitted them to make astounding discoveries in the field of science and to make great progress in a material way. Instead of thanking Him, they took all the credit to themselves.

"The sovereign majesty of God has tumbled," said Cauchy, the great mathematician who died in 1857. "Only the material exists. . . . Reason alone can and has the right to explain everything. The supernatural order is impossible. Religion and faith are superfluous; they are burdens which encumber the human spirit. . . . Science . . . alone reigns victorious; it alone emancipates man, releases him from his chains, permits him to reach his full height and to search all horizons."

The ordinary people of the world read statements such as this and decided these great men knew what they were talking about. The peasants of La Salette cursed and swore and defiled the Sabbath because the men they respected said there was no longer a need for God. There were probably no intellectuals in the mob that stabbed Count Rossi and drove the Pope from Rome in 1848, but the writers, the scientists, the college professors were as much responsible for these actions as if they themselves had paraded through the streets with the bloody knife. And the anti-God movement was growing. There is no telling where it might have ended if it had been allowed to go unchecked.

But our Lady had no intention of letting it go unchecked. Her appearances in Paris and at La Salette and the definition of her Immaculate Conception had started a countermovement in the world. In 1858, the movement was spurred on by the most challenging series of apparitions that had taken place up to that time.

Since the revolt against God was led by such brilliant men, we might expect Mary to combat it by raising up a saint of great intellectual powers—a saint who would lead people back to God by the very brilliance of his arguments.

Instead, Mary chose Bernadette Soubirous, a poor, sickly, uneducated peasant girl, who at the age of fourteen did not even know her catechism.

Bernadette had gone with her sister and a friend to gather wood. The other two girls had run on, leaving her to follow as best she could.

Suddenly as she stooped over to take off her shoes before crossing a little millstream, there was a noise like a violent wind. Startled, Bernadette looked up and saw a golden cloud emerge from a grotto on the other side of the stream. This was followed by a beautiful Lady.

"She looked at me immediately," said Bernadette later, "smiled at me and motioned me to advance, as if she had been my mother. All fear left me; I seemed to know no longer where I was. I rubbed my eyes; I shut them; I opened them. But the Lady was still there, continuing to smile at me and

The Lady of the Grotto

making me understand that I was not mistaken. Without thinking of what I was doing, I took my rosary in my hands and went to my knees. The Lady made a sign of approval with her head and took into her hands her own rosary which hung on her right arm."

As Bernadette recited the Rosary, the Lady allowed her own beads to glide through her fingers. She joined only in the recital of the Gloria at the end of each mystery.

When the recitation of the Rosary was finished, the Lady returned to the interior of the rock, and the cloud went with her.

This happened near the town of Lourdes in the southwestern corner of France on February 11, 1858. It was the first of nineteen appearances which our Lady was to make to Bernadette Soubirous.

The people of Lourdes had never wavered in their faith from the time they were first converted. They had endured the persecutions of the Roman emperors, the Vandals, the Arians and the Albigensians. When many other people in southern France succumbed to the Protestant Revolt, they held fast. They did not fall prey to the madness that swept most of France at the time of the French Revolution. Nor did they join the revolt against God which was led by the nineteenth-century intellectuals and liberals. They were expecially devoted to the Blessed Virgin.

Perhaps it was because of all this that Mary chose Lourdes as the scene of her apparitions in 1858.

As news of the apparitions spread throughout the countryside, larger and ever larger crowds were attracted to the grotto. Only Bernadette saw the Lady. The others saw nothing but a big black hole in the rocks. But the people saw Bernadette in her ecstasy and knew when our Lady was there. Most of the people believed Bernadette's story. A minority, including the government officials and other members of the "intelligentsia," scoffed at it. This minority was to cause trouble.

During the third apparition, Thursday, February 18, Mary said to Bernadette: "Will you do me the kindness of coming here every day for two weeks?" Bernadette said she would come. Then the Lady said, "I do not promise to make you happy in this world but in the next." Bernadette was to have many occasions to recall these words before she died.

At the sixth visit the Lady looked sad and said, "Pray for sinners." Very quickly, however, she smiled again.

At La Salette, Mary had wept the entire time. At Lourdes, she looked sad part of the time, but she frequently smiled. Could it be that the increased devotion to her and the definition of the doctrine of the Immaculate Conception had caused this change? It seems possible, but we cannot be sure.

During the eighth apparition, the crowd saw the girl move on her knees to the rosebush upon which the Lady had been standing. She prostrated herself at each step. Then turning to the people, she cried, "Penitence! Penitence!"

Our Lady revealed a spring of water during the ninth apparition. This water was to become world famous for the miraculous cures worked through it.

On Friday, February 26, the Lady said, "Bend low and kiss the ground for the sake of sinners." Bernadette did, and so did most of the spectators.

On March 2, the Lady requested that a chapel be built at the place of her appearance. She also said that she wished processions to come there.

March 25 was the feast of the Annunciation. On this day Bernadette had an uncontrollable desire to ask her visitor her name. Others had freely been calling her the Blessed Virgin, but to Bernadette she had been "the Lady."

The girl made her request, and the Lady merely smiled. Bernadette repeated the question, and then she asked it a third time.

"The Lady was standing above the rosebush," Bernadette tells us, "in a position very similar to that shown on the Miraculous Medal. At my third request, her face became very serious, and she seemed to bow down in an attitude of humility. Then she joined her hands and raised them to her breast. She looked up to heaven. Then slowly opening her hands and leaning toward me, she said to me in a voice

The Lady of the Grotto

vibrating with emotion: 'I am the Immaculate Conception.'"

These momentous words meant nothing to the ignorant peasant girl. She repeated them to her pastor, Abbé Peyramale. This priest had been very skeptical about the apparitions, but now his skepticism began to fade. She could not have made up those words!

Thus our Lady put heaven's approval on Pope Pius IX's act of just a little more than three years before. The whole story of the Fall of man, the Incarnation and the Redemption are implicit in her words: "I am the Immaculate Conception." So we have a new summary of Christian revelation in our own day. It came at a time when the world had almost forgotten the original revelation.

The local politicians watched the proceedings at Lourdes with uneasiness. They saw that the crowds were getting larger and larger, and crowds made them nervous. Mobs in Paris had overthrown the government in 1789, in 1830, and in 1848. Who could tell what a crowd in Lourdes might do in 1858? Conditions in the Third Empire were none too stable anyway.

Most of these local politicians called themselves Catholics. They attended Mass every Sunday and made their Easter duty. But they scoffed at the idea that the Blessed Virgin might really be appearing. Such things just did not happen in the enlightened nineteenth century.

The officials questioned Bernadette and threatened her, but they could get nowhere. They even threatened her father who had once been in jail on an unproved charge of theft. This did no good either.

When all else failed, they put a fence around the grotto. Then they placed police on guard to see that no one broke the fence. This, they were sure, would end the nonsense.

The fence did not prevent the Blessed Mother from appearing once more. Bernadette had to kneel on the other side of the river, but that made no difference. "I saw neither the river nor the barrier. The distance between the Lady and me appeared no greater than usual. I saw nothing but the Blessed Virgin, and never had I seen her so beautiful."

Mary smiled a tender farewell. After that, Bernadette saw her no more.

But that did not end the story of Lourdes. That was just the beginning.

So devoted were the people to Our Lady of Lourdes that they kept contriving to get past the fence which the authorities had erected. Many of them would be caught and fined, but then they would go back again. Finally they appealed to Louis Napoleon, who by this time had made himself Emperor Napoleon III, and was vacationing at nearby Biarritz. The Emperor was playing a clever game of balancing the religious-minded people against the enemies of religion. Apparently he thought it time to make a gesture in the direction of religion. He ordered the grotto opened. The happy pilgrims flocked there in large numbers.

A commission appointed by the Bishop of Tarbes, the diocese in which Lourdes was located, investigated Bernadette's story thoroughly. Every witness was questioned again and again. Bernadette told her story over and over and answered the same questions so many times that she would surely have lost her patience if she had been less of a saint. On January 18, 1862, the Bishop gave his approval to the devotion which had sprung up at Lourdes.

The growth of the shrine was rapid after that. Three great churches were built, one above the other, and a hospital for sick pilgrims. Today it is one of the most famous shrines in the world. A million and a half pilgrims go there every year. The devotion of these pilgrims is inspiring. So many people are praying at the same time and with such intensity that the air seems to be charged with prayer.

Bernadette later entered the convent. As our Lady had warned her, she found no happiness in this world. She suffered from the curiosity of visitors who wished to see "the saint," from the strictness of her superior who was of the mistaken opinion that Bernadette needed humbling, and from the tuberculosis that racked her body. Hundreds of pilgrims were being cured at Lourdes, but for Bernadette there was no cure.

She died on the afternoon of April 16, 1879. On her lips was a final prayer to her Lady of the grotto:

"Holy Mary, Mother of God, pray for me, a poor sinner, a poor sinner. . . ."

She was canonized on December 8, 1933.

Louis Bourriette, a blind stonecutter of Lourdes, was the first to discover the miraculous properties of the spring which our Lady had disclosed. After the thirteenth apparition, he asked his daughter to bring him some water from the spring. He bathed his eyes in it, and he could see for the first time in twenty years.

From that time to today thousands of persons have been cured of their afflictions by means of this water. Bathhouses, or *piscines,* have been erected so that pilgrims can bathe in it. Here as J. K. Huysmans says, "the Virgin turned into a bath attendant works; it is in this damp den, and with this putrid water that she operates."

So the Blessed Mother is very much present at Lourdes even though no one sees her. The people then are forcibly reminded of her presence when a person thought to have been incurably afflicted is suddenly cured. And this is still happening with amazing frequency in our own day.

At first most of the cures took place in the baths. Since 1905, when Pope Pius X advocated the practice of frequent Communion, more cures have taken place during the procession of the Blessed Sacrament than in the baths. Our Lady seems to be giving her approval to the action of another Pontiff.

In 1882, the Medical Bureau was established to investigate the cures taking place at Lourdes. This Bureau is Mary's challenge to the scientists and other intellectuals who say there is no such thing as the supernatural.

The Medical Bureau is open to all doctors who care to visit it. These doctors are invited to examine any pilgrims who claim to have been cured and they are free to go through the files of the Bureau. The visiting doctors are of all nationalities and of all religious persuasions.

The pilgrim who claims to have been cured must have a certificate from his local physician saying that he suffers from an incurable malady. This is all important. If he does not have this, or if it is too vague, he is not examined at all.

If his certificate is satisfactory, the pilgrim undergoes a most intense examination. The Bureau can make four possible decisions regarding his case: (1) no cure has taken place; (2) there has been only a partial cure; (3) the cure is complete, but some natural explanation might be given; (4) the cure is complete, and no natural explanation can be given.

It is only the last class in which the Bureau is further interested. The cure is not certified, however, unless the pilgrim comes back a year later for another examination. The Bureau wishes to be sure that there has been no relapse.

The word *miracle* is never used by the Medical Bureau. It merely certifies that a case which had been considered incurable has been cured. The Church's position on miracles is simple: Miracles are perfectly possible. God made the natural laws, and He can set them aside any time He wishes. It is seldom, however, that the Church says, "This is a miracle." The cures that have taken place at Lourdes are not certified as miracles although people all over the world are accustomed to refer to them as such.

Madame Biré, in 1908, had her sight restored although her optic nerves were atrophied. Oculists testified that according to all laws of science she was blind. Yet she could read the smallest type in the newspapers.

In 1875, Pierre de Rudder had an inch of bone created instantaneously in his left leg. No law of science can explain this. It happened at a Lourdes shrine in Belgium.

Father McSorley in his book, *Outline of Church History*, says that, in the 50 years following 1858, some 4000 medically miraculous cures were recorded at Lourdes. They are still taking place at the rate of about 15 per year.

Particularly fascinating is the perpetual miracle of Lourdes. At the hospital, the patients are segregated according to sex but not according to disease. Persons with many different

The Lady of the Grotto

kinds of sickness are packed together in one room as close as the beds will fit. At the baths, the water is changed only twice a day. Patients with running sores, with cancerous growths, and with every kind of infectious disease are plunged in one after another. Yet, neither in the hospitals nor in the baths has there ever been a case of a patient becoming worse or contracting a new disease.

At the beginning of this century a group of doctors tried to close Lourdes on the grounds that it was unsanitary. Their attempt failed because they could not find a single case of infection resulting from a visit to the shrine.

"At Lourdes," an English nurse once said, "we find our Lady putting microbes and bacilli firmly in their place." This flouting of the microbe, the suspension of the usual laws of nature has been going on for over a century.

What do men of "science" have to say about all this? Most of them simply refuse to recognize Lourdes. "Miracles are impossible," they say. And that is that. The late Dr. Alexis Carrel was asked to leave the University of Lyons because he said that one of his patients had been cured at Lourdes. When Dr. Carrel's book, *Man the Unknown*, appeared, *The New York Times* carried letters from other doctors who seemed to think that Carrel was the victim of superstition or that he had lost his mind.

The amazing thing about this is that Dr. Carrel had visited Lourdes several times and had personally examined pilgrims before and after their cures, while his adversaries were not even acquainted with the story of the shrine. Ordinarily, the rule of the scientist is: investigate, investigate, investigate. In the case of Lourdes, however, they refuse to investigate. Lourdes causes the scientists to act in a strangely unscientific manner.

Our Lady's challenge to the irreligious intellectuals still stands. "Come to Lourdes and see for yourselves," she seems to say. But most of them refuse the invitation. In refusing, they make themselves look ridiculous in the eyes of all fair-minded people.

This refusal is probably one reason why these intellectuals

do not have the following today that they did in 1858. Our Lady has held in check a movement that was threatening to sweep the world. Today, an even worse threat faces the world, and once again our Lady is fighting it.

More wonderful than the cures of the body that have taken place at Lourdes are the cures of the soul. "The trip to Lourdes is never made in vain," is a common saying among the bath attendants, the stretcher bearers and the hospital workers of Lourdes. Among the uncured pilgrims this is especially evident. A person who comes to the shrine to ask his own cure usually ends up by praying for other pilgrims instead of himself.

Fred Snite, the "man in the iron lung," received a great amount of publicity when he went to Lourdes in 1936. He was not cured, but he said the time spent in Lourdes was a period of great spiritual consolation to him, and he named one of his daughters Bernadette. Today it would be difficult to find a case of more perfect resignation. As he lay on his back in his iron lung, in obvious discomfort, he said, "I feel that for some reason God has selected me to suffer. I look upon this as my ticket to heaven."

This is the typical attitude of the uncured pilgrims. It is our Lady's gift to them.

But the spiritual consolation is not confined to the physically afflicted. All pilgrims who approach the shrine and pray go away refreshed in spirit, more devout to our Lady, closer to her Son.

Why did our Lady make her nineteen appearances at Lourdes in 1858? The obvious and most certain answer is: to save souls. That is always her purpose.

As to more specific aims, there was her request, repeated by Bernadette, for "Penitence! Penitence!" These words emphasized the sinful state of the world and the need for penance. This was a repetition of the message of La Salette.

Very much the same idea was expressed when she said, "Pray for sinners!" This was also to be an essential part of the Fatima message some years later.

The Lady of the Grotto

Our Lady emphasized the value of the Rosary by allowing the beads to slip through her fingers at each apparition while Bernadette said the prayers. She joined in the Gloria at the end of each decade, but she could not say the Hail Mary, because she could not pray to herself.

She told us that she is the Immaculate Conception and thus emphasized this important doctrine while confirming the action of Pius IX who had defined the dogma.

In the marvelous cures of Lourdes, she confounds those who say there is no such thing as the supernatural.

Last, but not least, she has left us the great shrine that is visited by a million and a half pilgrims every year—a great powerhouse of prayer. The number of spiritual cures that have taken place there cannot be estimated. The amount of religious fervor that has been generated cannot be computed in statistics. The shrine has had a profound effect upon France and upon the world.

Although visited by many pilgrims each year, until World War II Lourdes was virtually unknown in many parts of the world. Millions of non-Catholics in the United States, for example, had never heard of the shrine. To other millions Lourdes was merely a name.

Of the thousands of articles listed in the *Reader's Guide to Periodical Literature* in the twenty-one-year period between 1924 and 1945, only three were about Lourdes. All of them were unsatisfactory. One of the writers told about the wonderful "psychic" healings at Lourdes and never mentioned God or the Blessed Mother. Lourdes, with its great number of amazing cures, should have been the object of great attention on the part of magazine editors seeking interesting and important subjects. Instead, the shrine was virtually ignored, simply because the cures could not be explained by natural means.

Then an amazing thing happened.

Franz Werfel, an Austrian Jew, found himself in Lourdes in 1940. The French army had collapsed, and Werfel knew he was a marked man with the Nazis. He and his wife fled toward the border of Spain, but they found the border closed. Forced to reside in Lourdes, in hourly danger of being apprehended, Werfel listened with wonder to the story of Bernadette and the apparitions. "One day in my great distress," said Werfel, a professional writer, "I made a vow. I vowed that if I escaped from this desperate situation and reached the saving shore of America, I would put off all other tasks and sing, as best I could, the song of Bernadette."

When he made this promise, it seemed impossible that he should escape the Nazi net that was closing in on him. Yet, escape he did. He made good his promise and wrote the novel, *The Song of Bernadette*.

Amazingly, the book became a best seller overnight although the usual best seller in America was a novel of lust and illicit sex. Even more amazing, a movie was made from the book, and millions of people in America and other parts of the world sat in darkened theaters and watched the wondrous story of Bernadette unfold before their eyes.

The majority of people who read the book and saw the movie were not Catholics. A fair proportion of them were probably "moderns" who did not believe in miracles. What did these people think? It seems certain that the novel and the motion picture made a tremendous impression. For one thing, they prepared Americans for the story of Fatima which they were to hear soon afterward.

One cannot help but see the hand of God in all this: Of all the places in the world Franz Werfel might have chosen to visit, Lourdes would have been close to the bottom of the list. Although not a Christian, he was moved to write a story about the Mother of Christ. How could a nonbeliever write such a story with so much reverence? One searches in vain for an answer unless it is the one given by St. Louis Marie de Montfort: "God wishes that His holy Mother should be at present more known, more loved, more honored, than she has ever been."

10

Our Lady Hears Her Children
PONTMAIN, 1871

FOUR times within twenty-eight years our Lady had appeared in France. In Paris and at La Salette she had warned the people of calamities that would befall the country if they did not repent. At Lourdes she had made a moving request for "Penitence! Penitence!" Many of the French people heeded the warnings, but many more continued to go their sinful ways. Revolutions, crop failures, and famines came, but still the multitude did not get on its knees to pray.

Then, in 1870, came the worst disaster to befall France up to that time, the Franco-Prussian War. The Third Empire of Napoleon III was no match for the Prussians under Bismarck. Paris was surrounded on September 18, 1870. On December 27, its daily bombardment began. The Parisians were starving, desperate, in deadly fear of momentarily being blown to bits. People in other parts of France lived in terror of being invaded.

France was suffering for its impiety.

At last the people began to heed our Lady's repeated admonitions. In their hour of trial, millions of French people turned to Mary as their mother and protector. At Our Lady of Victories, La Salette and Lourdes they gathered by the hundreds to beg her to intercede with her Son for their beloved country. In their parish churches they prayed; in the privacy of their homes they said their Rosaries fervently, imploringly.

This does not mean that everyone in France became converted during this trying time. Most of those in positions of influence were still irreligious, and after the war they were to increase their hold on the country. But the ordinary people—peasants, workingmen, small shopkeepers—turned to Mary by the thousands. She heard their prayers and was touched.

The Barbedette family lived in the little village of Pontmain in the northwest corner of the department of Mayenne, on the borders of Brittany. There were three boys in the family. The eldest, Auguste, was with the army. The second, Eugène, was twelve years old; and the third, Joseph, was ten. The two boys rose at six o'clock every morning, did their household work, and then recited the Rosary for their absent brother. After breakfast they went to the village chapel to perform the Way of the Cross for their brother's intention. Then they served Mass. After Mass, they joined in the public prayers for France and her army.

Often the Curé prayed: "Let us add penance to our prayers, and then we may take courage. God will have pity on us. His mercy will surely come through Mary."

On the evening of January 17, 1871, a neighbor, Jeannette Detais, stopped to see the Barbedette family. She had received news of Auguste, the soldier. She found the father and the two boys working in the barn. While she was there, Eugène walked over and looked out the door. "I went just to see what the weather was like," was the only reason he could give later. Suddenly he stood transfixed. About twenty or twenty-five feet above a neighbor's house, he beheld what he called a *"grande, belle Dame."* Her dress was blue, much darker than the blue of the surrounding sky. It fell in loose folds; the sleeves were loose and hanging. She wore soft slippers fastened with golden ribbons. Over her head was a soft black veil and on that was a golden crown. Her face was small and beautiful. She appeared to be about eighteen or twenty years old. Her arms were at her sides and the palms of her hands were turned out. The Lady was smiling at the child.

As Eugène gazed in awe, Jeannette Detais, who had delivered her message, came to the door of the barn. Eugène said excitedly, "Look, Jeannette, and tell me what you see over Augustin Guidecog's house!"

"I can't see anything," she replied, gazing into the sky.

Eugène called his father and brother to come. The father could not see anything either, but Joseph exclaimed, "Oh, I see a beautiful Lady!" He described her dress in detail.

"My poor boys," said the father, "you don't see anything; if you did we could see it too." He told the boys to come back into the barn and finish their work. To Jeannette he said, "Be sure not to talk in the village of what the children say they see."

"Don't fear," answered Jeannette.

The boys returned to their work, but later they again looked out the door. The Lady was still there. Their mother was summoned, but she could not see anything. At her suggestion, the family knelt and said five Our Fathers and five Hail Marys. Then they went in to eat supper. As soon as supper was finished, the boys rushed back to the barn and fell to their knees.

"They still see the vision," said Mr. Barbedette.

Their mother asked them how tall the Lady was.

"Just the height of Sister Vitaline," they answered.

This gave Mrs. Barbedette an idea. "I'll ask Sister to come here," she said. "She is better than you. If you see anything, she will surely see it too."

The nun arrived, but she saw nothing unusual.

"How is it possible you don't see!" exclaimed Eugène. "The apparition is so brilliant. Don't you see those three bright stars forming a triangle?"

"Yes, I see them."

"Well, the highest star is right over the Lady's head; the other two are on a level with her elbows."

These three stars were seen by everyone that night. They were never seen again.

Mrs. Barbedette accompanied the nun back to the school. They found three little girl boarders sitting around the fire.

"Children," Sister said, "go with Mrs. Barbedette. She will show you something."

"What is it?" they inquired.

"I don't know, for I have not seen anything myself."

The three children set off. Before reaching the barn, eleven-year-old Francoise Richer exclaimed, "I see something bright above Augustin Guidecog's house!"

When they reached the barn door, Francoise and nine-year-old Jeanne-Marie Lebossè cried out together, "Oh, the beautiful Lady, with her blue dress and golden stars!" They described the vision exactly as the Barbedette boys had. The third child saw nothing.

The news spread rapidly, and soon about eighty people—virtually the entire population of the village—had assembled at the barn door. The Curé came with them. A delicate little six-year-old boy, Eugène Friteau, beheld the vision, but he was not allowed to stay long in the cold air. He died a few months later. A two-year-old girl—daughter of Boitin, the shoemaker—began clapping her hands as soon as she was in front of the barn door. "Le Jésus! Le Jésus," she exclaimed. These were the only words she knew how to describe such a sight.

A small red cross was formed over our Lady's heart. The apparition became surrounded by a frame or circle of a darker blue than the robe. Four sockets were attached to the inside of the frame. Each socket held an unlighted candle. The four children all related these wonders.

One man said that if he had a telescope he was sure that he too could see what the children were seeing. Mrs. Barbedette brought him one, but still he could see nothing.

The children announced that the Lady had stopped smiling and was looking sad. The Curé said, "If the children only are privileged to behold the celestial vision, it is because they are more worthy than we are."

He then suggested that they pray. Everyone knelt down, some in the barn, others outside. No one seemed to mind

Our Lady Hears Her Children

the cold or the deep snow. Sister Mary Edward led in the recitation of the Rosary.

Suddenly the vision began to grow larger. "She is twice as tall as Sister Vitaline now!" the children exclaimed. The blue circle extended in proportion. The stars of the sky appeared to move aside, as if to allow the Lady to rise. Then they ranged themselves beneath her feet, outside the frame. There were about forty of these stars, and they were visible only to the children. Soon other stars appeared at a distance from the apparition and they fastened themselves on the dress.

"Oh, there are so many stars the Blessed Virgin will soon be gilt all over," one of the children exclaimed.

Our Lady smiled during the recitation of the Rosary. Sometimes her mouth opened and the children could see her teeth which were brilliantly white.

When the Rosary was completed, Sister Mary Edward began the *Magnificat*. Before the first verse was sung the children cried out, "Something new is coming!"

A plain white band had unrolled itself. It was about a yard wide and it extended the length of the roof of the house. The first stroke of a letter appeared, then the entire letter. The letter was in gold.

"It's an M!" the children cried. "And now there is another letter—it is an A!"

The word *Mais* was formed. Other letters appeared. Before the *Magnificat* was concluded the children read *Mais priez, mes enfants* (But pray, my children).

A villager returning from a neighboring town heard the singing and exclaimed, "You do well to pray to the good God! The Prussians are at Laval!"

"If they were at the entrance of the village," several villagers answered, "we should have no fear now!"

When the man was told of the apparition, he joined the group in their prayers.

They sang the litany and more letters appeared. The new message was, *Dieu vous exaucera en peu de temps* (God will hear you in a little while).

Next the *Inviolata* was sung. A second line of letters began to appear on the band. The children read *Mon fils* (My Son).

"It is really the Blessed Virgin," they cried. "Yes, yes, it is Mary! It is Mary!"

The emotion that filled the hearts of all present cannot be described. Many shed tears.

When the sentence was completed it was *Mon fils se laisse toucher* (My Son permits Himself to be moved).

This was Mary's message of hope and consolation to her afflicted children of France. No words could have been more welcome.

At the Curé's suggestion the people sang the canticle *Mère de l'Espérance* (Mother of Hope). At the end of the canticle, the words faded away.

After another canticle, the vision changed again. A red crucifix appeared near our Lady. She took it in her hands and held it out toward the children. At the top of the cross appeared the words *Jésus Christ* in red letters on a white band. A star shot up from beneath the Virgin's feet, lighted the candle at the lower left, then the top one, and then it passed over her head and lit the two candles at the right side. It rose again, passed outside the blue circle and came to a stop over Mary's head. As the crowd sang another hymn, the crucifix disappeared and the vision assumed the attitude of our Lady on the Miraculous Medal. On each of the shoulders were seen a small white cross about eight inches high.

When the hymn was finished the Curé said: "Now let us all recite our evening prayers."

A white veil rose from beneath Mary's feet. Little by little, the vision was hidden from view. The children gazed lovingly as she disappeared.

"Do you still see anything?" asked the priest.

"No, Monsieur le Curé. All is over."

It was a quarter past nine. The apparition had lasted more than three hours.

The Prussians, who had been at Laval only a few miles

away, never reached Pontmain. For some unexplained reason, they turned back before they got there.

The armistice was signed on January 27, just ten days after the apparition. France lost the war and had to pay a heavy indemnity, but the bloodshed was over.

Eugène became a secular priest and was made rector of Chatillon-sur-Colmont. He lived until 1927. Francoise Richer, though not a nun, worked in the service of Abbé Barbedette. She died in 1915. Joseph became an Oblate of Mary Immaculate, the order that was put in charge of the shrine at Pontmain. He died at the house of his Congregation in 1930. Jeanne-Marie became a religious of the Holy Family nuns and died at Bordeaux in 1933.

On February 2, 1872, the Bishop of Laval approved the devotion to *Notre Dame d'Espérance de Pontmain*. The barn was converted into an oratory. A great twin-spired church rose on the spot of the apparitions, and pilgrims went there in large numbers. As is usual in such cases, a number of cures took place.

Pontmain will always be remembered by great numbers of French people as the place where our Lady brought them her message of hope in the midst of their afflictions.

Today, the whole world can be compared to the France of 1871, with half of it conquered and the other half in terror of being conquered. But there is no need for fear, really. We can pray with perfect confidence to Our Lady of Hope.

11

"I Choose the Little Ones and the Weak"
PELLEVOISIN, 1876

ESTELLE FAGUETTE, lady's maid to the Countess Arthur de La Rouchefoucauld, became very ill in Paris in May, 1875. She was admitted to a hospital there, and the doctors diagnosed her illness as an advanced case of consumption. She was also suffering from a tumor which she had had for ten years. The doctors said there was no hope for her. Estelle was thirty-two years old at the time.

A short time later, she was moved to a house owned by her employers in Pellevoisin in the diocese of Bourges.

In September, 1875, Estelle wrote a letter to the Blessed Virgin. A new shrine to Our Lady of Lourdes had been erected near Pellevoisin. She asked a friend to take her letter to the shrine and hide it in the stones at the feet of the Virgin's statue.

For a long time she could not resign herself to the thought of dying. "It's not fair," she said to herself. "God can't take me now. I'm the only support of my mother and father and little orphan niece. How would they get along without me?"

After a long struggle with herself, she was able to make an act of complete resignation. "My God," she prayed, "in expiation of my sins, let me suffer. Behold, I am ready; strike as it shall please You; only give me courage, patience, and

"I Choose the Little Ones"

resignation to Your holy will. If groans escape from my lips, receive them as prayers from my heart to Yours."

On February 10, 1876, the doctor said she had only a few hours to live. When told that she could keep nothing on her stomach, he said, "It is useless to torture her for the short time she has to live."

She was still alive on Tuesday, February 15, although she was expected to die momentarily. That morning she told the priest that the Blessed Virgin had appeared to her during the night and that she would be either dead or cured by the following Saturday. The next day she told the priest that she had seen the Virgin again and that she would be cured Saturday. On Thursday morning she emphatically repeated the statement to the priest and to several other people.

On Friday night she seemed to be in her last agony. The priest wished to hear her confession, but she said she would wait until the next day when she would be well. He was very uneasy about this, but he left without hearing her confession.

On Saturday morning she told the priest that she felt as if she had been cured but that she could not move her right arm. She had lost the use of it four or five days earlier. The priest gave her Holy Communion. Then he said to her: "My poor Estelle, you have edified us by your courage and resignation. Be full of confidence now, and to prove to us that what you have said is not illusion, make the Sign of the Cross with your right hand."

Estelle raised the hand, and the seven or eight people present saw her make the Sign of the Cross without the least difficulty.

Later that day she got up, dressed herself, ate a meal, and talked happily with her friends. The consumption was gone. The tumor, which had grown larger during her illness, had disappeared completely. The doctors who had been attending her said the cure could not have come from natural causes.

Estelle lived for many years after that and never had a relapse. In fact, her health remained better than it had been before her illness.

The next day Estelle wrote her account of the five apparitions. On the night of the 14th, she says, she was trying to get some rest "when suddenly the demon appeared at the foot of my bed. He was horrible and at once began to make grimaces at me. Scarcely had I seen him when our Blessed Lady appeared on the other side at the corner of my bed. She wore a pure white woolen veil, which fell in three folds. I can never describe how beautiful she was. Her features were regular, her color white and rose tint, rather pale. Her large gentle eyes reassured me somewhat but not completely. The demon, perceiving the Blessed Virgin, drew back, dragging the curtain and the iron rod of my bed. This increased my terror which became unendurable. I crouched down in bed. He did not speak but turned his back to me.

"The Blessed Virgin said to him sharply: 'What brings you here? Do you not see that she wears my livery, and that of my Son?' He disappeared gesticulating. Then she turned to me and said gently, 'Fear nothing; you are my daughter.' Then I remembered that from the age of fourteen I have been a Child of Mary. I now felt less fear.

"She said to me gently: 'Have courage; be patient; my Son will allow Himself to be prevailed upon. You will suffer five days longer in honor of the five wounds of my Son. On Saturday, you will be either dead or cured. If my Son restores you to life, I wish you to publish my glory.'"

Our Lady told Estelle the next night that she was to be cured on Saturday. "If my Son has allowed Himself to be prevailed upon, it is because of your resignation and your patience." Then our Lady reproved Estelle for the faults she had committed during her past life. They had seemed to be very small faults when she committed them, but now she saw that any sin is big in the eyes of God.

"I would have longed to cry out for pardon, but could not; my grief overcame me. . . . Oh, how sad I felt."

The next night our Lady reassured Estelle. "By your resignation you have expiated your faults. . . . I am all merciful. . . . Your good works and fervent prayers have touched my mother's heart. Among others that little letter you wrote to me in September. What moved me were the words: 'See the sorrow of my parents. If I fail them they are on the eve of begging bread. Remember, then, what you suffered when your Son Jesus was stretched out upon the Cross.'"

The fourth appearance was much like the first three.

Estelle asked our Lady on the fifth if she should change her state in life. "One can be saved in every state," was the answer. "Where you are, you can do a great deal of good, and you can publish my glory. What afflicts me most is the want of respect shown by some people to my divine Son in Holy Communion and the attitude taken for prayer, when at the same time the mind continues occupied with other things. I say this for people who pretend to be pious."

After our Lady disappeared that night, Estelle was cured.

On July 1, Estelle was kneeling in front of the fireplace when our Lady appeared for a sixth time. "What beauty! What sweetness! The ends of her cincture nearly reached the hem of her dress. She was all in white and remained standing.... When I first saw her, she had her arms stretched out and from her hands there fell drops like rain. She looked at something fixedly, then taking one of the tassels of her cincture, she raised it to her breast on which she crossed her hands. She smiled, and, looking at me, said: 'Be calm, my child; have patience; you will have sorrows, but I will be with you.'"

The following night, our Lady said that the Heart of her Son bears so much love for her "that He cannot refuse me any requests." She also said, "I have come especially for the conversion of sinners."

On July 3, our Lady returned, but her visit was short. She did not come again until September 9. "For a long time, the treasures of my Son have been open," she said. "Let them pray." Here Estelle said she was given to understand that Jesus had shown, through St. Margaret Mary, the glory and the power of the devotion of His Most Sacred Heart.

The Blessed Mother raised a small piece of woolen cloth which she wore on her breast. Estelle saw a red heart on it.

She knew it was a Scapular of the Sacred Heart. Our Lady said, holding it up, "I love this devotion." She paused and added, "It is here I will be honored."

A week later the Blessed Virgin again paid Estelle a short visit. "Let them pray," she said. "I show them the example."

"In the Church there is not the calm I desire," our Lady said on September 15. She sighed and shook her head. "There is something else, then." Estelle understood that there was some discord. Our Lady continued, "Let them pray and let them have confidence in me."

She looked very sad as she added, "And France, what have I not done for her? How many warnings, and yet she refused to listen! I can no longer restrain my Son." She appeared deeply moved as she said, "France will suffer." She put special emphasis on these words.

Estelle was struck by the thought that if she repeated these words no one would believe her. The Blessed Virgin knew what she was thinking.

"I have arranged all beforehand. So much the worse for those who may not be willing to believe you. Later on, they will recognize the truth of my words."

The twelfth apparition took place on November 1. "She appeared as usual, with her arms stretched out and wearing the scapular she had shown me on September 8. As usual, also, she gazed intently at something I could not see, then looked around on all sides. She did not speak, but at last, casting her eyes on me, with an expression of great kindness, she disappeared."

"I choose the little ones and the weak for my glory," said our Lady during the thirteenth apparition, November 5.

"You have not lost your time today; you have worked for me," she said on November 11. Estelle had made a scapular that day.

The fifteenth and last apparition took place on the feast of the Immaculate Conception, 1876.

"Recall to mind all my words," said our Lady.

Through Estelle's mind flashed everything Mary had said.

"My child, remember my words. Repeat them often. They

will strengthen you and console you in your trials. You will see me no more."

In the distance, to the left of the Blessed Virgin, Estelle saw a crowd of persons of all classes who threatened her and made angry gestures at her. She felt a little frightened.

Our Lady smiled. "You have nothing to fear from these. I have chosen you to publish my glory and to spread this devotion." She held out the scapular. "You will go to the prelate. You will present to him the model scapular you have made. Tell him that he is to help you with all his power and that nothing will be more acceptable to me than to see this livery on each of my children, and that they all endeavor to repair the outrages received by my divine Son in the Sacrament of His love. See the graces I will bestow on those who will wear it with confidence, and who will assist in propagating it."

"While speaking," said Estelle, "the Blessed Virgin stretched out her hands and from these there fell drops of rain. In each drop I seemed to read such graces as piety, salvation, confidence, conversion, health."

Our Lady said: "These graces are from my divine Son; I take them from His Heart; He can refuse me nothing."

A few minutes later she disappeared, and Estelle saw her no more on this earth.

In May, 1894, Pope Leo XIII approved the Archconfraternity of Our Mother All Merciful of Pellevoisin. The Congregation of Rites approved the Scapular of the Sacred Heart in a decree dated April 4, 1900. The rights concerning the scapular were conferred on the Superior-General of the Oblates of Mary Immaculate, with the power of delegating those rights not only to priests of his congregation but to all others who might apply for them.

The devotion to Our Lady of Pellevoisin came to the United States in 1934, when a confraternity was established at St. Paul's Church, East 117th St., New York City. On November 18, 1934, the Shrine of Our Lady of Pellevoisin was blessed at St. Paul's and the first public services were held.

Estelle Faguette continued to live at Pellevoisin after the apparitions. The bitter trials foretold by our Lady came to pass. About 1900, the whole story of Pellevoisin was bitterly attacked, and this caused Estelle much anguish. Long afterward, the man behind the attack confessed and retracted. Estelle lived until 1929.

It is remarkable that the apparitions of Pellevoisin are not more widely known. Our Lady covered a large number of subjects, and her words deserve close study.

"I wish you to publish my glory," she said. Mary, the maid of Nazareth, was the humblest of creatures. At first it seems strange that she should ask to have her glory published. When we reflect upon the matter we realize it is not for her own sake that she wishes this; it is for our sakes. She wishes to become better known that she might lead us to her Son.

A series of sermons could be preached on every sentence she uttered.

"If my Son has allowed Himself to be prevailed upon, it is because of your resignation and patience."

"I am all merciful. . . . Your good works and fervent prayers have touched my mother's heart."

"One can be saved in every state (of life)."

"What afflicts me most is the want of respect shown by some people to my divine Son in Holy Communion and the attitude taken for prayer when at the same time the mind continues occupied with other things. I say this for people who pretend to be pious."

"His heart bears so much love for me, that He cannot refuse me any requests."

"I am come especially for the conversion of sinners."

"For a long time the treasures of my Son have been open; let them pray."

"I love this devotion," she said of the Scapular of the Sacred Heart.

"And France, what have I not done for her? How many

warnings, and yet she has refused to listen! I can no longer restrain my Son. France will suffer."

And so we find that in the seventh of our major series of apparitions, our Lady was still concerned about France. She had indeed warned the country many times, and many punishments had come. Her Son had allowed Himself to be touched during the Franco-Prussian War, but now only five years later, France was offending Him again. The words "I can no longer restrain my Son" are strikingly similar to the words she had used at La Salette.

"I choose the little ones and the weak for my glory," our Lady also said at Pellevoisin.

We know how true this is when we consider the persons to whom she had appeared in our times: Estelle herself, Catherine Labouré, Sister Bisqueyburu, the two cowherds of La Salette, Bernadette of Lourdes, the simple villagers of Pontmain, the shepherd children of Fatima. No one who was rich and powerful or high in the world's esteem. Always "the little ones and the weak."

At Paris and at Blangy, Mary had pictured her graces as rays of light; at Pellevoisin, she showed them as drops of rain. Both figures represent her role as Mediatrix of All Graces and emphasize the fact that she is ready to shower her graces on all of us. All we need do is ask.

12

The Picture from the Secondhand Store
POMPEII, 1875-1876

POMPEII was a great and prosperous city in Roman times when it was destroyed by an eruption of Vesuvius. It was far from that in October, 1872, when Bartolo Long went there to attend to property owned by his wife, the Countess of Fusco. The region was described in the official record as "a most dangerous resort of bold and infamous robbers."

Bartolo Long had been raised and educated as a Catholic, but he had become involved with spiritualism. Weak as he was in his own faith, he was appalled by what he saw at Pompeii. There was only one little chapel and one parish priest for the entire region, yet this was sufficient for the few people who still went to church. Most of the inhabitants had fallen victim to superstition; fear of the evil eye was rampant.

On October 9, Bartolo was walking through one of the most desolate parts of the desolate region. His own doubts were assailing him again. Should he give up the faith in which he had been raised? Suddenly he became aware that a voice was speaking to him:

"If you seek salvation, promulgate the Rosary. This is Mary's own promise."

Bartolo answered: "If it is true that thou didst promise St. Dominic that whosoever should promulgate thy Rosary should

The Picture from the Secondhand Store 73

be saved, then shall I be saved, for I will not leave this valley until I have propagated thy Rosary."

The angelus rang out from the distant church, and Bartolo fell to his knees to confirm his pledge.

Bartolo's attempts to found a Rosary confraternity met with little success at first, but by 1875 he had made a promising start. In that year the Bishop of Nola was won over. Visiting the little chapel, the Bishop said, "You wish to raise an altar here in honor of the Rosary? I propose we raise not an altar but a church!" Then pointing to a field opposite he added, "That is where a basilica will be raised for Pompeii!"

Bartolo wished to find a picture that would encourage the peasants in the daily recitation of the Rosary. He told the people that he would have a picture for them by the time they completed a three-day mission. He found a picture of Our Lady of the Rosary which he liked, but he was very much disappointed when he learned that the picture did not meet the requirement of Canon Law. Bartolo hurried to Naples to secure another picture. He could find none that cost less than 400 francs, a price which he could not afford. What would he do? He had promised his people a picture.

A friend in Naples gave him a picture which he had bought in a secondhand shop for three francs. Bartolo looked at it with a sinking heart. It met the requirements of Canon Law all right, but it violated every aesthetic principle.

"Not only was it worm-eaten," said Bartolo, "but the face of the Madonna was that of a coarse, rough country woman ... a piece of canvas was missing just above her head. . . . Her mantle was cracked. Nothing can be said of the hideousness of the other figures. St. Dominic looked like a street idiot. To our Lady's left was a St. Rose. This later I had changed to a St. Catherine of Siena. . . I hesitated whether to refuse the gift or to accept. I had promised a picture unconditionally for that evening. I took it."

The picture was too big for Bartolo to carry by hand, so he gave it to a delivery man who made regular trips between Pompeii and Naples. The picture, wrapped in a sheet, was carried to the chapel on top of a load of manure which was to be delivered to a nearby farm. Thus, Our Lady of Pompeii arrived at her chosen shrine. For this picture became the focal point of devotion at the chapel.

Bartolo bought the picture in November, 1875. In January, 1876, it was partially restored in time for the canonical foundation of the Confraternity.

In Naples, meanwhile. Clorinda Lucarelli, a child of twelve, lay at the point of death. She was a victim of epilepsy and had been given up by the doctors. Clorinda's aunt and guardian heard of the new Rosary Confraternity and promised to help in the building of a new church if the child got well. The girl was restored to complete health on the very day the picture was re-exposed for veneration. Doctors who had examined her previously said that her recovery was not due to any medical treatment.

The relatives of Concetta Vasterilla, who was dying in agony, made a similar promise to Our Lady of Pompeii. She too recovered swiftly and completely.

Father Anthony Varone was cured of a fearful gangrenous malady the same day that he put his trust in Our Lady of Pompeii. All his symptoms vanished at once, and the next morning he rose to say Mass.

All of these cures took place in the early months of 1876.

The cornerstone of the new church was laid on May 8 of that year. Exactly a month later, Madame Giovannina Muta, who lay in the last stages of consumption, appealed to Our Lady of Pompeii. As she lay in bed she saw an exact replica of the picture in the chapel, although she had never seen the original. Our Lady gazed upon her and then threw toward her a kind of white ribbon on which was the message: "The Virgin of Pompeii grants your request, Giovannina Muta." She was cured immediately.

The cures attributed to Our Lady of Pompeii could be extended indefinitely. There is one, however, that deserves special mention.

The Picture from the Secondhand Store

Fortuna Agrelli, a girl of Naples, had been ill for thirteen months. She suffered intense pain. Her father had called in the most celebrated doctors but they had declared her incurable. On February 16, 1884, she and some of her relatives began a novena of Rosaries.

On March 3, our Lady appeared to Fortuna as the Virgin of Pompeii. She was sitting on a high throne, and the infant Jesus was on her lap. She held a rosary in her hand. She was accompanied by St. Dominic and St. Catherine of Siena. The throne was profusely decorated with flowers. The beauty of our Lady was marvelous. She looked at Fortuna with motherly tenderness.

"Queen of the Holy Rosary," Fortuna said, "be gracious to me; restore me to health. I have already prayed to thee in a novena, O Mary, but have not yet experienced the aid. I am so anxious to be cured!"

"Child," said the Blessed Virgin, "thou has invoked me by various titles and hast always obtained favors from me. Now, since thou hast called me by the title so pleasing to me, 'Queen of the Holy Rosary,' I can no longer refuse the favor thou dost petition; for this name is most precious and dear to me. Make three novenas, and thou shalt obtain all."

Fortuna obeyed, and she was cured.

Soon after that, our Lady appeared again. This time she said, "Whosoever desires to obtain favors from me should make three novenas of the prayers of the Rosary in petition and three novenas in thanksgiving."

This was the origin of the devotion of the Rosary Novenas to Our Lady, sometimes called the Irresistible Novena. The devotion calls for five decades of the Rosary each day for 27 days in petition to be followed by five decades a day for 27 days in thanksgiving—54 days in all. It is a powerful form of prayer; we have our Lady's word for it.

The new church at Pompeii was completed and then enlarged. In May, 1891, it was consecrated by Cardinal La

Valletta, as Papal Legate for Pope Leo XIII. A large orphanage was built beside it and a hospice for pilgrims.

In 1906 Bartolo Long, who lived to see the marvelous results for the Confraternity he had originated, deeded his property at Pompeii to the Holy See. Under the Lateran Treaty of 1929, the church and surrounding property became directly subject to Vatican City State. In 1934, at the command of Pope Pius XI, a new basilica was begun on the spot that had been pointed out by the Bishop 59 years before. The basilica was completed in 1939.

The picture from the secondhand store is today enshrined in a frame of gold and encrusted with diamonds and gems which hide all but the faces of our Lady, the saints and the Holy Child. Crowds pray before it each day, beseeching our Lady for her graces. Pilgrims were especially fervent in the trying days of World War II and during the troubled years that have followed. Our Lady of Pompeii has been a great consolation to the Italians in their troubles.

Pompeii, like the other principal manifestations of our Lady since 1830, seems a forerunner of Fatima. The Rosary is the central devotion of Pompeii, and at Fatima the Blessed Mother came to ask us to "say the Rosary every day."

The Rosary will be a powerful weapon in restoring the world to Christ.

13

Our Lady in Ireland
KNOCK, 1879

It RAINED all day in the little village of Knock in County Mayo, Ireland, on that memorable twenty-first day of August in 1879.

At seven o'clock that evening, fifteen-year-old Margaret Beirne was sent to lock up the church. After she had done so, she noticed a brightness over the building. This was most strange, especially on a rainy day, but Margaret was not curious enough to investigate the matter.

A little later Mary McLoughlin, the priest's housekeeper, passed within a short distance of the church. She was on her way to see Mrs. Beirne and her daughter Mary, both of whom had just returned from a short trip. Miss McLoughlin noticed a strange light at the south gable of the church. In the light she saw three figures representing the Blessed Virgin, St. Joseph and a bishop. Standing beside the figures was an altar on which were a cross and a lamb. She decided that the pastor had probably bought some new statues in Dublin. She did not mention the incident while at the Beirne home.

About eight or a quarter after, she decided that it was time to go home. Mary Beirne, Margaret's older sister, offered to walk part way with her. When they came within view of the church gable, they saw the light and the figures.

"Oh, look at the statues!" Mary Beirne exclaimed. "Why didn't you tell me that Father got new statues for the chapel?"

Mary McLoughlin answered that she knew nothing about them.

When they came closer, Mary Berine cried out, "They're not statues. They're moving. It's the Blessed Virgin!" And she ran home to get her mother and her brother.

The news spread and other people also came to see. Fourteen persons in all saw the figures. A fifteenth witness, Patrick Walsh, lived half a mile from the chapel. From his fields he saw a large globe of golden light at the southern gable. He had never before seen such a brilliant light. The next day he inquired about it and learned of the apparitions.

The other fourteen people all testified that they saw the Blessed Virgin clothed in white garments, wearing a large brilliant crown. Her hands were raised as if in prayer and her eyes were turned toward heaven.

At Mary's right was St. Joseph. His head was inclined toward the Blessed Virgin as if paying her respect. He was somewhat aged, with a gray beard and grayish hair. At Mary's left stood St. John the Evangelist, vested as a bishop, his left hand holding a book and his right hand raised as if in preaching. To the left of St. John was an altar on which were a cross and a young lamb. One witness said he saw angels' wings hovering about this altar.

The figures stood out from the gable wall and were about a foot and a half or two feet above the ground. The gable was bathed in a cloud of light.

The vision lasted for about two hours. The rain was falling all the while, but the figures and the spot above which they stood were perfectly dry.

Fourteen-year-old Patrick Hill, one of the witnesses, tells us that "the figures were full round as if they had a body and life. They said nothing; but as we approached them they seemed to go back a little toward the gable."

Of our Lady he says: "I distinctly beheld the Blessed Virgin Mary, life size, standing about two feet or so above the ground, clothed in white robes that were fastened at the neck; her hands were raised to the height of the shoulders, as if in prayer, with the palms facing one another, but slanting inward toward the face. . . . Her eyes were turned toward heaven. She wore a brilliant crown . . . and over the

Our Lady in Ireland 79

forehead where the crown fitted the brow, a beautiful rose. The crown appeared brilliant and of a golden brightness. . . . The upper parts of the crown appeared to be a series of sparkles, or glittering crosses. I saw her eyes, the balls, the pupils and the iris of each. I noticed her hands especially, and face. . . . The robes came only as far as the ankles. I saw the feet and the ankles; one foot, the right, was slightly in advance of the other.

"At times . . . all the figures appeared to move out and again to go backward. I went up very near. One old woman went up and embraced the Virgin's feet, and she found nothing in her arms or hands. They receded, she said, from her."

Patrick Hill also tells us that he came so close to the figure of St. John "that I looked into the book. I saw the lines and the letters."

Mary McLoughlin ran to tell the priest, Archdeacon Bartholomew Cavanagh, about the figures. He understood her to say that they had disappeared, and he did not go out to look. "I have regretted ever since that I neglected to do so. I shall always feel sorry that a sight of the apparitions has been denied me, but God may will that the testimony to His Blessed Mother's presence should come from the simple faithful and not through priests."

Mary came to a country which had remained faithful through centuries of trials and persecutions. Ireland was poverty stricken, with most of its people living in almost unbelievable squalor. The Catholic Emancipation Act of 1829 had officially ended three centuries of persecution of the Church. During that time thousands of persons had been put to death for their religion. After 1829, the persecution simply took a more insidious form. Catholics were no longer slaughtered, but they were offered bribes of food and money to abandon their religion and to send their children to non-Catholic schools. It must have been difficult for a man to refuse such a bribe in the famine years when he saw the thin emaciated faces of his wife and children, but the vast majority of people preferred starvation to renouncing their faith.

The year 1847 was one of the blackest in Ireland's history. That was the year of the dread potato famine, when thousands died of starvation and thousands of others were forced to leave the country. When it was over, the population of Ireland was half of what it had been, and even today it is much smaller than it was before 1847. There were failures of the potato crop again in 1877, 1878, and 1879.

Typhus fever struck down many of those who escaped death by starvation. At the Cross graveyard in north Mayo there were from five to fifteen funerals a day. Because the people were so poor and because so many died, most of them had to be buried without coffins.

Famine, fever, abject poverty, cruel persecution—surely a nation could bear no more. It seemed that the Irish race was destined to be wiped out.

Just when conditions were at their worst, Mary appeared at Knock.

The Church has not yet pronounced upon this apparition. The facts related at the beginning of this chapter are from purely human testimony. The testimony seems most convincing. The fact that the Knock devotion is still growing after a century is a fair indication that it is not based on a delusion. So is the fact that many remarkable cures have taken place at the shrine and are still taking place.

Within seven weeks of the apparition, the Archbishop of Tuam, the Most Reverend John MacHale, appointed a commission of three priests to investigate. They questioned the witnesses separately and found that their stories agreed in practically all details. The witnesses ranged in age from six-year-old John Curry to seventy-five-year-old Bridget Trench, the lady who had tried to kiss the feet of the Virgin. All were known to be of good character and not the kind who would manufacture such a story. The commission reported that "the testimony of all, taken as a whole, was trustworthy and satisfactory."

Our Lady in Ireland

Despite this favorable report, the Archbishop decided to wait. In 1936, Archbishop Gilmartin appointed another commission. Evidence was taken from the two surviving witnesses as well as from persons claiming to have been cured at the shrine. A full statement was forwarded to Rome, but as yet there has been no formal sanction of the shrine.

One of the witnesses who lived long enough to testify before both commissions was Mrs. O'Connell, the former Mary Beirne. She was always ready to talk to any visitors and was interviewed numerous times through the years. She talked to newspaper correspondents, archbishops, bishops, and ordinary pilgrims. All were impressed by her candor and her sincerity. In 1936, in a sworn statement, she confirmed her story of 1879. She was grievously ill at the time. After her statement was read to her, she made this addition: "I make this statement on my deathbed, knowing I am about to go before God."

She died six weeks later, on October 19, 1936.

Every possible natural explanation of the figures has been investigated. It was thought that perhaps someone had projected them with a magic lantern. A commission tried this out but could find no possible way of projecting the images into the air. It will be remembered that they stood out a short distance from the gable.

Newspaper correspondents from England also tried out the magic-lantern idea. They were fair enough to admit that "in the situation a magic lantern was not possible."

It was suggested that the figures might have been the work of an artist who used phosphorescent paint. When the vision was first seen, however, it was still daylight, and phosphorous would not have been visible.

A story that gained wide circulation was that one of the witnesses was addicted to drink. This was proved to be false. It would not have explained anything anyway. There were fifteen witnesses to the apparition, and no one has suggested that all fifteen were under the influence of alcohol.

Cures began taking place at Knock soon after the apparition, and Archdeacon Cavanagh kept a record of them. Here is his account of the first recorded cure:

"On the 31st of August 1879 (ten days after the apparition), a girl aged twelve years was cured while attending Mass at Knock. Her parents, Mr. and Mrs. P. J. Gordon of Claremorris, attested that Delia had suffered intensely all her life from deafness and violent pains in her left ear. Several times each week they had to get up in the night to try to relieve the awful pain by various remedies. They took her on a pilgrimage to Knock. While attending Mass there, the pain attacked Delia so badly that she began to cry, and Mrs. Gordon had to bring her outside where they knelt in prayer before the place where the apparition was seen. Mrs. Gordon picked out a piece of cement from the gable, made the Sign of the Cross over it and placed it in the afflicted ear. Almost immediately the pain completely disappeared never to return and no trace of deafness remained. Her general health improved rapidly and in a very short time she became the picture of health and strength."

There were thousands of such cures, but they were not scientifically investigated until 1936. In that year the Medical Bureau was established. This Bureau is modeled after the one at Lourdes. Now the world is offered scientific proof of the cures that take place at Knock. Doctors who have no religion at all have admitted that the Bureau is run in an impartial manner and that every case is investigated carefully.

Pilgrimages to Knock began soon after the apparition and have continued ever since. About 250,000 pilgrims go there every year. This is a remarkable number in view of the fact that Knock has no train or bus service and that the shrine has not been formally approved by the Holy See. During World War II, 10,000 Masses were offered in honor of Our Lady of Knock for the intention of keeping Ireland at peace. Many of the people credit Our Lady of Knock with keeping Ireland out of the war just as the Portuguese people give credit to Our Lady of Fatima for keeping their country at peace.

Our Lady in Ireland

What did the apparition mean? At Paris, La Salette, Lourdes, and Fatima, our Lady spoke. We have her own words on record. At Knock, she said nothing. Yet we can be certain that she did not appear without an important purpose.

In most of Europe—in most of the world, for that matter—the majority of people had turned away from God. Even in such supposedly Catholic countries as Spain, France, Italy and Portugal, men were worshiping reason and science instead of God. But in Ireland, the people had clung to their faith despite three and a half centuries of bitter persecution. They had retained their love for the Mass during all the years that the Mass had been officially outlawed. They had never faltered in their devotion to the Blessed Mother, a devotion that had been brought to them by St. Patrick himself. Every night, in thousands of miserable huts all over the island, families had knelt on the dirt floors to say the Rosary together.

So it seems likely that Mary appeared in Ireland to reward the people for their devotion and to comfort them in their afflictions. Most authorities on Knock point out that Mary was wearing a crown. Thus, they say, she represented herself as Queen of Heaven, Queen of Ireland, Mediatrix of All Graces.

"The mission of Mary to Knock was not one of rebuke or complaint against our people, as was the case at La Salette and Lourdes, against the prevailing vices and abuses that were shaking the very foundations of the faith in France in those days," says the Very Rev. Jarlath Royanne, O.Cist. "Neither was it a call to do penance as on those occasions. No, Mary's mission to her faithful Irish people that day was rather one of compassion and comfort, with an implied admonition, no doubt, of dangers ahead, and the imperative need of prayer."

Every early account of the apparition points out that it occurred on the eve of the octave of the feast of the Assumption.

Did Mary intend to establish this connection between Knock and Fatima? At any rate, the coincidence is interesting. It reminds us that Mary, our Queen, has an Immaculate Heart filled with an almost infinite love for us.

The two saints who appeared with Mary were the two people—next to our Lord Himself—who were most closely associated with her while she was in this world. St. Joseph cared for her before Jesus was born, and he watched over her and Jesus for some years after that. As head of the Holy Family, he is the model husband and father. He is also the Patron of the Universal Church. In the apparition he was looking at her in a reverential manner. It seems likely that he represented all families and also the Universal Church in paying homage to the Queen of Heaven.

St. John was Mary's guardian after our Lord's death. He stood with her beneath the cross while Jesus was giving His life for the world. It was to him that our Lord almost with His dying breath said, "Behold thy mother." St. John represented all of us that day.

So St. John, by his presence, reminds us that Mary is our spiritual mother. But he does more than that. He was garbed as a bishop and was reading from a Mass book. He stood next to the altar on which was the sacrificial lamb. St. John was our Lady's priest. After the Resurrection he celebrated Mass for her, renewing the sacrifice of Calvary, bringing her Son down upon the altar. It is also interesting to note that in the Apocalypse, St. John refers to our Lord as a lamb twenty-seven times.

"A meditation on Knock," says Rev. Patrick O'Carroll, C.S.Sp., "will ultimately lead us to the Lamb of God, who for us was slain on Calvary, and by whose Precious Blood our souls that have been defiled by sin are washed white as snow. Our attention is above all turned to the same Lamb of God that is mystically immolated on every altar, when the Holy Mass is celebrated. Knock, then, calls for a fuller appreciation of the Mass."

Virtually all authorities agree on this, that the Mass is the central feature of Knock. Our Lady herself seems to bear this out. Most of the cures that have taken place there have occurred during Mass. At Lourdes, the Blessed Sacrament is emphasized; at Knock, the Mass.

14

Other Manifestations of Our Lady

1841-1906

THE MANIFESTATIONS of our Lady between 1830 and 1917 are not limited to the ones described in the preceding chapters. Some of the others are described in this chapter. Not all have been pronounced upon by Church authorities, but those related here seem to have reliable human testimony. For the sake of simplicity, expressions such as "she appeared" are sometimes used instead of "she is believed to have appeared." This is done with the realization that the final decision in such cases rests with the Church.

In 1841, eleven years after our Lady had given us the Miraculous Medal and one year after she had given us the Green Scapular, Father Pierre de Smet, Apostle of the Rockies, established a mission on the Bitter Root River, in what is now the state of Montana. He named it St. Mary.

On Christmas Eve, an Indian orphan named Paul came to Father de Smet with a strange story. He had entered his tepee, and there he had seen—he could not tell whether it was a man or a woman, but he rather thought it was a woman. The clothes were not like the ones worn by either the men or the women in the Flathead tribe. "Her feet did not touch the ground; her robe was white as snow; she had a star above her head, and under her feet a snake gnawing at a fruit that I don't know. From her heart there came forth rays of light which came toward me. When I saw that, at first I was afraid; then I wasn't afraid. My heart was burning, my head clear. I don't know how it came about, but suddenly I knew my prayers."

What had the visitor said? Just one thing. She was glad that the mission of the Flatheads was called St. Mary.

About the beginning of 1845 Sister Apolline Andriveau, of the Daughters of Charity, was making the Stations of the Cross in the chapel of the Sisters' house at Troyes, in France. At the thirteenth station, Sister said later, "it seemed to me that Our Blessed Lady placed the body of Our Divine Lord in my arms, saying: 'The world is drawing down ruin upon itself, because it never thinks of the Passion of Jesus Christ. Do your utmost to bring it to meditate thereon, to bring about its salvation.'"

Our Lord appeared to Sister Apolline in a series of apparitions from July 26 to September 14, 1846. He revealed to her the Red Scapular of the Passion. Pope Pius IX approved the scapular in a rescript dated June 25, 1847. Great indulgences are attached to its use, including a plenary indulgence every Friday for those who meditate upon the Passion.

The scapular and bands must both be of red wool. On one woolen segment our Lord is represented on the Cross; at the foot of the Cross are the implements of the Passion and about it are the words: "Holy Passion of Our Lord Jesus Christ, save us." On the other are the hearts of Jesus and Mary; above these is a cross with the inscription: "Sacred Hearts of Jesus and Mary, protect us." These images are essential to the scapular.

The last of the Red Scapular apparitions took place just

Other Manifestations of Our Lady

five days before the one and only apparition of Our Lady of La Salette. Sister Apolline belonged to the same order as St. Catherine Labouré to whom the Miraculous Medal had been revealed in 1830. This was also the order to which Sister Justine belonged; the Green Scapular had been revealed to Sister Justine in 1840. There is a marvelous unity about all these apparitions. At Troyes and at La Salette our Lady said that the world was drawing down punishment on itself. The Heart of Mary, and sometimes the Heart of Jesus, was prominent in all the manifestations taking place at this time: the Miraculous Medal, Our Lady of Victories, the Green Scapular, the Red Scapular. The Indian boy who said he saw the vision in 1841 also spoke of the heart from which came rays of light.

So many scapulars have been revealed to us that a troubling thought comes to mind: how can a person possibly wear them all? The *Catholic Encyclopedia* tells us that several scapulars may be attached to the same pair of strings or bands. If the Red Scapular is one of these, the bands must be of red wool. We are also told that "since 1910 . . . it is permitted to wear, instead of one or more of the small scapulars, a single medal. . . . If the medal is to be worn instead of a number of different scapulars, it must receive the blessing that would be attached to each of them. . . . This medal must be worn constantly, either about the neck or in some other seemly manner, and with it may be gained all the indulgences and privileges of the small scapulars without exception. . . ."

The Blessed Virgin is believed to have appeared near Green Bay, Wisconsin, in 1858, the same year she appeared to Bernadette at Lourdes.

The young lady to whom she is believed to have appeared was Adele Brisse, who was born in Belgium in 1831. Adele had a great devotion to the Blessed Virgin. She wished to become a nun and work in the foreign-mission field. She did not wish to accompany her parents to America. Her confessor said: "Go with your parents, and you will be rewarded for your obedience. If God so wills, you can become a Sister in America. I shall pray for you." The Brisse family arrived in the Wisconsin wilderness in the early 1850's.

There were few priests on the Wisconsin peninsula. The Belgian immigrants who had settled there were so busy clearing the land that they had little time for instructing their children in religion. It seemed that in two or three generations the people of the region would lose their faith completely.

Twice in 1858, while she was trudging along a forest path, Adele saw the vision of a lady in white. The third time, acting on the instructions of her confessor, she asked: "In God's name, who are you and what do you desire of me?"

"I am the Queen of the Heavens, who prays for the conversion of sinners, and I wish you to do the same," the Lady answered.

"You were at Holy Communion this morning?" she continued in her soft sweet voice.

"Yes, dear Lady," answered Adele.

"You have done well, but I wish you to do more. Pray for nine days. Go and make a general confession and offer your Holy Communion for the conversion of sinners. If they do not convert themselves and do penance, my Son will be obliged to punish them."

Adele's three companions wanted to know to whom she was speaking.

"Kneel," said Adele. "The Lady says she is the Queen of the Heavens."

"Oh, why are we so unhappy not to see her as you do?" asked one of the women.

"Blessed are they that believe and do not see," answered the Lady.

Then, turning to Adele, she said, "What are you doing here in idleness, while your companions are working in the vineyard of my Son?"

"What more can I do, dear Lady?" asked Adele, weeping.

"Teach the children."

Other Manifestations of Our Lady

"How shall I teach them who know so little myself?" pleaded Adele.

"I do not mean the science of the world; teach them their catechism, that they may know and love my Son; otherwise, the people here will lose their faith."

"With God's grace, and the help of your intercession, I promise, dear Lady, to be faithful to do what you bid me," answered Adele.

"Go and fear nothing," said the Lady. "I will help you."

Raising her eyes and hands, the Lady rose slowly. She seemed to be asking a blessing on the little group kneeling below. Adele fell in a faint from which she had to be revived by her comrades.

Adele devoted the remainer of her life to the education of the young. To her must go much of the credit for keeping alive the spark of faith in the Belgian settlers. To help her in her work Adele founded a religious community of women who followed the rule of the Third Order of St. Francis but took no vows. In 1871, a great forest fire swept much of the peninsula destroying everything except Sister Adele's community. This left the people impoverished and made it more difficult than ever for her to secure funds for her work. She was forced to go on begging trips to distant cities.

In addition to her difficulties of carrying on her work in a backwoods region with few resources, Adele also faced the opposition of some members of the clergy. Seemingly because of their unfavorable reports, the Bishop put an interdict on the chapel built on the site of the apparitions and he told Adele to close her school. The school was allowed to reopen after two weeks, and the interdict was later removed. The whole affair seems to have been based on an unfortunate misunderstanding, but the difficulties may account for the fact that the apparitions have never secured ecclesiastical approval.

Today, a brick chapel stands on the spot where the Blessed Virgin appeared. This adjoins a home for crippled children which was completed in 1842.

Father Luke Desilets was sent to the little town of Cape de la Madeleine on the St. Lawrence River in the Province of Quebec. His new parish was rich in history but poor in faith. His church, built in 1714, was a century and a half old and it had replaced the original chapel built in 1659. By the middle of the nineteenth century, the people of the district had grown extremely lax.

One evening Father Desilets went into his church and found, before the statue of the Blessed Virgin, a small pig with a rosary between its teeth. "There!" he said. "Men drop their beads, but the very beasts pick them up!" He knelt before the statue and promised to spend the rest of his life spreading devotion to the Rosary. Immediately afterward, there was a remarkable rebirth of piety among his people.

In time, there was need for a larger church at Cape de la Madeleine. The men of the parish crossed the river and quarried and prepared the stones for the new edifice. The parish could not afford a barge to bring the stones across the river, and the river is so wide and swift at that point that it does not freeze every year. Beginning in November, 1877, the parishioners recited the Rosary every Sunday after High Mass in petition for freezing weather. At the beginning of March they became discouraged, but the pastor himself continued to pray.

On the evening of March 14, a warm wind began breaking up the ice farther up the river. It came floating down in huge chunks. Ice accumulated behind the cape. By March 16 it formed a mass reaching almost from shore to shore.

All that night, in the bitter cold, more than fifty men worked to reinforce the causeway. The work was dangerous because the current was swift and much of the ice was soft. Far into the morning a dim light shone from one of the rectory windows. "There is nothing to fear," the men said to each other. "The Curé is reciting his beads. His Aves are holding us up." From then on, the causeway of ice was called the Bridge of Rosaries.

For eight days the men brought the stones over the Bridge of Rosaries on their sledges. There were swirling pools

Other Manifestations of Our Lady 91

just a few feet from the path across the ice, but there were no accidents. On the eighth day, the weather turned warmer. Most of the stone had been hauled by this time, and Father Desilets ordered the work to stop. That very afternoon the passage was swept away.

The new parish church was built, and Father Desilets was able to see his ancient chapel dedicated to the Queen of the Holy Rosary. This dedication took place on June 22, 1883.

On the evening of the dedication Father Desilets and two other priests knelt in the chapel. The statue of the Blessed Virgin had that day been moved from the side altar to the main altar. As they knelt there, the three priests saw the downcast eyes of the statue open wide and look up to heaven!

Father Desilets died a month later, his life's work accomplished.

The miraculous statue, now known as Our Lady of the Cape, was crowned in 1904 by the authority of Pope Pius X. In 1909, the Bishops of Canada proclaimed the chapel to be a National Shrine to the Blessed Virgin.

The shrine is visited by about 230,000 pilgrims each year.

Two country women were looking for some sheep on a hill near Castelpetroso, Italy. They returned home, crying, sobbing and trembling. They said they had seen a light issuing from some fissures in the rocks. When they approached, they saw distinctly the image of the Sorrowful Mother—a lady, young, very beautiful, pale, with disheveled hair and bleeding from the wounds received from seven swords.

At first everyone scoffed at the story, but more people saw apparitions in the same spot. Some saw the Blessed Virgin as Our Lady of Mount Carmel, others as Our Lady of Grace, others as Our Lady of the Most Holy Rosary, but most often she appeared as the Sorrowful Mother.

The local pastors did not believe the story at first, but soon many of the priests themselves beheld the apparitions.

Pope Leo XIII asked the bishop of the diocese to investigate the occurrences, and on September 26, 1888, the bishop saw our Lady three times.

These apparitions differ from others in several respects. They were seen by a great number of people, about 500 in all. They were seen by priests, and it has been a characteristic of most of the apparitions of our times that no priests have been able to see them. In most cases, the bishop is very reserved in his opinion and withholds recognition of the devotion for some time. In this case, the bishop himself beheld the vision and became one of the most fervent advocates.

A picture of Our Lady of the Seven Dolors hung on the wall of the dining hall at *Colegio San Gabriel,* a boarding school conducted by the Jesuits in Quito, Ecuador.

On the evening of April 20, 1906, the thirty-six students of the *Colegio* had just finished their supper. The prefect, Father Andrew Roesch, came into the hall. He talked with some of the older boys about the San Francisco earthquake while the younger boys played.

James Chavez, one of the smallest boys, looked up at the picture of our Lady. To his amazement, the Blessed Virgin seemed alive. She was opening and closing her eyes!

The other boys also saw the eyes moving. Father Roesch saw the wonder, too, but he prudently pretended that it was just an illusion. He led the boys to the chapel where they recited the Rosary.

Soon after that the picture was taken to the chapel. One evening when the boys had finished saying the Rosary in the chapel, they cried out together: "She is moving her eyes."

These events were carefully investigated by a commission appointed by the Vicar-Capitular.

On June 3, the Vicar-Capitular ruled that the wonder first seen by James Chavez had really taken place, that it could not be explained by natural laws, and that it could not be attributed to the power of the devil. Therefore, the faithful could believe the story with a purely human faith and

Other Manifestations of Our Lady

could pay public honor to the picture and pray before it with lawful confidence.

The picture was moved to a larger church where a solemn triduum was celebrated. Thousands of people attended the triduum and many saw the miracle repeated. A novena was held after that, and more people saw the miracle.

On July 6 the new Archbishop of Quito came to take possession of his see. At two o'clock, the very moment he was entering the city, the Blessed Virgin slowly moved her eyes. Suddenly the background of the picture disappeared and the figure stood out as if in relief. The complexion was that of a living person.

The Blessed Virgin opened and shut her eyes. Twice she lifted them toward heaven. Sometimes she seemed to be making an effort to repress the tears. Then she became pale, her face waxlike as if she was going to expire. Many of the people sobbed. They begged pardon and mercy. Then the Blessed Mother resumed a serene face and her natural color.

After the picture was taken back to the chapel three children entered one day and found the Blessed Virgin weeping. The last time the wonder took place, toward the end of July, our Lady did not show any sign of suffering. She turned her eyes toward the Tabernacle.

The Miraculous Picture is still kept in the chapel of the *Colegio*. Every Thursday the chapel is open to the public. Around April 20 the picture is moved to a large church where a novena is held in honor of Our Lady of Quito. Several times the picture has been carried in triumph through Ecuador.

The enemies of religion were in control of Ecuador in 1906. The legislature had gone through the motion of repealing the consecration of the country to the Hearts of Jesus and Mary. Religious communities had property taken from them. Many Catholic schools were closed. Most of the bishops had been expelled from the country. The leaders of Ecuador boasted that they intended to destroy belief in God. It seemed that they would go a long way toward making good their boast. The people seemed too tired and too confused to resist.

It was then that the Sorrowful Mother intervened miraculously. After the manifestation in the *Colegio* there was a great reawakening of the Faith in Ecuador. The enemies of religion were not able to stem the tide, and they went down before it. Religious communities regained their property. Bishops came back to their sees. The schools that had been closed were reopened and many new ones were built. In 1949 a great National Eucharistic Congress was held in Ecuador.

The men who had set out to destroy belief in God had been utterly defeated.

The Woman had conquered.

15

"France Will Suffer"
WORLD WAR I, 1914-1918

"I can no longer restrain my Son!" Our Lady had declared sadly to Estelle Faguette at Pellevoisin in 1876. The world continued to ignore its Mother's warnings and to bring ever closer the great punishment that was to befall it.

Two years after the apparitions at Pellevoisin, the frail sixty-eight-year-old Cardinal Pecci became the new Pontiff, Pope Leo XIII. "It is not the tiara you are giving me, but death," the Pope said to the Cardinals who elected him. It is true that the papal tiara has been a heavy burden in these days when the devil is "every day redoubling his efforts." Nevertheless, Pope Leo XIII reigned for twenty-five years, until 1903. He thus became the first Pontiff of our twentieth century.

Pope Leo XIII earned the title "Pope of the Workingman" because of his great encyclical *Rerum Novarum*. Like Karl Marx, the Pontiff recognized the great abuse that had been brought about by the Industrial Revolution. But his solution, based on the teachings of Christ, was vastly different from the class warfare advocated by Marx. Employers who were making large profits were slow to follow the Pope's plan of granting justice to the workingman. Some even denounced him as a socialist. Had Pope Leo XIII been heeded, Communism would not be the threat that it now is.

As a protest against Italy's unjust seizure of the Vatican, Pope Leo followed the example of his predecessor and did not leave the Vatican during his entire reign. Relations improved slightly with some countries, but only slightly. Germany, under Chancellor Bismarck, engaged in a persecution of the Church. France, now in the firm grip of the anticlericals, passed law after law to hamstring the Church.

When Estelle Faguette had an audience with Pope Leo XIII in 1900, she said, "Holy Father, the Blessed Virgin said that France will have to suffer."

"Yes," said the Pontiff sadly, "France will have to suffer."

Fourteen years later, World War I broke out, and most of the battles were fought on French soil. This war was even more devastating than the one of 1870-1871 had been.

Cardinal Sarto was elected to succeed Pope Leo XIII. "Since I must suffer I will take the name of those who have suffered," he said, "I will be called Pius."

France caused Pope Pius X great anguish, as it had his predecessors. In 1904, the government declared that the concordat which had been in effect with the Holy See for a century was at an end. The Law of Separation was passed the following year. By this law, the government confiscated all possessions of the clergy as well as of charitable institutions. Religious congregations were disbanded. Many of the religious were forced to leave the country. Nuns were driven from their work in schools and hospitals. Churches were looted.

Many of the French people protested. The men sent to despoil the churches were often attacked by the infuriated peasants, and many of them had to have guards to protect them. Nevertheless, the sacrilegious work went on. "And France," our Lady had said at Pellevoisin, "what have I not done for her? How many warnings and yet she refused to listen!"

The misnamed liberalism which was scourging France spread to Spain and—this is interesting in light of later developments—to Portugal. The king and his son were murdered in Portugal. The next king was forced to abdicate. A republic was established. A Law of Separation, based on the one in France, was passed, and the Church was in for a long period of persecution.

In the dark days in which we are now living, the most encouraging signs we behold are increased devotion to Mary and increased devotion to her Son in the Eucharist. It is largely to Pope Pius X, "Pope of the Eucharist," that we owe the latter. It was he who urged frequent Communion and permitted children to receive Communion as soon as they reached the age of reason.

In 1916, two years after the death of Pius X, an angel appeared to three children near Fatima in Portugal. They were aged nine, eight, and six. The angel placed a Host on the tongue of Lucia, the oldest. To Francisco and Jacinta, who had not made their first Communion, he presented a chalice, and they drank from it. The angel said: "Take the body and blood of Jesus Christ, horribly outraged by ungrateful men. Make reparation for their crimes and console your God." He seemed to be expressing at the same time displeasure with the state of the world and approval of the early Communion advocated by Pius X.

It was to these same three children that our Lady was later to appear.

The war clouds were gathering in the last part of the

reign of Pope Pius X. Men were about to reap the terrible punishment that was due them for having "horribly outraged" their God. The Pontiff tried in every way possible to avert the war, but he saw that he was doomed to fail. He told his Secretary of State that a war would break out in 1914. Early in May, 1914, he said to a South American who was returning home, "How fortunate you are that you will not be here when war breaks out in a very short time."

When he heard that Archduke Ferdinand of Austria had been assassinated, he knew that the conflict had begun. "Oh, my poor children!" he cried. "This is the last affliction which the Lord is sending me! Willingly would I sacrifice my life to ward off this terrible scourge!"

Twice the Austrian ambassador asked Pope Pius to bless the armies of that country. He was told, "I bless peace."

Austria declared war on Serbia. Russia joined the conflict on the side of Serbia. Germany came to the aid of Austria. France and England declared war on Germany and Austria.

Pope Pius was stricken by what the physicians thought to be a minor illness, but he died August 10, 1914. Those about him knew that he died of a broken heart.

Pope Pius X was declared a saint. He was beatified June 3, 1951, and was canonized May 29, 1954.

The new Pontiff, Benedict XV, strove valiantly to bring an end to the war. The leaders on both sides were convinced that they could win, however, and they were in no mood to stop fighting when victory seemed within their grasp. Never before had there been such destruction. This was the first war in which airplanes were used, and death rained from the skies. Ships were sunk; cities leveled. Women and children were victims along with the fighting men.

The Pope tried to arrange a truce on Christmas Day. Great Britian, Germany, and Belgium seemed sympathetic, but France and Russia said no. Cannons continued to roar, and blood continued to flow on the birthday of the Prince of Peace.

When Italy entered the war, she made the Allies promise that the Pope would not be allowed to take part in the peace negotiations. She was afraid the matter of the Papal States might be brought up.

The Pope's efforts for peace went on constantly. On March 6, he said to his Vicar-General, Cardinal Pompili: "A father whose sons are engaged in a violent conflict is not at liberty to cease his pleadings for peace, even though they disregard his tears and exhortation. . . . Therefore, we must again raise our voice against this war which appears to us as the suicide of civilized Europe."

Far from diminishing, the war, like a giant conflagration, was spreading throughout the world. Portugal was engulfed in 1916, the United States in April, 1917. By this time almost every country in the world was involved.

In Russia, events of sinister and far-reaching importance were taking place. The war was going badly for that country which had been misruled for so many years by the czars. A revolution broke out in March, 1917, and Czar Nicholas II abdicated.

An unstable provisional government was set up in Russia. It was not to last for long. Conditions were in a state of chaos, and the followers of Karl Marx thrive on that sort of thing. On April 16, Nikolai Lenin and Leon Trotsky, leaders of the Communists, arrived in Petrograd to make their plans for taking over the country.

In May, 1917, the month of our Lady, the world situation seemed hopeless. The war had been going on for almost three years, and no end was in sight. If it had lasted much longer, European civilization would have succeeded in committing suicide.

On May 5, 1917, when everything appeared darkest, Pope Benedict XV addressed a letter to his Cardinal Secretary of State in which he recounted his unsuccessful efforts to bring about peace. Then he said:

"Because all graces . . . are dispensed by the hands of the most holy Virgin, we wish the petitions of her most afflicted children to be directed with lively confidence, more than ever in this awful hour, to the great Mother of God.

"We charge you, then, Lord Cardinal, to communicate to all the bishops of the world our ardent desire that recourse be made to the Heart of Jesus, Throne of grace, and that to the Throne recourse be made through Mary. . . .

"To Mary, then, who is the Mother of Mercy, and omnipotent by grace, let loving and devout appeal go up from every corner of the earth. . . . Let it bear to her the anguished cry of mothers and wives, the wailing of little ones, the sighs of every generous heart, that her most tender and benign solicitude may be moved and the peace we asked for be obtained for our agitated world."

The Pope also directed that "Queen of Peace" be added to Mary's titles in the Litany of Loreto.

Eight days later—as if in direct answer to the Pope's appeal—the Mother of God appeared to the three shepherd children of Fatima.

16

"Men Must Offend Our Lord No More"

FATIMA, 1917

THROUGH the shepherd children of Fatima, our Lady spoke to us who are living today.

Her words are just as pertinent today as they were in 1917. In fact, many parts of her message seem to be meant specifically for us. "If my requests are granted, Russia will be converted, and there will be peace" means infinitely more to us than it did to the world of 1917. At that time, Russia had just undergone a revolution and was so weak that she had been forced out of World War I. Who at that time, when the Allies were deeply embroiled in a war with Germany, could foresee that Russia would ever be a threat to the peace of the world? Now the fact is pounded home by each new day's headlines.

That the message of Fatima is directed to us is also emphasized by the fact that much of the message did not become known until 1942.

This latter fact has puzzled a great many people. It puzzled the Rev. Thomas McGlynn, O.P., and, in 1947, he had an opportunity to ask Lucia about it. Lucia is the one living survivor of the children of Fatima. When Father McGlynn had the privilege of interviewing her, she was a Dorothean Sister. Since then, she has joined the Carmelites.

"It seems," Father McGlynn said to Lucia, "from the words of our Lady in 1917, that the war of 1939-1945 was threatened as punishment for sin. But the warning was not generally known until 1942, after the punishment had begun. How is this explained?"

Lucia replied that, in 1917, the people knew the important part of our Lady's message, that is, that men must amend their lives, that they must not offend God, that He was already much offended.

In other words, our Lady let the people of 1917 know what she wished them to know at that time. They should have carried out her requests even though they did not know the punishment that awaited them if they failed.

Today, we not only know her requests, but we see that World War II was inflicted on the world as punishment for its sins. And we know that if we do not heed Mary's requests, there will probably be a World War III.

The three children were watching their flocks as usual. They were ten-year-old Lucia dos Santos and her two cousins Francisco and Jacinta Marto, nine and seven respectively. They were in a natural depression among the hills which was called the Cova da Iria. They had said their Rosary, as was their custom, and they had begun building a stone playhouse.

Suddenly, a brilliant shaft of light pierced the air. Frightened, they looked about them. The sun shone brightly, and there was not a cloud in the sky. How could there have been lightning? Just the same, they decided that they had better go home. They gathered the sheep and started down the hill.

When they were halfway down, another shaft of light filled the air. Panicky, they turned toward the right, and there, standing above a small holm oak they saw a beautiful Lady.

"It was a Lady dressed all in white," Lucia says, "more brilliant than the sun; shedding rays of light, clearer and stronger than a crystal glass filled with the most sparkling water, pierced by the burning rays of the sun."

Her hands were joined in an attitude of prayer. From her right arm hung a string of pearly white beads ending in a cross of burnished silver. Her feet were bare and rested on a cloud that just touched the little evergreen.

"Do not be afraid," the Lady said in a sweet voice, "I will not harm you." (How similar to the first words spoken to the children of La Salette!)

The words and the voice were both reassuring, and Lucia summoned enough courage to ask, "Where are you from, Madam?"

"I am from heaven."

"What do you wish of me?"

"I come to ask you to meet me here six months in succession at this same hour, on the thirteenth of each month. In October, I will tell you who I am and what I want."

Francisco could see the Lady but he could not hear her, nor could he hear her in any of the subsequent apparitions. Jacinta could both see and hear the Lady, but Jacinta did not talk to her. All conversation during the series of apparitions was between the Lady and Lucia.

"And I, am I, too, going to heaven?" Lucia asked.

"Yes, you shall."
"And Jacinta?"
"She, too."
"And Francisco?"
"He, too, but first he must say many Rosaries."

Father John De Marchi in *The Immaculate Heart* says that here the Lady's beautiful and compassionate glance rested for a little while on Francisco. "For reasons we are not qualified to fathom, it held a shade of sadness and disapproval. Somewhere in his little heart the Lady must have read a fault that others could not see."

Lucia thought of two girls who used to come to her house to learn sewing from her sisters. Both girls had died only recently.

"Is Maria Nevers in heaven?"
"Yes, she is."
"And Amelia?"

The documents give three different versions of our Lady's answer to this question: "She is in purgatory"; "She is still in purgatory"; and "She will be in purgatory till the end of the world."

Many people have objected to the third version, but Lucia has insisted that it is the correct one. She says there is nothing strange about it; a person can go to hell for all eternity for missing Mass on Sunday.

The Lady then said to the children: "Do you wish to offer yourselves to God to endure all the suffering that He may choose to send you, as an act of reparation for the sins by which He is offended, and to ask for the conversion of sinners?"

"Yes, we do!" Lucia answered eagerly.

"Then you will have much to suffer, but the grace of God will assist you and always bear you up."

She opened her hands. From each palm came a stream of light which shone on the children and seemed to penetrate to the depths of their souls. Moved by an inward impulse the children fell to their knees and prayed: "Most Holy Trinity,

"Offend Our Lord No More"

I adore You! My God, my God, I love You in the Most Blessed Sacrament."

The Lady spoke again. "Say the Rosary every day to obtain peace for the world and the end of the war."

"She began to elevate herself serenely," Lucia says, "going in the direction of the east until she disappeared in the immensity of space."

This was not the children's first experience with the supernatural. An angel, "the Guardian Angel of Portugal," had appeared to them three times. On one occasion, as was mentioned in the preceding chapter, he had brought them Holy Communion. After each visit of the angel, they had felt heavy and tired. The Lady, however, left them with a feeling of lightness, of peace and of joy. After the Lady had disappeared, they knelt for a while having no desire to move or to speak or to do anything but meditate on the beautiful vision they had seen.

After a time, they rose to their feet and began to look for the sheep. They found them grazing quietly on the grass.

They spent the rest of the afternoon in the fields talking about the wonderful visit from our Lady. Francisco, who had not heard anything, wanted to know everything the Lady had said. When told that he would go to heaven but that he must say many Rosaries, he almost burst with happiness.

"Oh my Lady," he exclaimed, "I will say all the Rosaries you want."

The children agreed that our Lady had seemed unhappy about something, and this was the only thing that marred their very great happiness. They were too young to comprehend fully the fact that only one thing can make our Lady unhappy, and that is sin. They were to realize this, however, before the series of apparitions was over. In 1846, Mary had wept because of the sins of the world; in 1917, sins were still making her very sad.

The Lady returned every month as she had promised. The children underwent great suffering and had many occasions to remember her words, "Then you will have much to suffer." Lucia's mother thought the girl was lying. The pastor of their church suggested the apparition might be the devil. They had trouble with the authorities, just as Bernadette had had. The civil administrator of their district arrested the children and kept them in jail so that they missed the apparition scheduled for August 13. In that month, the Lady appeared to them on the 19th.

But these sufferings were not enough for them. They gave their lunches to poor children, and they ate bitter acorns and unripe olives. Each wore under his clothes a shaggy rope which itched and chafed. Our Lady had asked for sacrifices, and they delighted in thinking up new ones to offer her.

On June 13, the Lady told the children to "say the Rosary always." To Lucia she said, "I want you to learn to read. Then I will tell you what else I want."

When Lucia asked that the three of them be taken to heaven, our Lady said: "I will take Jacinta and Francisco soon. But you must remain longer here below. Jesus will use you to make me better known and more loved. He wishes to establish throughout the world the devotion to my Immaculate Heart. I promise salvation to those who embrace it and their souls will be loved by God as flowers placed by myself to adorn His throne."

"Then I am to stay here alone!" Lucia said, sad at the thought of being left behind.

"No, my child. You are suffering very much, but do not be discouraged. I will never leave you. My Immaculate Heart will be your refuge and the way that will lead you to God."

Once more she parted her hands, and the children were enveloped by the light from her palms. Francisco and Jacinta were in a stream that went toward heaven, and Lucia was in a stream that spread over the ground. A heart surrounded by thorns was in front of the right palm. "We understood," says Lucia, "that this was the Immaculate Heart of Mary, so offended by the sins of mankind, desiring reparation."

Four or five thousand people were on hand for the apparition of July 13. When our Lady appeared to the children, the crowd saw that the sun became dimmer and that a little cloud stood over the holm oak.

"Offend Our Lord No More" 105

The Lady told the children to continue to say the Rosary. "Say it with the intention of obtaining the end of the war. The intercession of the Blessed Virgin alone can obtain this grace for men."

Lucia, thinking of her mother and of all the people who doubted her story, said, "Will you please tell us who you are and perform a miracle so that everyone will believe that you really appear to us?"

"Continue to come here every month. In October I will tell you who I am and what I desire, and I shall perform a miracle so that everyone will have to believe you."

Lucia requested the cure of some sick people. She was told that some would be cured and others not.

"Sacrifice yourself for sinners," the Lady said, "And say many times, especially when you make any sacrifices: 'O Jesus, it is for Your love, for the conversion of sinners, and in reparation for sins committed against the Immaculate Heart of Mary.'"

As our Lady said these words she parted her hands as she had done the two previous months. The light from her palms seemed to penetrate the earth. The children saw a great sea of fire. "In this sea," says Lucia, "were immersed black and burning demons and souls in human forms, resembling live transparent coals. Lifted up into the air by the flames, they fell back on all sides like sparks in a conflagration, with neither weight nor balance, amid loud screams and cries of pain and despair which horrified us and shook us with terror. We could tell the devils by their horrible and nauseous figures of baleful and unknown animals, but transparent as the black coals in a fire."

Pale with terror the chilldren raised their eyes to our Lady for help.

"You have seen hell," said the Lady, "where the souls of poor sinners go. To save them, our Lord wishes to establish throughout the world devotion to my Immaculate Heart. If people will do what I tell you, many souls will be saved and there will be peace in the world. The war is coming to an end, but if the offenses against God do not stop, another and worse one will begin in the reign of Pius XI.

"When you see a night illumined by an unknown light, know that it is the great sign that God gives you that He is going to punish the world for its crimes by means of war, of hunger and of persecutions of the Church and of the Holy Father.

"To prevent this, I shall come back to ask the consecration of Russia to my Immaculate Heart and the Communion of Reparation on the First Saturdays. If my requests are granted, Russia will be converted and there will be peace. If not, she will scatter her errors throughout the world, provoking wars and persecutions of the Church. The good will be martyred; the Holy Father will have much to suffer; various nations will be annihilated.

"But in the end my Immaculate Heart will triumph. The Holy Father will consecrate Russia to me; it will be converted, and a certain period of peace will be granted to the world.

"In Portugal, the dogma of the faith will be kept always."

These grave words, the Lady said, were not yet to be revealed to the world. The girls were to repeat them to no one except Francisco.

She then told them another secret which has not as yet been revealed. Lucia has written it down and delivered it to the bishop of Leiria.

On August 13, the children were in jail in Ourem. The civil administrator threatened to boil them in oil if they did not tell the Lady's secret. Though badly frightened, they could not think of disobeying our Lady. In disgust, the administrator finally freed them. A large number of people, not knowing that the children had been kidnaped, went to the Cova for the scheduled appearance of the Lady. At noon, there was a loud clap of thunder. Then, according to an eyewitness:

"Right after the thunder came a flash, and immediately we all noticed a little cloud, very white, beautiful and bright, that came and stayed over the holm oak. It stayed a few minutes, then rose toward the heavens where it disappeared. Looking about, we noticed a strange sight that we had already seen and would see again. Everyone's face glowed, rose, red, blue, all the colors of the rainbow. The trees seemed to have no branches or leaves but were all covered with flowers; every leaf was a flower. The ground was in little squares, each one a different color. Our clothes seemed to be transformed also into the colors of the rainbow. The two vigil lanterns hanging from the arch over the holy spot appeared to be of gold.

"When the signs disappeared, the people were sure that our Lady had come, and, not finding the children, had returned to heaven. They felt that our Lady was disappointed. . . ."

The August apparition took place on the 19th, while the children were tending sheep in a hollow called Valinhos. The Lady appeared over a holm oak slightly taller than the one in the Cova. "I want you to continue to come to the Cova da Iria on the thirteenth and to continue to say the Rosary every day," the Lady told them.

"What do you wish us to do with the money and the offerings that the people leave at the Cova da Iria?" Lucia asked.

"Two litters should be made; you and Jacinta are to carry one with two girls dressed in white; Francisco is to carry the other with three boys also dressed in white robes. The money placed on the litters is for the feast of Our Lady of the Rosary."

Our Lady repeated her promise of a miracle. "In October, I shall perform a miracle so that all may believe in my apparitions. If they had not taken you to the village, the miracle would have been greater. St. Joseph will come with the Baby Jesus to give peace to the world. Our Lord also will come to bless the people. Besides, Our Lady of the Rosary and Our Lady of Sorrows will come."

Lucia asked for the cure of some sick persons and was told that some of them would be cured within the year. Our Lady made it plain, by her next words, however, that her principal concern is for souls.

"Pray, pray a great deal and make sacrifices for sinners," she said gravely, "for many souls go to hell because they have no one to sacrifice and pray for them."

Many of the people who were present for the apparitions of September 13 saw a luminous globe cross the sky and stop over the holm oak. Then later it rose and disappeared toward the sun. Monsignor John Quaresma, who was one of the many to behold this phenomenon, said: "The three little shepherds had seen the Mother of God herself; to us had been given the grace to see the chariot that had borne her from heaven to the barren and inhospitable hills of Aire."

There was another unusual feature of this apparition. Many people saw white flowers which seemed to shower from the sky and disappear before they touched the ground.

While the crowd was seeing these things, our Lady was saying to the children, "Continue to say the Rosary to bring about the end of the war."

She repeated her promise of a miracle the following month. Then she said, "God is content with your sacrifices, but does not wish you to sleep with the rope. Wear it only during the day."

Someone had given Lucia a bottle of cologne with the request that it be presented to our Lady. It was probably the nicest gift a Portuguese peasant woman could think of. Our Lady graciously refused the gift, saying: "That is not necessary for heaven."

In July, August, and September, our Lady had promised a miracle in October. Lucia had told a number of people about this promise, and the word spread rapidly through Portugal. Unbelievers scoffed at the idea and waited confidently for October 13. They were sure that there would be no miracle and that the entire story of Fatima would be exposed as a hoax. Those who believed talked the matter over excitedly. Think of it! A miracle promised in advance and in their own country of Portugal!

Several days ahead of the promised date, the roads became clogged with people making their way toward Fatima. "Nearby communities, towns and villages, emptied of people," said the Lisbon newspaper *O Dia*. ". . . They came on foot, by horse or by carriage. They travelled the highways and the roads, between hills and pine groves. For two days these came to life with the rolling of the carriages, the trot of the donkeys and the voices of the pilgrims."

Lucia's mother tried to get the girl to retract her story. Other people warned her that something very serious would happen if there were no miracle. It was said that there would be bombs in the crowd. The families of the children were very much frightened, but the children themselves were calm and serene.

"There will be a miracle, because our Lady promised it," Lucia said.

On the night of the twelfth, a cold wind came out of the north bringing with it a chilling rain. This caused the most acute discomfort to the pilgrims who had to sleep in the open, but it did not dampen their ardor.

The next day was cold and rainy, but the pilgrims were not daunted. By 11:30, more than 70,000 of them had gathered at the Cova. They sang hymns, recited prayers and said the Rosary. Seldom has there been a more striking demonstration of faith. Our Lady must have been very much pleased with the Portuguese people that day.

A path had to be cleared through the throng for Lucia, Francisco, and Jacinta. "Put down your umbrellas," Lucia said. The word spread throughout the crowd, and all umbrellas were lowered. Lucia does not know now why she made this request.

At two o'clock wartime, noon sun time, Lucia saw the flash of light that always preceded our Lady's appearances.

"Silence, silence, our Lady is coming," Lucia cried.

Our Lady came out of the east and again stopped above the holm oak.

"Who are you, Madam, and what do you want of me?" Lucia asked.

"I am the Lady of the Rosary, and I desire a chapel built in my honor in this place.

"People must continue to say the Rosary every day. The

war will end soon, and the soldiers will return to their homes."

"I have so many things to ask you," Lucia said.

"I will grant some of them, the others, no."

Assuming a sadder air, the Lady said, "Men must offend our Lord no more, and they must ask pardon for their sins, for He is already much offended."

The children could never forget the sad look on her face as she said these farewell words. Lucia says that they are the very essence of the message of Fatima. "Men must offend our Lord no more, and they must ask pardon for their sins, for He is already much offended." It was the same as the message of La Salette but in different words: "If my people will not submit, I shall be forced to let go the hand of my Son. It is so strong, so heavy, that I can no longer withhold it."

Our Lady stretched forth her hands, and the light again shone from her palms. She pointed toward the sun which seemed dim in comparison with the light from her hands. Then she seemed to disappear in her own radiance.

High up in the sky appeared a representation of the Holy Family. St. Joseph held the Child Jesus on his left arm. To the right was the Blessed Virgin dressed in the blue and white robes of Our Lady of the Rosary. St. Joseph and the Child Jesus made the Sign of the Cross over the world three times.

The vision faded, and then Lucia alone beheld our Lord dressed in red as the divine Redeemer. He blessed the world. Beside Him stood Mary dressed in the purple robes of Our Lady of Sorrows.

In the third and last of these visions, Lucia saw the Blessed Virgin clothed in the brown robes of Our Lady of Carmel.

The 70,000 pilgrims did not see any of this, but they were seeing something very spectacular. Our Lady did not forget that she had promised them a miracle.

The crowd heard Lucia shout, "Look at the sun!" (She does not remember saying this.) At that moment, the clouds parted suddenly and revealed the sun which looked like a phosphorescent disk. Everyone could look at it without blinking, although there was no fog and the clouds no longer obscured it.

The testimony as to what happened after that differs greatly. Most persons saw the sun spin about in the sky, throwing off rays of light in all directions like a gigantic pinwheel. This light, they say, was yellow, red, green, blue and violet successively. The people stood spellbound as they beheld this manifestation of God's power.

Then the sun suddenly detached itself from the sky and plunged toward the earth. The terrified people thought they would be crushed by it. Most of them fell to their knees in the churning sea of mud.

"Save us, Jesus!" went up the cry from hundreds of throats. "Our Lady, save us!"

Many fervently said the Act of Contrition.

Just when it seemed certain that the world would be destroyed, the sun stopped its downward plunge and climbed back to its accustomed place in the sky. It again became the brilliant sun of every day.

Some witnesses declare that the sun spun in the sky, stopped for an instant, then spun in the other direction and that this process was repeated. Others say its spinning was one continuous motion with no stopping. Many are sure that the sun plunged toward them in a straight line; many are equally sure that it came toward the earth in a zigzag path. Estimates of the length of time the display lasted vary from a few seconds to twelve minutes.

When a number of people have seen a very important event, it is only natural to expect some variations in their stories. Carlos de Azevedo Mendez, however, has an account that is at complete variance with most of the others. Here is his version as told to Father McGlynn: "The rain stopped; the clouds split open into tatters—thin transparent strips. The sun was seen as a crown of fire, empty in the middle. It went round on itself and moved across the sky. It could be seen behind the clouds and in between them, rolling around and moving horizontally. Some cried, 'I believe!'; others 'Forgive!' The crowd prayed in terror."

Senhor Mendez saw clouds, while practically all the others declare the sun spun around in a cloudless sky. For him the sun moved horizontally across the sky; for others it came rushing toward the earth. To him the cloud was a crown of fire, empty in the middle, to others it was a disk. He did not see the colored lights mentioned by others.

One woman to whom Father McGlynn talked did not see the sun at all. She saw nothing unusual except the sudden stopping of the rain. She was a rare exception. Practically everyone else in that crowd of 70,000 persons agree that something wonderful and awe inspiring happened to the sun although they do not agree as to the details of what happened. It seems that each person saw what God deemed best suited to his particular needs. The fact that impressions were so different forestalls any interpretation of the miracle as a natural phenomenon. So does the fact that it was not registered on any scientific instruments anywhere.

Was it mass hypnosis? Did the people just *think* they saw the sun behave in such a peculiar manner? This is rendered extremely unlikely by the fact that the rain had been pouring down until the minute the miracle occurred. In that cold drenching rain, a solar display is the last thing the people would have imagined.

If the mass-hypnosis idea is rendered unlikely by the rain, it is rendered impossible by the fact that people as far as twenty miles away from the Cova da Iria saw the phenomena.

One of the best proofs of the reality of the miracle is the space given to it by the Portuguese newspapers. The intellectuals of Portugal were infected with the same materialism as their counterparts in other countries. They had declared that miracles were impossible. But there was no denying what they had seen with their own eyes. Page after page in the daily newspapers was devoted to the wondrous occurrence.

Lucia dos Santos, a poorly educated ten-year-old girl, had announced three months in advance that a miracle would take place at noon on October 13, 1917, and that miracle had taken place. This was God's sign that the message of

Fatima was genuine, a message that should be studied and carried out by everyone.

"I shall perform a miracle so that all will believe," our Lady had said to Lucia, and she had carried out her promise.

17

"The Little Saint"
JACINTA MARTO, 1910-1920

"I WILL take Jacinta and Francisco soon," our Lady had said to Lucia on June 13. The final illness of the two children began with the influenza epidemic that swept the world in 1918. They were both stricken. Complications set in, and neither recovered, although Jacinta lingered on longer than her brother.

One day when Lucia came to visit her sick cousins, Jacinta had great news for her.

"Lucia," she cried, "our Lady came to see us and said she was coming soon for Francisco. She asked me whether I wanted to convert more sinners. I said yes. Our Lady wants me to go to two hospitals, but it is not to cure me. It is to suffer more for the love of God, the conversion of sinners, and in reparation for the offenses committed against the Immaculate Heart of Mary. She told me that you would not be with me. My mother will take me there, and afterward I am to be left there alone."

Jacinta was happy to undergo any sacrifice for the conversion of sinners. Francisco, too, underwent great suffering without the least complaint. His desire was to console our Lord and our Lady. It seemed to him that they were very sorrowful.

In April, Francisco asked to be allowed to make his First Communion. His request was granted. It was also his last Communion. He died April 4, 1919. He was not yet ten years old.

Jacinta missed her brother very much even though she knew he was happy in heaven. "I think of Francisco and how I'd love to see him," she told Lucia. "But I also think of the war that is going to come. So many people will die, and so many will go to hell. Many cities will be burned to the ground, and many priests will be killed. Look, Lucia, I am going to heaven. But when you see that night illumined by the strange light, you also run away to heaven."

Lucia said that would be impossible, and Jacinta agreed. "But don't be afraid. I'll pray a lot for you in heaven, and for the Holy Father also, and for Portugal, for the war not to come here and for all the priests."

Her influenza grew worse and an abscess formed on her chest. Her suffering was great, but she was glad that she could offer it for the conversion of sinners. She was taken to a hospital at Ourem, but the doctors there could do nothing for her. After two months she was returned to her home.

A priest who visited her at her home said: "She was all bones. It was a shock to see how thin her arms were. She was running a fever all the time. Pneumonia, then tuberculosis and pleurisy, ate away her strength. I remembered as I saw her, that our Lady had promised Bernadette of Lourdes that she would not be happy in this world but in the next. I wondered whether our Lady had made the same promise to Jacinta."

We know now that the Lady had made the same promise, in slightly different words. She had said, "You will have much to suffer." She had also promised that Jacinta would go to heaven.

Despite her illness she made several painful trips to the Cova, and she also went to Mass.

"Don't try to come to Mass," Lucia said one day. "It's too much for you. Besides, it isn't Sunday."

"The Little Saint" 115

"That doesn't matter. I want to go in place of the sinners who don't go even on Sundays."

These words from the lips of a favored child of Mary remind us that the desecration of the Sabbath was one of the sins against which our Lady had protested at La Salette.

"Look, Lucia," Jacinta continued, "our Lord is so sad and our Lady told us that He must not be offended any more. He is already offended very much, and no one pays any attention to it. They keep committing the same sins."

This also recalls Mary's words at La Salette: "And as for you, you take no heed of it."

Another time Jacinta said to Lucia:

"Soon I shall go to heaven. You are to stay here to reveal that the Lord wants to establish throughout the world the devotion to the Immaculate Heart of Mary. When you start to reveal this, don't hesitate. Tell everyone that our Lord grants us all graces through the Immaculate Heart of Mary; that all must make their petitions to her; that the Sacred Heart of Jesus desires that the Immaculate Heart of Mary be venerated at the same time. Tell them that they should all ask for peace from the Immaculate Heart of Mary, as God has placed it in her hands. Oh, if I could only put in the heart of everyone in the world the fire that is burning in me and makes me love so much the Heart of Jesus and the Heart of Mary."

The Blessed Virgin appeared to Jacinta again and told her that she would die in a hospital in Lisbon. Soon after that a specialist told her parents that she should be taken to a hospital in Lisbon. They protested that there was no point in making such a trip if the Blessed Virgin had told her that she was going to die. The doctor replied that the only way they could be sure the Blessed Virgin wanted to take the girl was to go to all lengths to save her. This argument convinced them, and so they took her to Lisbon.

The hospital had no vacant room, and no one wanted to take such a sick girl into a private home. Finally, she was given room in an orphanage. A chapel adjoined the orphanage and Jacinta was happy to be under the same roof with the

Blessed Sacrament. The superior, Mother Godinho, was very kind to the girl. Our Lady appeared to Jacinta several times during her stay in the orphanage.

Jacinta made many statements that were far beyond the ordinary girl of her years. Mother Godinho kept a record of them. She asked Jacinta where she learned these things and was told that our Lady taught her some of them and that others she had thought out for herself. "I like to think very much."

"Wars are only punishments for the sins of the world," she said one time. "Our Lady cannot stay the arm of her beloved Son upon the world any more. It is necessary to do penance. If the people amend themselves, our Lord shall still come to the aid of the world. If they do not amend themselves, punishment shall come."

Again one is struck by the similarity between Jacinta's words and the words of Our Lady of La Salette. "If my people will not submit, I shall be forced to let go the hand of my Son."

"If men do not amend their lives," said Jacinta on another occasion, "Almighty God will send the world, beginning with Spain, a punishment such as never has been seen." She spoke of "great world events" that were to take place around 1940. She cried when she thought of the catastrophe that was coming and when she thought of the way men were offending Jesus and Mary.

"My dear Mother," she said at another time, "the sins that bring most souls to hell are the sins of the flesh. Certain fashions are going to be introduced which will offend our Lord very much. Those who serve God should not follow these fashions. The Church has no fashions. . . . If people only knew what eternity is, they would do everything to change their lives. People lose their souls because they do not think about the death of our Lord and do not do penance.

"Many marriages are not good; they do not please our Lord and are not of God.

"Pray a great deal for governments. Pity those governments which persecute the religion of our Lord. If the governments left the Church in peace and gave liberty to the Holy Religion, they would be blessed by God.

"Do not give yourself to immodest clothes. Run away from riches. Love holy poverty and silence. Be very charitable, even with those who are unkind. Never criticize others and avoid those who do. Be very patient, for patience brings us to heaven. Mortifications and sacrifices please our Lord a great deal.

"The Mother of God wants a large number of virgin souls to bind themselves to her by the vow of chastity. I would enter a convent with great joy, but my joy is greater because I am going to heaven. To be a religious one has to be pure in soul and in body."

"Do you know what it means to be pure?" Mother Godinho asked.

"Yes, I do. To be pure in body means to preserve chastity. To be pure in soul means to avoid sin, not to look at what is sinful, not to steal, never lie and always tell the truth even when it is hard. Whoever does not fulfill promises made to our Lady will not be blessed in life."

On February 2, 1920, Jacinta was admitted to the hospital. She was examined by many doctors. Most of these were concerned only with science and medicine and had no thought of God. Jacinta knew this and the thought saddened her. "Pity doctors. They have no idea what awaits them. Doctors do not know how to treat their patients with success because they have no love of God."

In these three sentences ten-year-old Jacinta protested against the materialism of our times. She saw that men were putting their trust in science and ignoring God. But she was not angry with them; she pitied them.

All of Jacinta's words are worth great consideration. We are not bound to believe private revelations, and some of Jacinta's remarks were not even private revelations. The Blessed Virgin told her some things, and others she "thought out" for herself. We do know, however, that Jacinta was very saintly and that she had been promised by our Lady that she would go to heaven. Her words are not to be dismissed lightly. And her prediction of a great punishment being visited on the world, beginning with Spain, came only too true!

So when Jacinta tells us that "the sins that bring most souls to hell are sins of the flesh" her words carry great weight. And there seems little reason to doubt them, when we behold the Sixth Commandment held up to ridicule in Broadway plays, in magazine fiction and in best-selling novels; when in some parts of the United States one marriage in three ends in a divorce, a flagrant disregard of God's laws.

"Certain fashions are going to be introduced which will offend our Lord very much" seems meant for our own day. Was Jacinta thinking of us when she uttered these words back in 1920?

"Wars are only punishments for the sins of the world" is a sentence that should be broadcast to the world. Our day-to-day actions are more important to the keeping of the peace than all the maneuverings of the world's diplomats.

On February 10, two of Jacinta's ribs were removed. Because of her weakness, she could not be given a general anesthetic, and the local one did not take away her pain. "It is for love of You, my Jesus," she murmured. "Now You can convert many sinners, for I suffer much."

For six days the agonizing pain lasted. Then on the night of February 16, our Lady appeared to her and told her that her suffering was at an end. The pain stopped. On February 20, she asked for the Last Sacraments. The priest heard her confession and said he would bring her Communion in the morning. She asked him to bring it at once because she was going to die soon. She died before her wish was fulfilled. A young nurse, Aurora Gomes, was the only person present when Jacinta quietly breathed her last.

Crowds flocked to the undertaking parlor where Jacinta was laid out in her white First Communion dress with a blue sash, our Lady's colors. The people were sure that Jacinta was already in heaven with our Lord and our Lady, and they wanted to see "the little saint." Although her body had been filled with poison, she was beautiful in death. Her lips were red, her cheeks rosy and a pleasant aroma came from her body. "I have seen many bodies, in my business, young and old," the undertaker said later. "Never did a thing of this sort happen to me before or since."

Jacinta's body was placed at first in a vault at Ourem. In 1935 the Bishop of Leiria requested that it be taken to Fatima and buried in the church yard beside the body of Francisco. Her casket was opened at that time and the body was found to be whole and incorrupt.

In April, 1951, the remains of Francisco and Jacinta were moved to the basilica which had risen above the Cova da Iria. Jacinta's body was examined again. It was found to be partly corrupted but still in a remarkable state of preservation.

The cause of the beatification of Francisco and Jacinta is now being considered.

18

The Heart Encircled With Thorns

REVELATIONS TO LUCIA, 1925-1929

"You must remain longer here below," our Lady said to Lucia. "Jesus will use you to make me better known and better loved."

So Lucia had remained on this earth long after her two cousins had been taken.

In January, 1918, the Holy See re-established the diocese of

Leiria, after a lapse of sixty years. Fatima is a part of this diocese. The Reverend Joseph Correia da Silva was named Bishop and took possession of his diocese August 5, 1920. The new Bishop considered it one of his most important duties to investigate the complete story of the Fatima apparitions. He interviewed Lucia on June 13, 1921. He told her that he thought it would be best if she entered a convent school. The purpose of this was to take Lucia away from the devout people and curiosity seekers who were constantly around her and to give her a chance to forget the apparitions should they prove to be imaginary. The Bishop also wished to determine whether the many cures and conversions which were taking place at the Cova were induced by hysteria caused by her presence there. He wished to see whether the cures and conversions would continue to take place in her absence.

"You must not tell anyone when or where you are going," the Bishop said.

"Yes, Bishop."

"You must not tell a soul at school who you are."

"Yes, Bishop."

"And you must not utter a word about Fatima."

"Yes, Bishop." Lucia would do whatever she was commanded.

It was not easy to leave her home and her mother, but she offered the sacrifice to save souls from hell. She entered a school conducted by the Sisters of St. Dorothy. She was given a new name, Maria das Dores, and only the superior knew who she was.

When she completed the course of studies, she asked whether she might be admitted to the order. She entered the convent in 1925, became a novice on November 2, 1926, and two years later made her vows as a lay Sister. On October 3, 1934, she made her perpetual vows. She was known in the order as Sister Dores. This word means sorrows and is not a proper name in English. The nearest thing to it is Dolores.

On December 10, 1925, our Lady came back, as she had

The Heart Encircled With Thorns

said she would, to request Communions of reparation on the First Saturdays. Lucia was praying in her cell at the convent when our Lady appeared, together with the Child Jesus elevated on a cloud of light. Our Lady rested one hand on Lucia's shoulder. In the other, she held a heart surrounded with sharp thorns. The Child Jesus spoke first:

"Have pity on the Heart of your Most Holy Mother. It is covered with the thorns with which ungrateful men pierce it at every moment, and there is no one to remove them with an act of reparation."

Then our Lady said:

"My daughter, look at my Heart encircled with the thorns with which ungrateful men pierce it at every moment by their blasphemies and ingratitude. Do you at least try to console me and announce in my name that I promise to assist at the hour of death with the graces necessary for salvation all those who, on the first Saturday of five consecutive months, go to Confession and receive Holy Communion, recite the Rosary and keep me company for a quarter of an hour while meditating on the mysteries of the Rosary with the intention of making reparation."

The request for the First Saturday devotion was repeated in 1926 and 1927.

In 1927 our Lord spoke to Lucia from the tabernacle, while she was praying in the convent chapel in Tuy, Spain. He gave her permission to reveal two parts of the July apparition which had been kept secret until that time. These were the vision of hell and the long message beginning, "You have seen hell where the souls of poor sinners go. To save them, God wishes to establish throughout the world devotion to my Immaculate Heart. . . ." This was the message which said that if people did not stop offending God another and worse war would begin in the reign of Pius XI. It was also the message in which our Lady said, "If my requests are granted, Russia will be converted and there will be peace. If not, she shall spread her errors throughout the world, promoting wars and persecutions of the Church. . . ."

For some reason, the authorities did not allow this message to be made known to the world until 1942.

The third part of the July message has not yet been revealed. Acting on instructions from heaven, Lucia has written it down and the Bishop of Leiria has placed it in his archives.

In 1929, our Lady came to ask the consecration of Russia to her Immaculate Heart. In the July apparition she had said that she would come back to make this request. She asked that the consecration be made by the Holy Father in unison with all the bishops of the world.

Three years passed and nothing was done. Lucia again wrote to the Bishop. She quoted our Lord as saying, "The Holy Father will consecrate Russia to me, but it will be late."

On October 13, 1930, the thirteenth anniversary of the Miracle of the Sun, the Bishop of Leiria published a pastoral letter in which he said that the apparitions of Fatima were worthy of belief. The investigation had been under way since 1922.

19

"I Will Convert Sinners"

BEAURAING, 1932-1933

THE STORY OF FATIMA does not end with the revelations to Lucia in the convent. It is a story that goes on and on. In order to keep events in their proper chronological order, however, it is necessary to interrupt the story of Fatima at this point and to come back to it later.

Since Fatima, our Lady is reported to have appeared in many parts of the world. In the vast majority of cases, the

Church authorities have not had the time to make the full painstaking investigation that is necessary. Experience has proved that it is extremely dangerous to report such alleged apparitions, even the ones which seem most authentic according to human testimony. A "vision" which seems completely authentic to the lay observer today may be condemned tomorrow. The unauthenticated visions reported earlier in this book, such as Knock, seem at least to have stood the test of time.

By 1951 there was such a furor over unproved visions in various parts of the world that Monsignor Alfredo Ottaviani, Assessor of the Holy Office, issued a warning which appeared on the first page of *Osservatore Romano*, Vatican City daily:

"Swarms of the faithful run to a place of presumed visions . . . deserting . . . the Church with its sacraments, preaching, and instruction. . . . No one would dare to build a house by himself, to make a suit or a pair of shoes, or cure himself of illness. Yet, where a matter of religious life is concerned, all authority is rejected. . . . Why present the spectacle of fatuousness or insane overexcitedness to him who fights and despises us?"

Monsignor Ottaviani contrasted conditions today with those of fifty years ago. At that time there was a widespread feeling that belief in miracles or visions was superstition, a "relic of the Dark Ages." Fifty years ago the Church was constantly defending miracles against the attacks of atheists, agnostics and cynics. Today, the Church must curb excesses in the opposite direction.

In an article in *Life* magazine, the British novelist Graham Greene gives an example of a case that has been condemned. This was the "moving statue" in Assisi. This stone statue stands above the main door of a church. Somebody noticed that the statue seemed to breathe and move its arms. Thousands came to see the "miracle." Greene and a friend paid a visit to the church. "My companion and I were both skeptics, but from the first glance we took, the statue seemed to move; sometimes the breast, sometimes the hands, sometimes the whole statue seemed on the point of toppling into the square.

It was probably, we thought, the movement of our own heads that produced the illusion, so we lay flat on our backs on the gravel and shut our eyes and rested them. We opened our eyes and immediately the statue breathed and moved above us."

Despite the fact that so many people had testified to seeing the statue move, the Bishop condemned the "miracle." After that, says Greene, the pilgrimage should have stopped if the Communist mayor of Assisi had left well enough alone. "But he came down to the Church and attacked Our Lady in an address to the crowd and had a paralytic stroke then and there."

"Even with that assistance," Greene adds, "the legend is dying out. Its death is one more support for the legends that do not die. We are forced to ask ourselves: 'Is there any explanation but that some are true?'"

Of all the visions that have been reported since Fatima, we shall confine ourselves to the two series that have received full ecclesiastical approbation. These are the apparitions of Beauraing and Banneux. The two series are closely associated in time and in place.

Beauraing and Banneux are both small towns in the Walloon, or French-speaking, section of Belgium. The two towns are less than a hundred miles apart. The first apparition at Banneux took place just 12 days after the last one at Beauraing.

At Beauraing, our Lady appeared to a group of five children. At Banneux, she appeared to one child. Thus, all the approved apparitions of our Lady in the twentieth century have been to children: Fatima, Beauraing and Banneux. Three of those in the past century were also to children: La Salette, Lourdes and Pontmain. It is as though our Lady would lead us back to her divine Son through innocent children who have not succumbed to the evils of the world.

Beauraing is a town of about 2000 people in the southern part of Belgium, five miles from the French border. The

"I Will Convert Sinners"

people of this district had once been staunch Catholics, and they had remained such in the early half of the nineteenth century when their neighbors in France had turned away from religion. It was almost in our own century that religious indifference began to set in among the Walloons, but by 1932 the inhabitants of Beauraing were, on the whole, indifferent or even hostile to the Catholic faith. Most of them were very poor, and in their desperate economic plight had been at least half converted to the teachings of Karl Marx. The Socialists carried the district in most elections.

Three of the five visionaries of Beauraing belonged to the Voisin family. There were Fernande, 15, Gilberte, 13, and Albert, 11. The latter was the only boy among the five. The other two children were Andree and Gilberte Degeimbre. They were 14 and 9. Two of the girls, it will be noted, were named Gilberte. It will simplify matters if we call them Gilberte V. and Gilberte D.

Gilberte V. was a day student at a school taught by the Sisters of Christian Doctrine. Her father, a railway official, allowed her to receive her education from the Sisters despite the fact that neither he nor his wife went to church. Gilberte, a very religious girl, had long been praying that her parents would return to the Church.

On the evening of Tuesday, November 12, 1932, Fernande and Albert started to the convent to walk home with their sister. They were joined by Andree and Gilberte D. The two older children walked on arm in arm while Albert and Gilberte D. amused themselves by ringing the doorbells of the houses they passed.

At the convent, they rang the bell and waited for Gilberte V. to come out. On the railroad embankment near the convent, Albert beheld "the figure of a Lady, dressed in a long robe of pure white." "Look!" he exclaimed. "The Blessed Virgin walking on that bridge!" The other children saw the figure, too.

Gilberte V. came out the door and wondered what they were looking at. Then she, too, saw the vision.

More frightened than anything else, the children ran home.

No one believed their story. They began to doubt it themselves when everyone told them that their imaginations were deceiving them.

The next night, the four children returned to the spot and were again met by Gilberte V. Once more they saw the figure in white walking back and forth on the embankment.

The mother of the two Degeimbre children was a widow; her husband had died the year before. Mrs. Degeimbre did not believe that her two younger daughters had really seen the Blessed Virgin. She thought they were suffering delusions or that someone was playing a trick. On December 1, she accompanied the four children when they went to the convent.

This time the figure appeared in the convent garden near a grotto of Our Lady of Lourdes. The children could now make out that it was a beautiful Lady dressed entirely in white and with a crown of golden rays. She appeared to be standing on a cloud. Her feet were not visible. She extended her arms slowly and then disappeared.

Mrs. Degeimbre, who could see nothing, sent the children to get Gilberte V. Then, armed with a stick she thrashed about in the bushes for the person who was playing tricks on the children. Her search was in vain. Gilberte V. and the other children returned, and immediately they beheld the vision again. Gilberte D., the youngest, was so overcome with emotion that she was taken home and left with Gilberte V. The other children returned and beheld the vision for the third time that evening. This time our Lady appeared near the lowest branch of a hawthorn tree. This was the place where she appeared during all the remaining apparitions.

The next day Mother Theophile, superior of the convent, forbade the children to speak of the apparitions, and she told them not to come to the convent garden again.

That evening the children's mothers asked them to go to the school to meet Gilberte V., so they did not think they were being disobedient in doing so. Again they saw the vision. Albert asked, "Are you the Immaculate Virgin?" The Lady smiled and nodded her head.

"What do you want?" Albert asked.

Then came the first words uttered by our Lady at Beauraing: "Always be good."

The parish priest, Abbé Lambert, when informed of this, thought that the message sounded like something that originated with the children rather than with the Blessed Virgin. He could not bring himself to believe that the Virgin would make such a trite remark. At home, the parents still disbelieved the children and threatened them with punishment if they did not tell the truth. As for Mother Theophile, she ordered the gates of the convent garden locked at dusk and put two fierce dogs inside.

On Saturday, in obedience to the Superior, the children stayed away from the garden. They were very sad at not seeing their Lady. When Mother Theophile went out to lock the garden gate, she found a crowd of 150 persons waiting. She told them to go home, that there was nothing to see. One member of the crowd said, "See what a Socialist we have in this woman. She has even less belief in this business than we have."

The next day Mother Theophile relented. She said that because the children had obeyed her they would be allowed to come to the grotto. The apparitions continued. Our Lady told the children on several occasions that she wished them to be present on the feast of the Immaculate Conception. Because that day had been specifically mentioned, many people hoped that there would be some great sign at that time. About 15,000 people were present. The five children fell into a profound ecstasy when they beheld the Lady. They did not respond when doctors stuck pins into their flesh, placed flames under their fingers, and shined flashlights into their eyes. Gilberte V. said later, "Just think of it! They tried to tell me that they had pricked and burned me!"

On December 17, our Lady asked for a chapel on the spot where she appeared so people might come there on pilgrimage.

Four days later, she said: "I am the Immaculate Virgin." A few days after that she said, "Soon I shall appear for the last time."

On December 29, the Blessed Virgin opened her arms in the usual gesture of farewell and in so doing exposed her Immaculate Heart, a heart of radiant gold. Once again there was the emphasis on the Immaculate Heart of Mary which has been so prominent in many modern apparitions.

The next day, she said, "Pray! Pray very much!" and again revealed the brilliance of her heart. This was displayed for a third time on the last day of the year.

On January 1, our Lady said "Pray always." She also said that her final appearance would take place two days later.

A great crowd was on hand for the last appearance. Four of the children gave a joyous shout as the apparitions began. Fernande sobbed because she did not see the vision. Our Lady talked to each child separately. To Andree she said: "I am the Mother of God, the Queen of Heaven. Pray always. Good-by." Gilberte V. was told "I will convert sinners. Good-by." To Albert and Gilberte D. she simply said, "Good-by."

When the vision was over, Fernande steadfastly refused to leave the spot, so disappointed was she at not seeing her Lady. Suddenly she heard a loud crashing noise, and she saw a great ball of fire on the tree. Then she saw the Blessed Virgin.

"Do you love my Son?" our Lady asked.

"Yes."

"Do you love me?"

"Yes."

"Sacrifice yourself for me."

Extending her arms, she shone more brightly than ever. Then she showed Fernande her heart and said, "Good-by."

Realizing that she would never again see the Lady in this world, Fernande wept.

Afterward, the three youngest children said that our Lady had entrusted to each of them a secret which might not be told to anyone.

The story of the apparitions caused a great sensation all

over Europe. Many people were sure the appearances were authentic. Others were equally sure they were not. There had been no great sign for everyone to see, such as the Miracle of the Sun at Fatima. In 1934 and 1935, many books and magazine articles dismissed the apparitions as hallucinations. Little by little, the opposition lost its force. The father and mother of the Voisin children returned to the sacraments, as if in answer to Gilberte's prayers and our Lady's promise that she would convert sinners. Mrs. Degeimbre became convinced that her children were telling the truth. It was noted that they never contradicted each other even when questioned separately about the most minute details.

Pilgrims from Belgium and from many other parts of Europe visited the shrine. There were two million pilgrims in the first year. Many cures and temporal favors were reported. More amazing were the conversions which resulted. These conversions are called "Beauraing's Greatest Invisible Treasure." Our Lady had said, "I will convert sinners."

The people of Beauraing returned to the sacraments, and the Socialists lost their grip on the district.

When World War II began, people from other countries could no longer visit the shrine. As if to make up for this, Belgians came in larger numbers than ever.

When Belgium was conquered by Germany, many German soldiers visited the shrine. There they recited prayers which had been taught to them by their mothers long before the Hitler movement had torn them from church and family. The Belgian people respected their right to do this as members of the Universal Church and children of Mary even though they wore the hated enemy uniform.

After the Allies had driven the Germans from Belgium, American soldiers mingled with the Belgian pilgrims. They poured out their homesick hearts in prayers. Many of them made their "return" to the Church at Beauraing.

In 1934, the Bishop of Namur appointed an Episcopal Commission to investigate the events. The Bishop died, and the investigation continued under his successor.

The new Bishop received from Rome a decree dated December 7, 1942, and approved by Pope Pius XII, which granted him full liberty to proceed toward canonical recognition. On February 2, 1943, the Bishop published a decree with authorized public devotions to "Our Lady of Beauraing." This was during the dark days of the German occupation of Belgium, and the people took great comfort from this development. In 1946, on the feast of the Immaculate Heart of Mary, the Bishop blessed the official statue of Our Lady of Beauraing.

On July 2, 1949, the Bishop released two important documents. One was an episcopal decree recognizing as authentic miracles two of the many cures credited to Our Lady of Beauraing. The cures took place in June and July, 1933, in the interval immediately following the apparitions.

The other document was a letter to the clergy of the diocese. In it, the Bishop said: "We are able in all serenity and prudence to affirm that the Queen of Heaven appeared to the children of Beauraing during the winter of 1932-1933, especially to show us in her maternal Heart the anxious appeal for prayer and the promise of her powerful mediation for the conversion of sinners."

A remarkable feature of Beauraing is the fact that, although our Lady appeared at least thirty-three times, she said very little. It would seem that at Fatima she had already given her great message to the world. At Beauraing she again asked for the three things she had requested at Fatima: prayer, sacrifice, devotion to her Immaculate Heart.

20

Virgin of the Poor
BANNEUX, 1933

THE BISHOP of Liége knelt in his cathedral before the exposed Blessed Sacrament. Bishop Kerkhofs had made a decision to consecrate his diocese to the Immaculate Heart of Mary in accordance with the requests made by Our Lady at Fatima. Now he was putting his seal on that decision. This was the evening of January 15, 1933. The apparitions at Fatima had been approved less than three years before, so Bishop Kerkhofs was among the first to follow our Lady's request in this regard.

The apparitions at Beauraing had been concluded two weeks before and all Belgium was in a turmoil about them. Atheists scoffed, and Catholics were divided. All over the country, Catholics were praying for a sign which would indicate whether the apparitions were true or false.

While the Bishop knelt in his cathedral, an eleven-year-old girl, Mariette Beco, pressed her nose against the window of her home. The Beco family lived in a poor section on the outskirts of Banneux, ten miles east of Liége. Mariette was waiting for her brother Julien to come in. It was seven o'clock and she had to keep his supper warm. Her father, who had put in a long working day, had gone to bed early. The younger children were asleep. Mrs. Beco was working in a back room.

It was Sunday, but none of the Becos had attended Mass that morning. The father was a badly lapsed Catholic, and he had not encouraged the Becos to perform their religious duties. Like Beauraing, Banneux is in the Walloon section of Belgium and, as in Beauraing, most of the people were Marxian Socialists at that time.

Mariette looked out upon a dark, moonless night. The flickering light of the oil lamp sent shadows scampering up and down the wall of the kitchen.

Suddenly Mariette called, "Mother, there is a Lady in the garden."

Mrs. Beco came running into the kitchen. Who could it be? Visitors were rare at the humble cottage. The family was poor and hard working, and had no time for entertaining.

Mrs. Beco looked out the window and saw a vague form moving about. "Maybe it's a witch," she said in a frightened voice.

Mariette thought that the figure might be an illusion caused by the lamp. She put her head first on one side and then on the other. The Lady was still there. Mariette noticed a blue girdle similar to the one on the statue in the village church. She knew the Lady was not a witch.

"Oh, no!" she said to her mother. "It is the Holy Virgin."

"As if that is likely," scoffed her mother.

Mariette picked up a rosary that she had found one day at the side of the road but which she had never used. She said six decades, keeping her eyes fixed on the Lady. Then the Lady beckoned Mariette to come out to the garden. The girl started to do so, but her mother would not let her. The mother bolted the door and put a sheet over the window.

Julien came soon after that. He had seen nothing in the garden. He was intrigued by Mariette's story and said the figure was probably the result of a reflection from the icicles. He tried in vain to reproduce it.

When Mariette's father heard the story the next day, he laughed and called his daughter a fool.

Meanwhile, Mariette had confided in her best friend, ten-year-old Josephine Leonard. Josephine ran to the pastor, Abbé Jamin. The priest was leaving the church when she came to him. He was just concluding a novena in which he

Virgin of the Poor

had pleaded that some sign, either of approval of disapproval, be given for Beauraing. He did not take Mariette's story as a sign, however. He supposed that she had heard about Beauraing and that her imagination was playing tricks on her. He knew that there had been an epidemic of "visions" throughout France after Bernadette had seen our Lady at Lourdes. Besides, the Becos did not seem to be the type of family that would be favored by visions from heaven.

The Abbé sent word to Mariette to forget her apparition and not to spread stories about it.

On Wednesday morning, the Abbé was amazed to see Mariette at Mass. She had quit school a few months before because she had failed for the third time to pass her examination for Holy Communion, and she had stopped going to Mass at the same time. This morning she not only attended Mass, but she went to school afterward. She knew her catechism lesson perfectly, probably for the first time in her life.

That same evening, January 18, 1933, at seven o'clock, Mariette went out into the garden before she could be stopped. Her father followed her. He found her kneeling by the gate saying her Rosary. It was cold and dark. Just as he reached the girl, she stretched forth her arms. She had again found her Lady.

Mr. Beco did not know what to do. No matter what he said, Mariette did not seem to hear him. He ran to the house, leaped on his bicycle, and rushed to town to get the pastor.

The priest was not in, but Mr. Beco found a friend who was a practicing Catholic. When they got back to the farm, they saw Mariette stand up and walk onto the highway.

"Where are you going?" they asked.

"She is beckoning me," Mariette answered.

The girl made her way along the road following the Lady who seemed to glide rather than walk. They reached a spring which was flowing out of a bank into a ditch by the side of the road. Obeying the Lady, Mariette knelt and plunged her hands into the water.

"This spring is set aside for me," the Lady said. "Good night."

Mr. Beco and his friend brought Mariette home where they found the Abbé waiting for them. They told him what had happened. Mariette was now able to give a better description of the Lady. Her robe was long and white. The right foot was bare. Under the right foot was a beautiful golden rose. She wore a blue girdle, and rays of light shone from her head. She was a little more than five feet tall. Her hands were raised to her breast and pointed upward. A rosary hung from her right arm. The description was similar to that of Our Lady of Lourdes.

When Mariette completed the story, Mr. Beco told the priest he would like to go to confession and receive Holy Communion.

The next day, the pastor called in a Benedictine for advice. This priest told Mariette to ask the Lady her name.

That evening the Lady again appeared and Mariette followed the instructions.

"I am the Virgin of the Poor," was the answer.

The Lady again led Mariette to the spring. Following the instructions of the Benedictine, Mariette asked, "Madame, you did say yesterday, 'This spring is set aside for me'?"

The Lady smiled, nodded, and said, "It is for all the nations . . . for the sick. . . . I have come to relieve the sick." She then added, "I shall pray for you. Au revoir." With that, she faded into the darkness of the night.

There were five other apparitions on January 20, February 11, 15, and 20, and March 2.

On January 20, Mariette asked if there was anything the Lady desired. "I would like a little chapel," was the answer. The Lady placed her hands on Mariette's head to bless her. Overcome with emotion, the girl fainted and was carried into the house.

On February 11, the seventy-fifth anniversary of the first apparition at Lourdes, the Lady showed her compassion for the world by saying, "I have come to relieve suffering."

On February 15, the child asked for a sign. The Lady said, "Have faith in me, and I shall have faith in you. Pray much." She told Mariette a secret, "something I mustn't tell anyone, not even Mama or Papa." After this visit, the girl wept for a long time. She has never told her secret.

The Lady led Mariette to the spring on February 20. This time she was not smiling. She said urgently, "My dear child, pray hard. Au revoir."

The most recent appearance of our Lady to receive official recognition took place on March 2, 1933. Mariette knelt in the pouring rain saying her Rosary. When she had reached the third glorious mystery, there was a gust of wind and the Lady stood before her. She stood before the girl as she had stood before St. Catherine Labouré, the children of La Salette, St. Bernadette, the children of Fatima, and the children of Beauraing. She looked at Mariette for a long time without smiling. Then she said: "I am the Mother of the Saviour, the Mother of God. Pray hard. Adieu."

Until this time, our Lady had said "au revoir" which means "until the next meeting." This time she said "adieu" which means "good-by."

She blessed Mariette and again the girl fainted. She did not see our Lady depart.

When the ecclesiastical investigation began, it was found that the Beco family had become model Catholics. Mariette told her story over and over and could not be made to contradict herself or to retract anything. She was examined by panels of doctors and psychiatrists, men of world-wide repute. So many cures have been reported that Banneux rivals Lourdes in this respect. In addition, there have been many conversions from schism, heresy and paganism.

The most spectacular physical cure has been that of Benito Pelegri Garcia, an anarchist of Barcelona, Spain. Garcia's right arm was so severely injured in a boiler explosion that he was not able to work. His wife, a Belgian, heard of the events at Banneux and insisted that they make a pilgrimage. They walked from Barcelona to Banneux, abstaining from wine and tobacco on the way. The journey was made under the pitiless mid-summer sun. The couple had little food and very poor lodging.

Benito put both hands into the spring at Banneux. His left

hand found the water pleasantly cool but his right hand found it boiling hot. Withdrawing his hands, he said, "If you are the Virgin of the Poor, prove it. Here is a man who has come all the way from Spain."

He thrust his right hand into the pool a second time. Then he drew the drain tube from the wound. Before the amazed eyes of everyone present, the wound closed, the flesh became sound, and the arm was completely normal!

Church officials and residents of Banneux are making the village a center of charity, with homes for the aged, orphanages, and hospitals for the poor. Abbé Arendt is compiling a Marian library at Banneux and is seeking everything that has ever been written about Mary. The International Union of Prayers, with headquarters at Banneux, has enrolled thousands of members.

In 1942, during the German occupation, the Bishop authorized the cult of Our Lady of Banneux, Our Lady of the Poor.

In 1947 he said, "Today, after five consecutive years of observation and prayer, we are happy to renew and confirm this approbation and declaration."

The chapel requested by our Lady was speedily constructed and was blessed on August 15, 1933. The cornerstone of a new basilica was laid in 1948.

During the war, Mariette married a Dutch salesman. In 1944, during the Battle of the Bulge, an American chaplain found them and their fifteen-month-old baby living in the cellar of a small home occupied by American troops.

Why are Beauraing and Banneux so closely connected in time and space? One could counter with another question: Who can explain the ways of God?

A priest who knows Belgium very well says: "Mary hovers in and around her beloved Belgium, a country so Catholic that she will not permit it to fall into the hands of scoffers and spiritual wolves who have tried all methods and means to dissuade the faithful from their original heritage."

Through most of her history, Belgium has been staunchly

Catholic, and this has included the royal family. Of all the countries of Europe, Belgium was one of the very few that resisted the materialism and indifferentism of the nineteenth century. Only in comparatively recent years have the industrial workers, in their great distress, begun to turn to the teachings of Karl Marx. Mary is apparently determined to save Belgium.

Banneux is one more reminder, in these days when the followers of Karl Marx seem to be sweeping everything before them, that our great hope—our only hope—lies in our carrying out the request our Lady has made at Fatima and other places. She prays for us without ceasing, she had told us, but she needs our help. She needs our prayers and sacrifices.

21

The Unknown Light
WORLD WAR II, 1939-1945

YEARS PASSED, and the consecration of Russia to Mary's Immaculate Heart was not made. Neither did men stop offending God, as our Lady had begged them to do at Fatima.

Man's pride in his own accomplishments which had been increasing for more than a century reached its zenith in the days after World War I. In much of the Western World the Armistice was wildly celebrated. "The war to end all wars" was over, and man had shown himself capable of solving all his problems.

Pride, greed and lust were man's answers to God's demand for prayer and penance. The newspapers mirrored the spirit of the twenties. It was a time of crime, luxury, vice, divorce and public scandal. In the United States it was the age of the bootlegger, flaming youth and falling public morality.

The thirties brought a world-wide depression, increased powers of dictators and the threat of another general war. The people of the Western World lost some of their optimism and their faith in inevitable progress. They decided they had not solved all their problems after all. They became more serious, more conscious of the need for reform. Their outlook, however, was a Godless one. They would reform, but they would do it in their own way.

Governments as well as individuals offended God. In Mexico there was a bitter persecution of the Church. Pope Pius XI, who had succeeded Pope Benedict XV in 1922, said of this country: "Priests and laymen, too, were pitilessly slain, at the crossroads, in the public squares, before their very churches." The best known of many martyrs of the Mexican persecution was Father Miguel Pro, who went down before the firing squad crying, "Long live Christ the King!"

Benito Mussolini and his Fascists came to power in Italy. They tried to bend everything, including the Church, to their will. They abolished religious schools and youth movements under religious auspices. Children were to be brought up with the idea that the State was supreme in all things and that they owed the State their undivided allegiance. Pope Pius XI said in an encyclical about Italian Fascism: "A conception of the State which makes the rising generation belong to it without exception, from the tenderest years up to adult life, cannot be reconciled either with Catholic doctrine or with the natural rights of the family." Because the Pope was sure that the Fascist authorities would try to suppress the encyclical, he had Monsignor Francis J. Spellman, later Cardinal Archbishop of New York, smuggle it out of the country and release it in Paris.

Adolf Hitler and his Nazis became masters of Germany and showed themselves to be even more ruthless than the Fascists of Italy. The bishops of that country said that the Nazis had embarked on a program that aimed at nothing less

The Unknown Light

than the complete extermination of the Church. Of the approximately 20,000 priests who were in Germany when Hitler came to power, 14,364 were killed, imprisoned or exiled by the Nazis.

Both Hitler and Mussolini used the threat of Communism as an excuse to seize power. Once they were in power, they adopted many of the same tactics as the Communists, including the persecution of religion.

As soon as the Communists were in control of Russia they began their campaign to conquer all Europe. The most direct way into western Europe was through Warsaw, the capital of Poland. They hurled their divisions at that seemingly defenseless city. When all the other diplomats fled the city the Papal Nuncio, Archbishop Ratti, later to become Pope Pius XI, stayed on. His prayers and courageous example so inspired the Poles that on August 15, feast of the Assumption, they gathered together the remnants of their retreating army. All day long the soldiers prayed to the Blessed Virgin. They attacked the vastly larger Russian army on August 16. By the 17th the Russians had been hurled across the border. Warsaw and Europe were saved from Communism, for a while.

Defeated in Poland, the Communists merely bided their time. In the 1930's they struck again, this time in Spain. The Communists gained a strong voice in the Spanish "republic" and were overthrown only after a long and bitter civil war. During this war, which started in 1936, more than 11,000 priests and nuns and 12 bishops were killed by the "Loyalists," as the supporters of the Communist-dominated government were called. More than 20,000 churches, convents and schools were sacked. In each church that was pillaged, the Communists seemed to wreak their special hatred on the statue of the Blessed Virgin.

These bitter persecutions, within the memory of most of us, bring to mind the words of St. Louis Marie de Montfort: "The devil, knowing he has but little time, and now less than ever, to destroy souls, will every day redouble his efforts. He will presently raise up cruel persecutions. . . ."

"When you shall see a night illumined by an unknown light, know that it is the great sign that God gives you that He is going to punish the world for its crimes by means of war, of hunger, and of persecution of the Church and the Holy Father."

On the night of January 25, 1938, Lucia looked out of the window of her cell in the convent and saw the entire sky aflame with a weird light. This phenomenon was seen all over Europe and in many other parts of the world. Astronomers called it an especially brilliant display of the Aurora Borealis. Lucia knew it to be the "unknown light" foretold in the July apparition.

The world could have been spared this punishment if it had heeded the warning of Fatima, if it had stopped offending God, but now the sign had been given that "another and worse" war was about to begin.

In September of the following year, Germany invaded Poland. This is generally regarded as the beginning of World War II. The Blessed Virgin had said that the war would begin during the reign of Pope Pius XI, and he had died just a few months before. When asked about this point, Lucia said: "The annexation of Austria gave occasion for the war." It might be noted that the Spanish Civil War in which the Russians had aided one side while the Germans and Italians had aided the other was fought during the reign of Pope Pius XI. The Japanese-Chinese War also had begun then. Either of these events could be regarded as the real beginning of World War II. Back in 1920, Jacinta had said: "If men do not amend their lives, Almighty God will send the world, beginning with Spain, a punishment such as has never been seen."

"When the Munich accord was made (in 1938) the Sisters rejoiced because they thought that peace was secured," said Lucia later. "Unhappily, I knew more than they."

Pope Pius XI died in the spring of 1939 and was succeeded by Pope Pius XII who worked day and night to avoid the war that was impending.

On March 19, 1939, Lucia wrote to her Bishop: "From

The Unknown Light

the practice of the devotion to the Immaculate Heart of Mary, together with the consecration, depends war or peace for the world. That is why I wish so much for this devotion to be propagated, and, above all, because it is the will of God and of our dear heavenly Mother."

Another letter, dater April 20, 1939, reads: "Our Lady promised to postpone for some time this scourge of war if the practice of this devotion will be propagated. We see her turning aside the chastisement in proportion as efforts are made to propagate this devotion; but I fear that we will not be able to do more than we are doing, and that God, being not well pleased, may lift the arm of His mercy and let the world be devastated by a chastisement that will be horrible like never before. It will be horrible ... horrible...."

The war started off in a horrible manner, with the Germans raining death on Polish cities and with the ruthless extermination of Polish Jews. Then it settled down to a quiet period in which French and German armies faced each other over the Maginot Line. This was the period of the so-called "phony war."

"Would that the world knew the hour of grace that is being given to it," Lucia wrote in 1940, "and would do penance."

Then, at the suggestion of her spiritual director, Lucia wrote to Pope Pius XII, telling him the exact request of our Lady. The Pope deliberated long and prayerfully over this request from heaven.

In the meantime, the "phony war" erupted into a very real war. France suffered once more. The country soon collapsed and had to submit to German occupation. Later, it once again became the chief battleground of the war.

Archbishop Saliege of Toulouse, in a pastoral letter, asked: "Did we really work and pray hard enough? Have we made up for sixty years of national apostasy; sixty years when the French spirit succumbed to every disease of the mind; when the French will relaxed, morality dropped and anarchy arose to unusual proportions?"

Destruction rained not only upon France but upon almost

every country of Europe and several in the Far East. It was, as Lucia had predicted, "horrible as never before." The Japanese bombed Pearl Harbor on the eve of the feast of the Immaculate Conception in 1941, and the United States declared war on the feast itself.

Writing about the war, in 1949, John Cogley said in *Today*: "Things have moved so fast since the war ended four years ago that the terror and misery of the short Nazi rule of Europe have been almost forgotten by many Americans. The handful of GI's who witnessed the liberation of living skeletons at Dachau and Buchenwald, who saw the fiendish efficiency of the concentration-camp ovens, and who knew the actual stench of Nazi death in their nostrils—these are likely to remember a little longer than most. But for the vast majority of us, the full horror of what Nazism meant is gradually fading away.

"It is, it seems to me, impossible for the human mind to imagine evil more thorough, malice more absolute than that symbolized and practiced by the Nazi party." Mr. Cogley pointed out that during their twelve years in power the Nazis killed six million Jews. Six million! The figure is too much for our imaginations. And the Jews are only part of the story!

"Just as it is easy to forget the horrible evil that was National Socialism, so is it easy to forget its millions of victims. They are remembered in mass terms—so many Polish Jews, so many French Catholics, so many German Communists, etc.—but rarely as men and women who might be living today, shaping the post war world, tending little European shops, lecturing in classrooms, editing magazines, sitting at factory benches, coming home at the end of a day to a wife and children. The history books will always remind us of the tragic mass of victims. It takes our imagination and our compassion to turn the mass into living people—husbands and wives torn from each others' arms, children snatched from their classrooms or their cradles, young people who might, during the summer of 1949, have known the ecstasy of first love."

The Unknown Light

The people of the United States and the other nations of the Western Hemisphere suffered little in comparison with the people of Europe. It is interesting to note that the story of Fatima did not become known in the Western Hemisphere until the end of the war. In Europe at least part of the story had been known for some time. If Europeans were more guilty than Americans of deliberately ignoring the message, they also suffered more.

In 1942, Portugal celebrated the twenty-fifth anniversary of the Apparitions at Fatima. This country had not been engulfed in the second World War as it had in the first. On the last day of October, the bishops of Portugal gathered at the shrine. They joined with the Holy Father, whose voice came to them by radio, in dedicating the world to the Immaculate Heart of Mary. The Pope made a special mention of Russia: "Give peace to the peoples separated from us by error or by schism and especially to the one who professes such singular devotion to thee and in whose homes an honored place was ever accorded thy venerable icon (today perhaps often hidden to await better days); bring them back to the one fold of Christ under the one true Shepherd. . . ."

Six weeks later, on the feast of the Immaculate Conception, the Pope repeated this consecration at St. Peter's in Rome.

Our Lady has asked for the consecration of Russia as one of the conditions for world peace. Would peace now be granted to the world?

The following spring, Lucia wrote to the Bishop of Gurza, her spiritual director: "The good Lord has already shown me His pleasure in the act of the Holy Father and the various bishops, although incomplete according to His desire. In exchange, He promises to bring the war soon to an end, but the conversion of Russia will not take place yet. If the bishops of Spain heed the desires of our Lord and engage in a true reform of the people . . . good; if not she (Russia) will again be the enemy with which God shall punish them once more."

World War II was to come to an end, but there was no guarantee of real peace. Before taking up the question as to why the consecration of 1942 was "incomplete" it might be well to give the rest of Lucia's statement:

"The good Lord is allowing Himself to be appeased, but He complains bitterly and sorrowfully about the small numbers of souls in His grace who are willing to renounce whatever the observance of His law requires of them.

"This is the penance which the good Lord now asks: the sacrifice that every person has to impose upon himself is to lead a life of justice in the observance of His law. He requires that this way be made known to souls. For many, thinking that the word penance means great austerities and not feeling in themselves the strength or generosity for these, lose heart and rest in a life of lukewarmness and sin.

"Last Thursday, at midnight, while I was in chapel with my superiors' permission, our Lord said to me: 'The sacrifice required of every person is the fulfillment of his duties in life and the observance of My law. This is the penance I now seek and require.'"

Our Lord's statement regarding penance is very important and will be treated later. The question that concerns us now is why our Lady considered the consecration of 1942 "incomplete according to His desire."

The answer usually given is that our Lady had requested the consecration of Russia, not the world, to her Immaculate Heart. She had also asked, according to some accounts, that the Pope make the consecration in union with the bishops of the world.

Father Thomas McGlynn questioned Lucia on this point and reports the interview in *Vision of Fatima*.

"Did the Holy Father consecrate Russia to the Immaculate Heart?" Father McGlynn asked.

"He included Russia in the consecration," she answered. Then she added, "In the official way that our Lady asked for it? I don't think so."

Father McGlynn says that she uttered the words very humbly as if wishing that she were wrong.

Father's companion and translator pressed the point. "Do you think that our Lady's request has been complied with?"

The Unknown Light 145

"As our Lady made it, no," she answered. "Whether our Lady accepted the consecration made in 1942, as fulfilling her wish, I do not know."

This interview took place in 1947 and was one of the last Lucia has ever given. In April, 1948, she entered the Carmelites and now leads a cloistered life as Sister Mary of the Immaculate Heart. It will be virtually impossible for anyone but the highest authorities to interview her now.

In 1952 came the welcome news that Pope Pius XII had dedicated and consecrated all the peoples of Russia to the Immaculate Heart "in a most special way." By this time Lucia was no longer available for comment, but there can be no doubt that this was a long step toward world peace. We'll read more about this consecration in Chapter XXVI.

It was in the spring of 1943 that Lucia said God would end the war soon. The war in Europe ended in May, the Month of Our Lady, 1945. The was in Asia ended with the surrender of Japan the same year. This happened on the eve of the feast of the Assumption in our Western World, on the feast itself in the Far East.

While we know that World War II fell upon us as a result of our sins, the war contains striking examples of the mercy our Lady always shows when we turn to her. Two examples come from such widely separated and vastly different places as the island of Ceylon and the city of Rome.

When Singapore fell to the Japanese, their next objective seemed to be the island of Ceylon off the southern tip of India. Nothing had stopped their victorious sweep thus far, and it seemed that nothing could keep them from overrunning Ceylon. The people were terrified. More than 6,000,000 people live on the island, the vast majority of whom are Buddhists. Less than 10 per cent of the people are Catholics.

Archbishop J. M. Masson went to the little town of Tewatte where there is a grotto of our Lady. As a member of the Oblates of Mary Immaculate, he had a profound devotion to our Lady and a childlike confidence in her.

The Archbishop told Mary that he was placing the island under her protection. He promised that if Ceylon were spared the horrors of attack and occupation he would build a shrine in her honor at Tewatte. He then went back to Colombo, the capital, and assured the people that the Japanese would not invade Ceylon. And they did not. Later, the Archbishop visited Rome and obtained from Pope Pius XII permission to proclaim the Mother of God as Our Lady of Ceylon.

Archbishop Masson died, and the work continued under his successor, Archbishop Cooray. A great basilica, made possible by the grateful Catholics of Ceylon, has risen at Tewatte. It is of Indian architecture and contains fifteen altars, one for each mystery of the Rosary. The basilica was dedicated in the Marian Year of 1954.

Few people outside Italy know the part our Lady played in saving the city of Rome in the perilous year of 1944. After Italy surrendered to the Allies, the Germans occupied Rome. Pope Pius XII could look out the window of his apartment and see German soldiers patrolling night and day in front of the piazza of St. Peter's. Meanwhile the Allies were slowly advancing up the Italian peninsula, in the direction of Rome.

The Germans declared that they would never withdraw from Rome unless the city had been reduced to ruins. They prepared to resist. Barricades were raised in the streets. Antiaircraft guns were placed in the church towers. Old Roman monuments were converted into fortresses. Plans were made to blow up the bridges that crossed the Tiber.

The people were thoroughly frightened. With the Germans determined to resist and the Allies determined to capture the Eternal City, it seemed it would be reduced to a mass of rubble. In their fright, the people turned to the Mother of God.

About ten miles south of Rome is a shrine to Our Lady of Divine Love. The people carried the statue of Our Lady of Divine Love into Rome. They placed it in the Church of St. Ignatius and began an octave to our Lady. In the morning, Mass was celebrated every half hour until noon. In the after-

The Unknown Light

noon and evening there was recitation of the Rosary, a sermon, and Benediction of the Blessed Sacrament. The church was always filled. During the last few days of the octave the people who were in the church could hear the bombardment of the surrounding cities.

On the last day of the octave the priest who delivered the sermon begged our Blessed Mother to ask her divine Son to save Rome. The people wept and prayed. They promised to amend their lives and to be more faithful in their religious duties.

As they came out of church, the heard the wondrous news that while the Allies were entering Rome from one side the Germans had hastily left from the other. Rome was saved. (This great event has since been commemorated by a bronze plaque at the entrance of St. Ignatius Church.)

The next day the people flocked to St. Peter's Square. Pope Pius XII came out on the balcony. He said: "With profound gratitude we pay our tribute to the Blessed Mother of God and our Mother, who has added a new proof of her motherly love to her famous title 'Mother of the Roman People.' It will be eternally remembered in the history of this city."

A week later the Holy Father went to the Church of St. Ignatius. For a long time he knelt in grateful prayer before the statue of Our Lady of Divine Love. Then he went into the pulpit to speak to the people: "During four long years we have shared in common the sufferings and anxieties of a cruel war. Your sorrows have been ours. But we have experienced great consolations as we watched your faith that brought you to the feet of Mary, Mother of Divine Love. Our Immaculate Mother has once more saved Rome from great danger."

22

The Light of the Atom
HIROSHIMA, 1945

FATHER HUBERT SCHIFFER sat in his room at the rectory of the Church of the Assumption of Our Lady in Hiroshima. He was a German-born Jesuit missionary, who had studied for the priesthood in Tokyo and had recently been ordained. Tokyo had been undergoing bombardment day and night, and Father Schiffer's superiors had sent him to the quiet town of Hiroshima for a rest. On this morning of August 6, 1945, he had said Mass and had eaten his breakfast. Now he was reading the morning newspaper.

Then suddenly there was a great light.

This was not the "unknown light" that Lucia had seen from the window of her convent seven and a half years before. Lucia's light had been heaven made and was a warning. This light was man made and was the terrible fulfillment of that warning.

It was a burning, blinding light, as though the world had been removed from around him, and for one moment Father Schiffer was adrift in a great ocean of white.

The next thing the young priest knew he was lying on the floor recovering consciousness. Father Schiffer had been through many bombings in Tokyo. He was not surprised to find that he could not see. He had expected a temporary blindness to follow a concussion. The wetness that he could feel all over him was the blood that he had known would come if he were ever hit. Only the deafness could not be explained.

The Light of the Atom

There was absolute deathly quiet where there should have been the sounds of more explosions, the cries of terror, the shouts of the people, the wailing of sirens. In that awful stillness it suddenly came to him that this was nothing like the "sound" of deafness. It was vaster than that . . . emptier.

The pastor and two other priests, who had been upstairs, rushed down to aid the injured man. No one understood what had happened. The rectory was earthquake proof, and its walls held. Father Lasalle, the pastor, had been only slightly injured. He went to get his Red Cross kit to aid Father Schiffer, but the kit had been demolished.

"You'll have to go to the doctor's," said Father Lasalle. "Do you know where he lives?"

Father Schiffer shook his head.

"Come with me," Father Lasalle said. They went to the door. "You go down the street . . ."

He stopped.

There was no street.

There was, in fact, very little city. Where the city had been, the two men saw nothing but desolation. Instead of the buildings of Hiroshima, there were the far-off hills, hills which the priests should not have been able to see. Only the rectory stood amidst the surrounding rubble. The Church next door had been demolished. Flames were leaping up everywhere.

Father Lasalle told Father Schiffer that he had better leave before the flames enveloped him. "Go any place. Probably it's best down by the river. And, Father," he added, "you will soon see the Blessed Mother in Heaven. Please tell her that we will rebuild her church on this spot as soon as we can."

Somehow, Father Schiffer made his way through the streets, avoiding the fires, the falling debris, stepping over bodies. He stumbled to the bank of the river where he fell unconscious. At eight o'clock that night, some students from the novitiate found him and put him on a stretcher. Every movement sent stabs of pain that brought him back to consciousness. The students were tired. They had been carrying the injured all day. One of them slipped, and Father went rolling to the road. They put him back on the stretcher, and another slipped. Again he crashed to the road.

Half a dozen times Father begged of the bearers, "Let me die here."

"No," they answered. "We have orders to get you back for a decent Christian funeral. If we leave you here, you'll be mixed up with the other corpses."

At 5:30 in the morning they reached the novitiate. The master of novices worked on Father with a scissors and razor blade, taking out slivers of glass.

Somehow, Father Schiffer did not die. Every day he spent an hour having glass and wood splinters removed. He had forty pieces in his collection when it was over. For a long time the wounds refused to heal, but eventually they did heal.

A few days after the bombing of Hiroshima, Nagasaki was hit. Then the people of Japan learned that it was the atom bomb that had devastated both cities.

In the twisted rubble and the maimed bodies of Hiroshima lay man's hopes for a better world.

Since the eighteenth century, man had grown steadily in his belief that utopia was possible on this earth. Scientific knowledge and technological improvements were to rid the world of its ancient scourges: war, famine, disease and poverty. In our twentieth century, scientific discoveries were so great that the coveted utopia seemed within our very grasp.

Then man made the greatest scientific discovery of all time, and that discovery turned all his hopes to ashes. Man stood appalled by what he had done. Instead of reaching the promised land, he stood on the brink of a horrible abyss, led there by his own incredible blindness.

Scientists, who had been in the vanguard of the march of progress, suddenly looked helplessly to politicians for protection. The politicians came up with nothing better than their old threadbare formulas which had failed over the centuries.

Not very many people turned toward God. It is strange

The Light of the Atom

that when man lost his faith in himself, he did not find faith in God. His unreasoning hope of the last two centuries gave way to unreasoning despair. He persists in his blindness.

Yet, the situation is not without hope. Nothing happens unless God permits it to happen, even the falling of the atom bomb. And out of the bombing, God, if He so wills, can bring much good.

Five years after the bomb fell on Hiroshima, Father Schiffer was in New York, studying labor relations at Fordham University. There he met Captain Robert A. Lewis, co-pilot of the B-29 that dropped the bomb. Lewis was then the personnel manager of a New York candy firm.

"For five years I have looked forward to meeting someone who saw it from the ground," said Captain Lewis.

"I have waited for five years to meet someone who was in the plane," said Father Schiffer.

Father Schiffer described his experience, and then Lewis described his:

"We made a sharp turn to the right, as the scientists had warned us to do. We were flying manually by instruments at about 30,000 feet. Forty-three seconds after we had dropped it, the A-bomb exploded, 1800 feet above the ground. My God! I felt a flash through my whole body . . . the scientists said later it was 'ozone effect.' Then there were two distinct slaps at the ship about 20 seconds after the flash.

"The light was at my back, but even so it stunned me. It was fiercer than the sun on that bright and sunny day. Yet by that time we were maybe eight miles from the explosion. We had to get away to avoid the bomb effect ourselves. But later we could look back and see the mushroom.

"It looked as if the whole city were covered with boiling smoke. In three minutes it got up as high as 30,000 feet. We could see flames crawling up the mountains and covering the bridges and tributary rivers. It seemed impossible to comprehend.

"I thought, 'My God! What have we done? If I live a hundred years, I'll never be able to get this thought out of my mind.' . . ."

Father Schiffer told Lewis that 200,000 people had been killed by the bomb.

"Good heavens," said the Captain. "That many?"

"Yes," said the priest. "The Japanese officials minimized the loss at the ridiculous figure of 80,000. We knew better."

"I went back to Japan after the war," said Captain Lewis, "and the Japs in Tokyo had the *damnedest* reaction to the bomb you ever heard. They called it 'God's wind' and said it had saved many lives by bringing an end to the war."

Father Schiffer nodded.

"I know it," he said. "We thought we knew the Japanese psychology well after fifteen years, but their reaction at Hiroshima amazed even us. The survivors felt that their city had been given a unique honor . . . that of suffering in order to bring peace to the world. They look upon their 200,000 dead as willing victims, sacrificed for world-wide peace."

Lewis asked about the effect of the bomb on the survivors. Father said that there were no lasting physical effects. Then he added that spiritually the survivors are far better off than they were before.

"And what do you mean by that, Father?" Lewis asked.

"Well," said the priest, "it's a happy ending. I'll tell you."

This is the story Father Schiffer had to tell Captain Lewis and which he also wishes to tell us.

Several months after the bombing, Father Lasalle and an assistant went to what had been Hiroshima. They erected a small wooden hut and on Christmas celebrated an open-air Mass.

One morning three leaders of the Buddhist religion, called bonzes, came to visit the priests. At first they talked of the terrible destruction. But soon the visitors changed to another subject; they praised the beauty of the Catholic liturgy, told the astonished priests how much they liked the Gregorian chant, and asked many questions about the monastic life, meditation and prayer. Then the chief bonze asked, "Would your priests and your faithful eventually be willing to say prayers for peace?"

Father Lasalle said that they were doing that every day.

"You see, Father, it's like this: we will build up a new Hiroshima, a better one. But most of all, the hearts of men should be made better. We don't blame anyone for what has happened here. After all, we Japanese started this war. But we survivors in Hiroshima have all seen the terrible consequences of modern warfare. We don't want that to happen again, anywhere on earth.

"Now you Christians, and we Buddhists likewise, know that it is impossible to preserve peace without religion and prayer. What we want is to have a memorial shrine for perpetual prayer right in the center of atom-bombed Hiroshima. We don't know your religion too well, but would it eventually be possible for you Catholics to set up a shrine for constant prayers right here in the center of our city?"

Hiroshima had always been a Buddhist stronghold. The amazed priests could not refrain from asking why the Buddhists did not build the shrine.

"Our prayers are not strong enough," the chief bonze replied. "I have read your Bible, and I know your prayers are better than ours. Besides, you Catholics have nuns who get down on their knees and pray to God all day. That's what we want: we need many powerful prayers."

"If we Catholics build this shrine," answered Father Lasalle, "we would like to dedicate it to the Assumption of our Blessed Mother into Heaven. Christ's Mother is always praying for us in heaven and she wants nothing more than world peace."

The bonze readily agreed to this. "Nothing in this world will be a better symbol for peace than the heart of a mother."

The largest Tokyo newspaper sponsored a contest for architectural designs for Hiroshima's memorial shrine. The Japanese parliament named Hiroshima "a national symbol of peace," to be rebuilt as a spiritual and cultural center.

Funds for the shrine came mostly from abroad, from the United States and South America, but the Japanese contributed a notable share, too. There was one anonymous donation of $50,000 from the United States. Many decorations and fixtures, including four great bells for the tower, an organ, a tabernacle and a number of statues, were donated by Europeans. The Germans were especially generous.

On August 6, 1950, fifth anniversary of the atomic blast, a Japanese priest blessed the cornerstone of Our Lady's Memorial Shrine for World Peace. Four years later, on August 6 of the Marian Year of 1954, the shrine was dedicated. It is a gleaming edifice with clean modern lines. It is 200 feet long and 80 feet wide. It has a bell tower 150 feet high. The shrine has seven altars. The sanctuary is draped with the flags of all the nations that took part in World War II. A set of golden books lists the names of thousands of war veterans from those countries.

A perpetual crusade of prayer before the Blessed Sacrament is conducted by cloistered nuns from the United States. Among other prayers, they say the Rosary every hour day and night.

Prayers and sacrifice are the keynotes of Our Lady's Memorial Shrine for World Peace.

"This," says Father Schiffer, "is Hiroshima's answer to the pleas of Our Lady of Fatima."

23

The Doves of Peace
PORTUGAL, 1946

THE events that have followed the end of World War II do not need detailed recounting: The Communist sweep through much of Europe and Asia, the hordes of homeless starving people afraid to return to their homelands, the treatment accorded Cardinal Mindszenty and other churchmen, the appalling slaughter in Korea, the massacre of millions in China. And over and above all is the feeling that with Russia in possession of the atomic bomb, the worst is still to come. *No Place to Hide* is the disquieting title of a book that looks into a frightening future.

All of this recalls the words of Our Lady of Fatima. She said that if her requests were not granted Russia would "spread her errors throughout the world, promoting wars, and persecutions of the Church. Many will be martyred; the Holy Father will have much to suffer; several nations will be destroyed."

It does not seem that her requests are being followed to any great extent. Cynicism, despair, secularism and materialism are the marks of the "free" world. These are worse threats than the threat of Communism. These are the reasons Communism is allowed to make such headway.

The United States, if we judge by what we read in the press and hear on the radio, is close to being a completely materialistic nation. The Supreme Court so twists the meaning of the First Amendment that God is virtually excluded from the public schools. There are shocking disclosures of corruption in public office, of delinquency among teen-age boys and girls. Many doctors are asking that they be permitted to murder patients they believe to be incurable. Birth-control groups have become "respectable" and even enjoy the support of certain clergymen. At least 1 million babies die each year from abortions. Our magazines are saturated with sex. Our best-selling novels are jammed with illicit love. Our newspapers have column after column of the very things St. Paul said "should not be so much as mentioned among you."

Is there, then, no hope for the world? Are people to go on offending God, and is the punishment to become more and more severe until the whole world goes up in one great atomic flash?

No, for Our Lady of Fatima has also told us: "In the end

my Immaculate Heart will triumph. The Holy Father will consecrate Russia to me; it will be converted, and a certain period of peace will be granted to the world."

We do not know how much more punishment is in store for the world. That depends upon our own actions. But this we know: Russia will be converted some day and there will be peace. Perhaps that day is closer than we think. The blood of the modern martyrs, the sufferings of cardinals and bishops, priests and Sisters, ordinary people in all walks of life, cannot but draw floods of grace upon the world. And in every country there are people who do not make the headlines, but who are making a sincere effort to carry out our Lady's requests.

The purpose of this book has been to tell the story of the Blessed Virgin in the modern world and to do so, as much as possible, in a chronological order. Ignoring reputed apparitions which have not been pronounced upon, and reporting only facts that are known to be true, the account of our Lady in our world ends on a note of hope. The incidents still to be related, all of which have happened since the end of World War II, seem to offer us hope and encouragement.

Perhaps this is an accident of timing. Perhaps when the reputed apparitions of recent years have been duly investigated, it will be found that our Lady is giving us graver warnings than ever before. On the other hand, our Blessed Mother is our Lady of Hope, and she wishes to encourage this virtue in us. She is always ready to help us when things seem the darkest.

The first story is a simple one about some doves.

The entire population of the little Portuguese village of Bombarral turned out to see the procession and to honor Our Lady of Fatima. It was December 1, 1946. The statue of Our Lady of Fatima was being carried in procession from the Cova da Iria to the cathedral in Lisbon. This was a distance of 90 miles. Bombarral was one of the villages on the way.

The Doves of Peace

Two girls, carrying a box, ran out from among the spectators and stood before the approaching statue. They opened a box, and out flew five doves. The villagers smiled approvingly. Doves were a symbol of purity and peace. It was fitting that they should be released in honor of the Virgin Most Pure, the Queen of Peace.

Two of the doves flew away immediately. To everyone's amazement, the other three flew to the statue and nestled in the flowers at its feet.

The men carrying the statue were annoyed. They were afraid the doves might soil the statue. The men tried to shoo the doves away, but the birds refused to leave. When forced out of the flowers, they fluttered about for a moment and returned. The crowd, impressed by their persistence, prevailed upon the men to leave the doves alone.

For five days the doves remained at the foot of the statue, leaving only for short flights in search of food. In various villages, the statue was welcomed by loud cheers from the spectators, by bands playing lustily, by exploding firecrackers. An airplane swooped down from time to time to drop flowers on the statue. The doves, ordinarily very timid birds, were not perturbed by any of this. They remained serenely in their places. Nor could cold, rain or wind force them to leave their post.

The occasion of this procession, which the doves were helping to celebrate, was the three hundredth anniversary of the declaration of Mary Immaculate as Queen of Portugal. In 1646, King João IV, in a solemn ceremony, had taken the crown from his head and had placed it at the feet of a statue of the Blessed Virgin. He declared her to be Queen of Portugal under the title of the Immaculate Conception. By oath, he bound himself and his successors to defend the dogma that Mary was conceived free of original sin. He ordered the event inscribed on stone tablets in every town and city of the land. The monarchs of Portugal never wore a crown after that. They regarded it as belonging to our Lady. Portugal had become *A Terra de Nossa Senhora,* the Land of Our Lady.

For most of the three centuries that had passed since then, Portugal had remained the Land of Our Lady. There had been a short lapse at the end of the nineteenth century and at the beginning of this one, but by 1946, it was plain that our Lady's rule was unquestioned. Civil and religious leaders paid honor to her. On May 13, 1946, a personal legate of Pope Pius XII placed a crown on the head of the statue of Our Lady of Fatima. The jewels of this crown had been donated by the women of Portugal. Seven hundred thousand pilgrims were present when our Lady's rule over Portugal was thus renewed.

The culminating event in the series of celebrations was this journey of Our Lady of Fatima to the capital city.

The first stop the statue made in Lisbon was at a new parish church, Our Lady of Fatima. The Cardinal Patriarch met the procession at the church door and welcomed the Queen to her capital. The doves left the statue and went over to where the Cardinal was speaking. They looked up at him as if they were listening to him.

The statue was kept in the church for two days, and the doves remained with it. On December 7, while Communion was being distributed, one of the doves perched atop the crown that had been placed on the head of the statue by the papal legate. It remained there with its little white wings wide open during the whole of Communion.

On the evening of December 7, when the statue was being removed from the Church of Our Lady of Fatima, two of the doves flew to the sill of a stained-glass window and sat there fixedly with their eyes on the statue.

It had been raining hard. When the statue was carried from the church, the rain stopped suddenly, the clouds rolled back and the moon shone brightly.

The two doves that had been on the window sill rejoined their companion as the statue was carried through three miles of Lisbon streets to the cathedral. Half a million people lined the streets. They shouted "Hosanna to the Queen of Portugal." Flower petals showered down from the buildings.

When the statue approached the floodlighted cathedral one

The Doves of Peace

of the doves flew to the topmost pinnacle. It remained there during the nightlong vigil.

In the afternoon of the feast of the Immaculate Conception, December 8, the Cardinal, the hierarchy of Portugal, the President of the country, the Premier, and members of the diplomatic corps were in the cathedral to renew the act of consecration of Portugal to the Immaculate Conception.

At six o'clock that evening the statue began its return journey to Fatima. About this time the doves disappeared.

Father McGlynn was in Portugal just two months after these events. He made extensive inquiries about the doves. He found they had been purchased by Dona Maria Emilia Martins Coimbra, a resident of Bombarral. Dona Maria's idea was to have a triumphal arch over the street. At the top of the arch there was to be a floral crown with six white doves concealed within. As the statue passed under the arch, a cord would be pulled, releasing the doves, and there would be a flutter of white wings as the statue passed.

Dona Maria sent to Lisbon for the six white doves. She paid 78 escudos for them. One of the doves died on the way to Bombarral.

The arch could not be built in time, so Dona Maria had the two girls release the doves in front of the statue.

The people of Portugal rarely use the word "miracle" in connection with the Doves of Bombarral, but, as Father McGlynn observes, Dona Maria Emilia Martins Coimbra certainly got much more than she expected for her 78 escudos.

When the statue was on its return journey a little boy, Bernardin Raposo, released four doves, three white and one black. The black one flew away. The three white ones went to the foot of the statue and remained there until it reached the Cova da Iria. Then two were caged and the third was left in an open cage in the chapel.

On May 23, 1948, the statue of Our Lady of Fatima left Portugal and went to Spain for a Marian Congress in Madrid. When it arrived at the gates of the city, doves were liberated. Some flew away, but others went to the foot of the statue. They remained there during the eight days of the Congress.*

Are the doves that attended our Lady's statue in Portugal and in Spain a sign that our Lady is pleased with these two countries that share the Iberian Peninsula at the western end of Europe?

The idea cannot be ruled out, because both Spain and Portugal—in entirely different ways—have heeded Our Lady of Fatima's call for prayer and sacrifice.

When, in 1936, it became apparent that the Communists were in almost complete control of Spain, General Francisco Franco led a military revolt against the government. The Communists seized the arsenals in Madrid and Barcelona. They threw open the jails and armed the criminals. The country was drenched in blood for three years. Devout Catholics prayed for deliverance from the Communist scourge. They made great sacrifices. They fought valiantly.

One story illustrates the heroic Christian spirit that dominated many of the Nationalists. In 1936 the Nationalist forces had retired into the citadel of Alcazar. The phone rang for General Moscardo. A voice demanded the surrender of the fort. The general curtly refused the request. Then he heard the voice of his young son: "Dad, what do you want me to do?"

"Son, die like a Christian," General Moscardo replied.

Through the phone came the sound of the shot that ended the boy's life.

The prayers and the sacrifices were rewarded. Madrid fell in March, 1939, and the Nationalist regime under General Franco became the government of Spain. The country remained Christian, and the Communists were foiled in all their efforts.

---

* Fourth Edition: Father John Ryan, S.J., editor of *Fatima Findings*, writes that the above stories may give the erroneous impression that the phenomenon of the doves occurred only in Spain and Portugal in the years 1946 and 1948. Actually, Father Ryan says, the phenomenon has occurred, and is still occurring, in many widely separated parts of the world, some of them in our own hemisphere. He sends pictures of doves at the feet of the Pilgrim Virgin in Puerto Rico, Cuba, Nicaragua, and Colombia.

The Doves of Peace 161

Portugal was also delivered from the enemies of religion but in a somewhat different way.

We have seen that the civil administrator at Ourem tried to keep Lucia, Francisco and Jacinta from going to the Cova in August, 1917. The administrator was typical of the men who were governing Portugal at that time. The men were not Communists, or most of them were not, but they were avowed enemies of religion. In this they resembled the men who ruled France. Religious orders were suppressed, priests were hampered in their duties, charitable works were made impossible, and the Catholic press was reduced to a few small weeklies with little influence.

This in a country where for more than two and a half centuries Mary Immaculate had reigned as Queen!

For some years the government had been very unstable. Revolutions were frequent. And in 1916 Portugal had been drawn into World War I. Thousands of her soldiers were killed on the battlefields; her treasury was empty, and no end was in sight. There were rumors of more revolutions. Communist leaders thought they saw their opportunity to seize the government.

Then our Lady appeared at Fatima. A great number of Portuguese people began to heed her requests. Conditions in the little country began to improve almost at once.

The antireligious forces fought Fatima, but their battle was a losing one. The government tried to keep the people from visiting the shrine; at times, bodies of troops were sent there. On March 22, 1922, the little chapel that had been built at the request of our Lady was destroyed by dynamite. All such occurrences only increased the devotion of the people.

The devotion was rewarded. Antireligious laws were gradually relaxed. The atheistic government was overthrown in 1926, and two years later, Oliveira Salazar, a Catholic university professor, became head of the government. Mr. Salazar has been called a dictator, but he was not a dictator in the totalitarian sense. He allowed complete religious freedom, and the progress of the Church in recent years has been amazing. Churches are crowded. There are a great number of religious vocations. The religious orders are back and are stronger than ever, and the Catholic press is flourishing. *La Voz da Fatima,* a paper published at the shrine and containing news of the shrine, has the largest circulation of any publication in Portugal.

When Spain became engulfed in civil war in 1936, it looked as if Portugal would be drawn into it, since it shares the Iberian Peninsula with Spain and is cut off from the rest of Europe. Communists have small regard for national boundaries, and they could reasonably be expected to try to take over Portugal as well as Spain.

It was then that the bishops of Portugal promised a national pilgrimage to Fatima, if the country could be saved from the threat of Godless Communism. The country was saved, and on May 13, 1938, the twenty-first anniversary of our Lady's first apparition at Fatima, 500,000 people took part in the pilgrimage of thanksgiving. This was one out of every twelve inhabitants.

Portugal was also spared the horrors of World War II, a fact which Pope Pius XII noted when he spoke to the nation by radio in 1942. It was on this occasion that the Holy Father dedicated the world to the Immaculate Heart of Mary.

The changes that have taken place in Portugal since 1917 are truly amazing. The credit for them goes to the Blessed Virgin and to the people who heeded her message.

People from other countries who visit Fatima are invariably impressed by the intense devotion of the Portuguese peasants. This is especially evident around May 13 and October 13, when vast numbers come to the shrine. Fatima is a small out-of-the-way place, 75 miles from any big city. Transportation is difficult and expensive, so thousands of the peasants walk every mile of the way, praying with every step. Many make the last few miles on their knees. There are few sleeping accommodations, and the night before one of the big ceremonies thousands sleep on the ground. If the

The Doves of Peace

ground is muddy, they stand and say the Rosary all night.

The stranger from another land sees all this and marvels. Our Lady asked for prayer, sacrifice and devotion to the Immaculate Heart, the stranger reflects. These people are certainly granting her requests. Such devotion cannot help but have a great effect upon the world.

On October 13, 1951, one million people gathered at Fatima for the ceremonies closing the Holy Year outside Rome and for the thirty-fourth anniversary of the final apparition. This was the largest crowd that ever gathered at Fatima, or at any shrine. Six hundred thousand of the people had stood all night in the rain.

Bishop Fulton J. Sheen, Auxiliary Bishop of New York, took part in the ceremonies and also mingled with the pilgrims. He gave his impressions in an article for the N.C.W.C. News Service:

"Communism was defeated last Saturday, but the news has not leaked out yet . . .

"One million penitent souls can certainly do for the world what ten just men could have done for Sodom and Gomorrah. . . .

"On October 13, 1917, when Our Lady appeared at Fatima, Communism was just beginning to gnaw into the vitals of the world. In another thirty-four years Communism will no longer be in existence. What will disappear will be a Red dictator reviewing his troops in the Red Square. What will survive will be Our Lady of the Kremlin reviewing in the White Square below her troops of the Legion of Mary. . . .

"Rain, mud, a night without sleep, and love of Our Lady—those things make Fatima. Most people want a bed for the night; at Fatima all one wanted was a rosary.

"Stalin once asked in ridicule: 'How many divisions has the Pope?' The answer was given at Fatima: 'A million.' Each is armed with fifteen decades of explosive love. . . . On that dark, damp night of October 12, hundreds of thousands of men and women were engaged in that battle against everything that was non-God, and when morning came one knew that God had won."

164 *The Woman Shall Conquer*

Bishop Sheen concluded his article with these words: "No one who was among those million penitents on October 13 will doubt that Our Lady of Fatima will bring peace to the world. If other nations besides Portugal do penance, there will be no catastrophe or war. If, however, penance is done by Portugal alone, then some kind of catastrophe may have to come briefly before peace will follow. A few all-night vigils might do much for America and the peace of the world. The future is known only to God, but what the future brings depends on how we spend our days and our nights."*

In 1945, the atom bomb fell on Hiroshima. In 1946, the Doves of Bombarral accompanied Mary, Queen of Portugal, on a tour of her realm. The atom bomb is war in its most horrible form. Doves have always been regarded as a sign of peace.

Peace or war. The atom bomb or the doves of peace. The choice is up to us.

Portugal has made its choice. It has chosen peace.

---

* In the same article Bishop Sheen said that our Lady's appearances at Fatima marked the turning point in the history of the world's 347,000,000 Moslems, the most difficult of all religious people to convert to Christianity. The Moslems occupied Portugal for centuries and have left their mark. Fatima was the name of Mohammed's daughter, and after her death Mohammed wrote of her that she "is the most holy of all women in Paradise, next to Mary." Bishop Sheen believes that the Virgin Mary chose to be known as Our Lady of Fatima as a sign and a pledge that the Moslems, who believe in Christ's virgin birth, will come to believe in Christ's divinity. He points out that the Pilgrim Virgin statues of Our Lady of Fatima were enthusiastically received by Moslems in Africa, India, and elsewhere, and that many Mohammedans are now coming into the Church. As director of the Society for the Propagation of the Faith, Bishop Sheen can speak with authority.

24

Our Lady Returns to England

WALSINGHAM, 1945
STOCKPORT, 1947
AYLESFORD, 1951

In the eleventh century, five years before the Norman Conquest, there lived in the little village of Walsingham, England, a pious widow, Richeldis de Faverches. One day, according to the ancient tradition, Richeldis had a vision in which the Blessed Virgin took her to Nazareth and showed her the Holy House of the Annunciation. It was here that the Angel Gabriel had announced to Mary that she was to be the Mother of God. In this house the Holy Family had lived until our Lord was ready to begin His public life. The vision was repeated three times. Each time, our Lady told Richeldis to note carefully the dimensions of the little house so she could build a replica of it on her estate on Walsingham.

Richeldis hastened to obey. Acting under her instructions, a group of workmen built a house similar to the one she had seen in her vision. After the house was constructed, Richeldis did not know where she should put it. Then she received what she considered a sign from heaven. A heavy fall of dew soaked the meadow where Richeldis had planned to put the house, but two small rectangles were left dry.

It was decided to erect a stone foundation on one of these rectangles. Try as they might, however, the workmen could not make the foundation fit the house. They worked all day and at night went home "all sorry and sad."

Richeldis spent the entire night praying that the difficulties might be solved and the shrine erected.

The next morning Richeldis and the workmen found that the house had been moved more than 200 feet to the other space and was on a stone foundation.

Thus, says the legend, England received its most celebrated shrine.

There is a great similarity between the story of Walsingham in England and that of Loreto in Italy. The Holy House of Loreto is said to be the very house in which our Lady lived, while the house at Walsingham was a replica of it. The house at Loreto was said to have been moved by the angels from Nazareth to various parts of Italy until it took up its present location. The house at Walsingham was moved 200 feet.

Of the two legends, that of Walsingham is the older. The date given for the foundation of Loreto is 1291, that for Walsingham is 1061. The first written record of the Loreto tradition dates from 1472; that of Walsingham, from 1465. Walsingham therefore was not a copy of Loreto. For at least two centuries before Loreto was heard of, thousands of pilgrims were making their way to Walsingham, or New Nazareth as it was called. Whether or not these legends are true, there is no doubt of the sanctity of both shrines nor of the number of miracles and favors granted there.

Richeldis died, and her son, before going off on one of the Crusades, put the house, which had by then become a shrine, under the protection of the Canons of St. Augustine. This was a religious order which has since become extinct. The canons built a large church around the house, and they erected many other buildings. There was also a hospice for sick pilgrims. The roads to the great shrine were marked by wayside crosses. There were also a number of wayside chapels at which pilgrims stopped to pray. Among the thousands who made the pilgrimage to Walsingham were many kings and queens of England. Nobles vied with each other in making generous donations to the shrine. Such was the love

Our Lady Returns to England

Englishmen had for our Blessed Mother in medieval times.

New Nazareth became known thoughout all Christian Europe. Because of it, England was called "the Holy Land, Our Lady's Dowry."

King Henry VIII at first had great devotion to the Blessed Virgin. He made a pilgrimage to Walsingham, walking the last mile barefooted in the snow. He also made many generous donations to the shrine. When he broke with Rome in order to take a new wife, he had the buildings razed. So the shrine was destroyed after being in existence almost 500 years.

An anonymous sixteenth-century author wrote this *Lament Over Walsingham*:

Bitter bitter Oh to behold the grass to grow
Where the walls of Walsingham so stately did show;
Such were the works of Walsingham while she did stand:
Such are the wrecks as now do show of that holy land.
Level level with the ground the towers do lie
Which their golden glittering tops pierced once to the sky....
Weep weep O Walsingham whose days and nights
Blessings turned to blasphemies holy deeds to dispites,
Sin is where Our Lady sat Heaven turned to Hell,
Satan sits where our Lord did sway, Walsingham O farewell.

As England became more firmly Protestant the memory of Walsingham faded from the minds of most men, but not all. Among those who cherished the tradition of Walsingham there was a saying: "When England goes back to Walsingham, our Lady will come back to England." That day, however, seemed very remote.

In the nineteenth century there was a reawakened interest in medieval times. Men began digging in the ruins of old churches and abbeys. England was rediscovering its Catholic past. Along with this came the Oxford Movement and its numerous conversions of prominent Anglicans to the Roman Catholic Church. Oustanding among these converts was John Henry Newman, later Cardinal Newman.

Excavations were made on the site of the old shrine. Remains were found which tallied with ancient descriptions. A pilgrim's badge was unearthed. Catholics began to yearn for a return to Walsingham, but such a return seemed impossible. All the land that had once belonged to the shrine now belonged to non-Catholics. There was, in fact, not a single Catholic resident in the village of Walsingham.

It was decided to build a shrine to Our Lady of Walsingham at the parish church of King's Lynn, some miles away. A statue blessed by Pope Leo XIII was enshrined in the new sanctuary on August 19, 1897.

Most of the wayside shrines had been destroyed, but one of the most important ones was still standing. This was St. Catherine's Chapel, which had popularly been known as the Slipper Chapel. This was the last chapel on the way to Walsingham. Here pilgrims stopped to remove their shoes or slippers in order to walk the last Holy Mile in their bare feet.

The Slipper Chapel was built in the middle of the fourteenth century and is a gem of Gothic architecture. It is built in such a way that the sun rises behind the east window on the feast of St. Catherine, according to the old-style calendar. The chapel is small, measuring only 28 feet 6 inches by 12 feet 5 inches.

After the destruction of the shrine proper, the Slipper Chapel was no longer needed. For a time it was used as a forge, then as a poorhouse, and finally as a barn in which cows were kept.

About 1894 this chapel was discovered by an Anglican woman, Miss Charlotte Boyd. She wished to purchase it and restore it. While negotiations were going on, she received the gift of faith. She completed the purchase and employed a noted architect to do the work of restoration. In 1897, the day after the inauguration of the shrine at King's Lynn, Walsingham had its first official pilgrimage since the Reformation. The Slipper Chapel, the entrance to the Holy Land of Walsingham, was reopened and in Catholic hands after a lapse of three and a half centuries.

Our Lady Returns to England

The Slipper Chapel was made a shrine in 1934. From that time pilgrimages have been made from every part of England. Many people traveled on foot from London, 117 miles away. In 1938, the fourth centenary of the desecration of Walsingham, Cardinal Hinsley led the gigantic pilgrimage of Catholic youth to the Slipper Chapel.

During the war Catholic men and women from many nations found refuge in England. Free French, Poles, Belgians, Dutch and many others prayed at our Lady's shrine. Italian prisoners of war gave thanks for the liberation of their country.

When the war ended, in 1945, a number of Catholics in the forces of the United States wished to give thanks, not at the Slipper Chapel, but at the site of New Nazareth itself. The owners of the property gave them permission to do this. This was the first Catholic ceremony held on the spot since 1538. Now Benediction is held there regularly. Little by little, England is returning to Walsingham.

Another place in England closely associated with the Blessed Virgin is the Carmelite monastery at Aylesford. It was here in 1251, according to tradition, that our Lady appeared to St. Simon Stock, the first Prior General of the Carmelites in the West. Holding a scapular in her hand she said, "This is a sign to you and to all Carmelites that whosoever dies wearing this scapular shall never see eternal fire." All privileges and indulgences that went with this large scapular of the Carmelites were later extended to the familiar small "brown scapular" and later to the Scapular Medal.

The monastery at Aylesford was confiscated by King Henry VIII and the Carmelites were exiled. In 1950, the Carmelites regained possession of the monastery, in time to celebrate the seventh centenary of the Scapular of Mount Carmel. The Carmelites were back in Aylesford after an exile of four hundred years. The body of St. Simon Stock was returned to Aylesford from France in 1951.

From the **England** of today there also comes the story of the famous **roses of** Stockport.

On the first Sunday of May, 1947, five-year-old Pauline Byrne placed a crown of roses on the statue of our Lady in St. Mary's Church, Stockport, England. The incident was similar to hundreds of May crownings taking place throughout the world.

Rev. James Turner, D.D., pastor of St. Mary's, says that 1947 was the golden jubilee of his church. When ordering the crown for the statue, he asked the florist to choose yellow tea roses, as being the color nearest to gold.

"When I received the crown on Saturday evening," Father Turner says, "it looked lovely but terribly frail. I did not think it would remain presentable till the next day.

"Toward the middle of May I was surprised to see the roses in the crown still intact and beautiful; in all previous years the roses had fallen out after a week or ten days.

"At the end of the month I always took the statue back to my bedroom, although the people always begged me to leave the statue in the sanctuary because they loved it so much. But I was always adamant and said that June was the month of the Sacred Heart and our Blessed Mother must give in to her divine Son.

"At the end of May the roses were still intact and beautiful. I said to my parishioners: 'Well, you have always asked me to leave the statue in the sanctuary. I will do so as long as the roses remain intact.' Half jokingly, I added, 'If our Lady wants to stay in her place of honor, well, it's up to her to keep the roses as they are.'

"Really, I do believe that our Blessed Mother took up the challenge, because month succeeded month, and there was still no change in the roses."

In October, a reporter heard about the roses, and the story went all over the world. Visitors came by the hundreds.

The following year, the same May queen deposited a second crown of 17 golden ophelias on top of the first. This crown also failed to fade. In May, 1949, seven-year-old Anne Carley placed a third crown on the statue.

"To this day," says Father Turner, "there has not fallen a single petal from any one of the 50 roses.

Our Lady Returns to England

"Personally I look upon the three crowns as being beautifully symbolic of our Blessed Mother being crowned by the Eternal Father as His Beloved Daughter, by the Eternal Son as His cherished Mother, and by the Holy Ghost as His chaste spouse. Again I look upon the 50 roses as symbolizing the 50 Hail Marys of the Rosary.

"For these reasons I did not wish to superimpose a fourth crown on Our Lady of the Roses, and so I decided to place a crown on Our Lady of Lourdes. To our amazement, this crown is following the example of the crowns on Our Lady of the Roses."

A woman reporter examined this fourth crown in June, 1950, when it was more than six weeks old. She rubbed the petals and the delicate ferns between her fingers. They were completely dry, completely dehydrated; but they retained their original shape and form and virtually their original color. They looked like living roses and living ferns, but they were not. From their dryness, one would have expected them to fall to the floor, but they did not.

The reporter could not feel the first three crowns, because they were too high. From their appearance, however, she judged them to be in the same condition.

The Church has not pronounced upon the roses of Stockport, so we do not know whether they can be considered miraculous. If the Church does declare that a miracle has taken place, England, and the entire would, will have cause for great rejoicing.

The stories of Walsingham and Aylesford and Stockport bring to mind a prediction which Dominic Savio made about England. The message was relayed to Pope Pius IX by St. John Bosco. Dominic Savio was born in 1842 and died in 1857, a month before his fifteenth birthday. He was declared Venerable in 1933 and was beatified in 1951.

Dominic told Don Bosco several times that he wished he could see the Pope. Don Bosco asked him why.

"If I could only talk to the Holy Father," Dominic replied,

"I would tell him that in spite of the great trials which he has to suffer at present, he should not lose heart in his solicitude for England. God is preparing a great triumph for Catholicism in that country."

"What makes you say such a thing?" questioned Don Bosco.

"I'll tell you," replied the boy, "but don't mention it to the others or they might think it foolish. But if you go to Rome tell Pius IX for me. This is why I think so. One morning, during my thanksgiving after Communion, I had a distraction, which was strange for me. I thought I saw a great stretch of country covered in a thick fog, and it was filled with many people. They were moving about, but like men not sure where to put their feet. Somebody nearby said, 'This is England.' I was just about to question the man when I saw His holiness, Pius IX, as I had seen him in pictures. He was richly dressed and carried a bright torch with which he approached the multitude as if to enlighten their darkness. As he drew near, the torch seemed to disperse the fog, and the people were left in broad daylight. 'This torch,' said the man near me, 'is the Catholic religion, which is to illuminate England.'"

Don Bosco told the Pope about the incident in 1858. The Holy Father said: "What you have told me confirms me in my resolution to do all that is possible for England, which has long been the object of my special care. What you have related is, to put it at its lowest estimation, the counsel of a devout soul."

It was Pope Pius IX who had re-established the hierarchy in England in 1850, after a lapse of 300 years.

In 1852, Dr. John Henry Newman, later Cardinal, delivered his famous sermon in which he referred to the restoration of the Church in England as "The Second Spring." In the course of the sermon he said: "Arise my love, my beautiful one, and come. It is time for thy Visitation. Arise, Mary, and go forth in thy strength to that north country, which once was thy own, and take possession of a land which knows thee not. Arise, Mother of God, and with thy thrilling voice, speak to those who labor with child, and are in pain, till the babe of grace leaps within them. Shine on us, dear Lady, with thy bright countenance, like the sun in his strength, *O stella matutina*, O harbinger of peace, till our year is one perpetual May. From thy sweet eyes, from thy pure smile, from thy majestic brow, let ten thousand influences rain down, not to confound or overwhelm, but to persuade, to win over thine enemies. O Mary, my hope, A Mother undefiled, fulfill to us the promise of this Spring."

When Newman preached his sermon, *The Second Spring*, in 1852, the position of the Church was just beginning to improve after centuries of suppression. The Church in England has had a remarkable growth since then. Some authorities say that one Englishman out of every ten today is a Catholic, although it is impossible to secure exact figures. If we count only practicing members, the Catholic Church is the largest religious body in England today, larger even than the Church of England. In the past century Catholics have wielded an influence out of proportion to their numbers. Newman has enriched our spiritual life and our literature. Chesterton has trumpeted gay defiance to modern paganism. Belloc, Knox, and many others have given us cause to be grateful. Three of the most prominent of all living novelists—Graham Greene, Evelyn Waugh and Bruce Marshal—are British Catholics. Yes, England is having its Second Spring.

Throughout the country devotion to the Blessed Mother has spread greatly. This is true not only among Catholics, but among Anglicans and other Protestants as well. For centuries our Lady was virtually exiled from England, but that is true no longer.

"When England goes back to Walsingham, our Lady will come back to England." England, it would appear, is well on its way back to Walsingham. We may hope that under our Lady's guidance and protection England's Second Spring will soon give way to full summer.

25

The Assumption
ROME, 1950

NINETY-SIX YEARS had passed since Pope Pius IX stood in St. Peter's and proclaimed the doctrine that Mary had been conceived without sin.

Now, on the feast of All Saints in 1950, another Pius, seated on a red damask covered throne set up before the obelisk in St. Peter's Square, was about to proclaim another doctrine that adds to Mary's glory. This was Pope Pius XII, who had come to the throne of Peter in 1939.

Some 36 cardinals, 600 archbishops and bishops, hundreds of noblemen and knights and statesmen, thousands of priests and Sisters from hundreds of religious communities, and hundreds of thousands of lay people surrounded the Holy Father. The crowd of 700,000 overflowed the huge piazza into the streets beyond. The sun shone brightly from a sky of deep blue.

As the Pope spoke in a loud clear voice, microphones carried his words to every part of the huge crowd in the square, to 80,000 people waiting inside St. Peter's, and by radio to every part of the free world. "By the authority of Our Lord Jesus Christ, of the Blessed Apostles Peter and Paul and by our own authority, we pronounce, declare and define that it is a divinely revealed dogma that the Immaculate Mother of God, ever Virgin Mary, when the course of her earthly life was finished, was taken up body and soul into heavenly glory."

The Assumption

Having defined the dogma, the Holy Father declared, "If anyone, which God forbid, should dare voluntarily to deny or to call into doubt what has been defined by us, let him know that he has fallen away completely from the divine and Catholic faith."

At the conclusion of these words, the bells of Rome's 400 churches rang out so loudly that they seemed to shatter the heavens. The Pope and his procession made their way into St. Peter's where the Pontiff was to say a Mass in honor of the Assumption. Great cheers came from the crowd as Pope Pius passed by. Tens of thousands of people then went to nearby churches to hear Mass at the same time the Pope celebrated Solemn Pontifical Mass within St. Peter's.

The fact that Mary's body had been assumed into heaven had been accepted by virtually all Roman Catholics and by many other Christians for centuries. It was not until our own day, however, that it was made a dogma of the Church.

From the earliest times Christians believed that the body of the Mother of God, who was never stained by original sin, had not been corrupted by death. There was a strong tradition that Mary died quietly and peacefully amidst the Apostles. Her death, according to this tradition, was not like other deaths which are accompanied by suffering, reluctance to leave this world, and a fear of the unknown. Her death, rather, was an act of pure love, an intense desire to be reunited with her Son. A short time after her burial, according to this tradition, the Apostles visited her tomb and found it empty. Her body had been taken to heaven to be reunited with her soul.

The formal declaration avoids the question of Mary's death. Most theologians accept the old tradition. A very respectable minority are inclined to believe that she never died, that her body and soul were assumed into heaven at the same time. At any rate, she is in heaven soul and body and there she reigns as Queen.

Petitions for a definition of the Assumption began to reach Rome only a few years after the Immaculate Conception had been proclaimed. Pope Pius IX, however, believed that the right time had not yet come. The petitions continued to pour in. In a period of 80 years they far exceeded the requests for a definition of the Immaculate Conception, although the latter had been spread over a period of 231 years.

In Chapter VIII it was noted that the doctrine of the Immaculate Conception was an especially appropriate one for the nineteenth century. In 1854, man had elevated himself to the status of a god and thought he could solve all his own problems. The doctrine of the Immaculate Conception reminded man that he was born with original sin on his soul and that he was absolutely dependent upon God.

Today the bland optimism of the nineteenth century has turned to bleak pessimism and despair. Instead of bringing us to a heaven on earth, science seems to have brought us to the gates of hell. Man no longer thinks he can solve his own problems; now he wonders whether his problems can be solved at all.

But Mary's Assumption reminds us that she who is in heaven body and soul is our Mother, the Mother of God, the Queen of Heaven and the eternal enemy of Satan. She loves us more than we can possibly love ourselves, and she is our powerful intercessor. What we ask in her name, she will obtain for us. With God everything is possible, and God can refuse His Mother nothing. There is no reason for despair so long as Mary reigns as Queen of Heaven.

The Assumption also reminds us that our final goal is not on this earth but in heaven. If we live according to God's laws, our body and soul will someday be reunited in heaven, as Mary's are. The troubles we face in this world will be forgotten in the eternal happiness of heaven.

Graham Greene, writing in *Life* magazine on the subject of the Assumption, says that the great heresy of our times is the unimportance of the individual: "Today the human body is regarded as expendable material, something to be eliminated wholesale by the atom bomb, a kind of anonymous carrion. After the first World War crosses marked the places where the dead lay, Allied and enemy; lights burned continually in the capitals of Europe over the graves of the

The Assumption 177

unknown warriors. But no crosses today mark the common graves into which the dead of London and Berlin were shoveled. . . . The definition of the Assumption proclaims again the doctrine of our Resurrection, the eternal destiny of each human body, and again it is the history of Mary which maintains the doctrine in its clarity. The Resurrection of Christ can be regarded as the Resurrection of a God, but the Resurrection of Mary forecasts the Resurrection of each one of us."

In proclaiming the doctrine of the Assumption, Pope Pius gave to us a solemn demonstration of the supreme spiritual authority of the Church, an authority which many men have ignored or forgotten. The action also attests to the unbroken link of faith that unites Catholics of this day with the faithful of ages past. Communism and secularism will pass away, but Christ's Church will live till the end of time.

There is a striking parallel between conditions in 1854, when the Immaculate Conception was proclaimed, and conditions in 1950, when the Assumption was proclaimed.

In 1854, as we read in Chapter VIII, the Church was beset by enemies on all sides, and many were freely predicting that its days were numbered. The Pope had numerous enemies in his own city of Rome. They had driven him from the city once, and were awaiting a chance to do so again. In the midst of these troubles the Church had one of her most glorious moments, the proclamation of the Immaculate Conception.

Pope Pius XII guided the Church through the most troubled times it had seen since the days of the catacombs. Wars, famines, and persecutions—the greatest in history—were the lot of the world during his reign. He saw the Iron Curtain clank down on one country after another.

In his own city of Rome, he faced all the three forms of totalitarianism which have plagued our century. The Italian Fascists, who were in power when he was elected Pope, succeeded in making life very trying for him. The German Nazis, who seized the city when Italy surrendered to the Allies, made the Pope a virtual prisoner within the Vatican. Then there were the Italian Communists who paraded outside the Vatican gates boasting of what they would do to the Church when they gained control of Italy. Thanks largely to the inspiring leadership of the Holy Father, the Communists lost the election of 1948 and failed to take over the country. They do not regard this defeat as permanent. They are waiting for another chance.

It was in this city of Rome, which has seen so much turmoil in recent years, that the Pope proclaimed the doctrine of the Assumption in 1950. Again, in the face of great trials, the Church had one of her most glorious moments.

THE "WEEPING MADONNA" — *Sicily, 1953*

The madonna is a small terra cotta bust of our Lady. She is depicted with a flaming Heart and a sad look. Antonia and Angelo Giusto received the statue for a wedding present in March, 1953. By summer, Antonia was pregnant and was feeling faint and dizzy most of the time. She was forced to lie idle for days. She lay on the bed and talked to the little statue which was on a wall shelf. On August 29 she was amazed to see tears coming from the eyes of the statue. Three women, friends of the family, were called, and they, too, saw the tears. Except for short intervals the tears continued to flow for four days. They stopped at 11:30 on September 1.

Word of the phenomenon spread throughout Sicily and all Italy. Huge throngs came to the house. The statue was placed in the public square not far from the Giusto home. Hundreds of physical cures have been claimed. The tears were analyzed and found to be the same composition as human tears.

On December 12, 1953, the hierarchy of Sicily issued a statement in which they "unanimously judged that the weeping cannot be held in doubt." They asked for a "sanctuary which will perpetuate the memory of the miracle." *Osservatore Romano,* Vatican City daily, printed the statement without comment. On the day the statement was issued the madonna was seen to weep twice.

26

The Pope of Our Lady

ROME, 1954

Pope Pius XII, deserved, in a very special way, to be called the "Pope of Our Lady." For he always had a very great devotion to the Blessed Mother, and her influence was very evident throughout his priesthood and pontificate.

He once said: "Joyfully and sincerely we testify that our priestly life began with Mary and has continued under her protection and guidance. In the course of our rather long life, if we have accomplished anything good, anything right, anything useful for the Catholic faith, not in ourselves do we glory, but in God and Our Lady."

Father Eugenio Pacelli—the future Pope Pius XII—offered his first Sacrifice of the Mass in the sanctuary of St. Mary Major, the most prominent church in Rome named for Mary. His ordination card read: "Sublime Mother of God . . . at whose altar I offered for the first time the Holy Sacrifice to the Eternal God, remain close to me and assist me."

On May 13, 1917, Mary chose the exact hour of Eugenio Pacelli's consecration as bishop to make her first appearance to the three children of Fatima. Remarking about this years later, the Holy Father said: "It is as if our Holy Mother wished to show us that in the troubled times of our pontificate, in one of the greatest crises of human history, we should be enfolded, protected, and guided by (her) motherly assistance...."

When he was elected Pope, he entrusted his pontificate to Our Lady of Good Counsel: "... under the protection of the Virgin of Good Counsel who was the patron of the conclave, we assume the government of the Bark of Peter...."

Throughout his reign, Pius XII manifested a special devotion to Mary and had the greatest confidence in her intercession. Again and again he exhorted the faithful to pray to her as Mediatrix. He mentioned her in encyclicals and in addresses to pilgrims, to Marian Congresses, to Catholic nations and to the world.

During World War II he said again and again that the only certain way to peace is to go to God through Mary. When peace came, he reminded his spiritual family to "thank Mary for having obtained, through her powerful intercession, the long desired termination of that great world conflagration."

He sent words of praise and encouragement to the pilgrims observing important anniversaries at Guadalupe and at La Salette. In his broadcast to the Marian Congress at Ottawa in 1947, he said: "If it is true, as Bousset has said, that 'when Jesus enters any land he enters with His Cross,' it is equally true that He never enters without Mary."

When he received members of the Sodality of Our Lady in audience, he said: "Consecration to Our Lady in her Sodality implies a complete dedication of ourselves for the remainder of our life and for all eternity." In an Apostolic Constitution of 1948, he definitely designated the Sodality as Catholic Action: "The structure and peculiar character of the Sodalities of Our Lady are no obstacle whatever to their being called with fullest right Catholic Action under the auspices and inspiration of the Blessed Virgin Mary."

Pope Pius XII made notable contributions to Marian theology. The epilogue of his encyclical *Mystici Corporis* (June 29, 1943) has been called "a complete treatise on Mariology

The Pope of Our Lady

in miniature." In this epilogue the Holy Father dwelt on three phases of Marian theology: Mary as co-redemptress of the human race, Mary as the spiritual Mother of all members of the Mystical Body, and Mary as the Mediatrix of All Graces.

Again in *Mediator Dei* (November 20, 1947), we find reference to the same attributes of Mary:

"Holier than the Cherubim and Seraphim, she enjoys unquestionably greater glory than all the other saints, for she is 'full of grace,' and she is the Mother of God, who happily gave birth to the Redeemer for us. She became our Mother also when the Divine Redeemer offered the sacrifice of Himself; and hence, by this title also, we are His children. She teaches us all the virtues; she gives us her Son and with Him all the help we need, for God 'wished us to have everything through Mary.'"

On October 31, 1942, in a memorable radio address to the pilgrims at Fatima, the Holy Father dedicated the world to the Immaculate Heart of Mary. Later, he urged that every diocese, every parish and every family be dedicated to the Immaculate Heart.

In 1945, Pope Pius extended the Feast of the Immaculate Heart of Mary, August 22, to the Universal Church.

The climax of his career as Pope of Our Lady came on the Feast of All Saints, 1950. On that day he defined the Assumption of the Blessed Virgin as a dogma of faith.

Did the Blessed Mother give a special sign to Pope Pius that she approved his action in defining the Assumption? Reliable sources close to the Holy Father say that on four occasions in 1950, while he was walking in the Vatican gradens, he beheld the Miracle of the Sun. This was similar to the Miracle of the Sun which was seen by 70,000 people at Fatima in 1917.

The story was first revealed by Federico Cardinal Tedeschini who was speaking during a Solemn Pontifical Mass at Fatima on October 13, 1951. The Mass marked the end of the Holy Year outside Rome and also the thirty-fourth anniversary of the last apparition at Fatima. Cardinal Tedeschini was the Papal Legate to the celebration. He made it clear that he was speaking "in my own name only":

"It was at four in the afternoon on October 30 and 31, and on November 1 of last year, 1950, and on the octave of November 1, the day of the definition of Mary's Assumption into heaven. From the Vatican gardens the Holy Father turned his gaze toward the sun and there before his eyes the wonder of this valley (the Cova da Iria at Fatima) and this day (October 13, 1917) was renewed.

"Who can gaze upon the blazing sun, with its corona? But he could! On all four days he was able to gaze upon the activity of the sun. Under the hand of Mary, the sun, agitated and entirely convulsed, was transformed into a picture of life, into a spectacle of heavenly movements, into a transmission of mute but eloquent messages to the Vicar of Christ.

"Is this not Fatima transported to the Vatican? Is this not the Vatican transformed into Fatima?"

On November 17, 1951, *Osservatore Romano,* Vatican City daily, repeated Cardinal Tedeschini's statement that the Miracle of the Sun had been performed four times for the Holy Father at the Vatican. These four repetitions, *Osservatore* said, took place "when the entire Catholic family was rejoicing in union with the Vicar of Christ over the dogmatic definition of Mary's Assumption into Heaven."

On June 7, 1952, Pope Pius XII made the long-awaited consecration of Russia to the Immaculate Heart of Mary.

Our Lady of Fatima had first mentioned the consecration on July 13, 1917. She said: "I shall come back to ask the consecration of Russia to my Immaculate Heart."

She also said: "In the end my Immaculate Heart will triumph. The Holy Father will consecrate Russia to me, it will be converted, and a certain period of peace will be granted to the world."

In 1929 our Lady came back, as she had promised, and asked for the consecration of Russia to her Immaculate Heart. Lucia has been quoted as saying that the consecration should be made by the Pope in union with all the bishops of the world. Lucia made our Lady's request known to her bishop.

The Pope of Our Lady

Three years passed and the consecration was not made. Lucia wrote to the bishop again. She quoted our Lord as saying, "The Holy Father will consecrate Russia to me, but it will be late." (Any consecration to Mary is a consecration to Christ.)

In 1942, as we read in Chapter XXI, Pope Pius XII consecrated the world to the Immaculate Heart with a special mention of Russia. The following spring Lucia said that our Lord was pleased with the 1942 consecration but called it incomplete. He promised to bring World War II to an end, although the conversion of Russia would be delayed.

After this long wait, devotees of Fatima were delighted to learn that in July, 1952, the Pope had consecrated Russia to the Immaculate Heart of Mary.

The consecration was made in an unprecedented apostolic letter dated July 7, feast of the Apostles to the Slavs, SS. Cyril and Methodius. The letter was unique in that it was addressed not to the hierarchy or a ruler, but directly to "the dearly beloved peoples of Russia."

In the letter the Pope stressed his special love for the Russian peoples. He recalled his 1942 consecration of the world to the Immaculate Heart. Then he wrote:

"Now, in a most special way, we dedicate and consecrate all peoples of Russia to that same Immaculate Heart."

In his encyclical *Fulgens Corona* (September 8, 1953), Pope Pius XII proclaimed a Marian Year to begin December 8, 1953, and to end December 8, 1954, the 100th anniversary of the defining of the dogma of the Immaculate Conception. This was the first Marian Year in the Church's long history.

Pope Pius XII helped to make Mary better known, more loved, and more honored than she has ever been. He moved us closer to the day when the Woman shall conquer.

He was the "Pope of Our Lady."

Mary's Role
in Our World

27

God's Mother Is Our Mother

WE HAVE READ about the appearances Mary has made since 1830, and we have studied the various parts of her message. We know that within the past century two of Mary's prerogatives have been made dogmas of the Church. We are familiar with St. Louis Marie de Montfort's statement that God wishes His Mother to be more known, more loved and more honored than ever before. All in all, Mary is coming into greater prominence than she has had since the Middle Ages. She seems to be claiming our atomic age as her own.

Now, it might be well to ask ourselves, "Who is Mary?"

The question is not as superfluous as it seems. Even people who have had a deep devotion to the Blessed Virgin all their lives cannot fully comprehend the great honor, the great power, the great glory that belongs to Mary. The human mind simply cannot grasp all this. We must make an attempt, however, to understand as much as we can of it. If we are to heed Mary's message to the modern world, we should know her position in regard to the modern world.

"No one can find Mary who does not seek her," says St. Louis Marie de Montfort, "and no one can seek her who does not know her. . . . It is necessary, then, for the greater knowledge and glory of the Holy Trinity, that Mary should be more than ever known."

Mary has innumerable titles and privileges. Ponderous volumes have been written about them and have in no way exhausted the subject. People who wish to make a study of the Blessed Mother can go on indefinitely. For our present purposes, the three titles that are most important are Mother, Mediatrix, and Queen. They will be treated very briefly in this chapter and the two to follow.

Mary is our Mother.

Most of us realize this fact in a vague sort of way. We have heard it since we were old enough to remember. We have been accustomed to referring to Mary as our Blessed Mother.

Yet, do we *really* believe it? We have a mother who brought us into the world. Perhaps she is still living. If not, we probably have vivid memories of her. We can't have two mothers, can we? Mary is our mother in a figurative sense; she is called our mother because she has taken such an interest in us.

That is the way many of us would express our thoughts on the matter if we should ever stop to analyze them.

This attitude, however, is not correct. We do have two mothers, a mother in the natural order and a mother in the supernatural order.

Mary is our mother in the supernatural order. She is really and truly our mother, just as much so as is our mother in the natural order.

A mother is one who gives life. Our earthly mother gave us our life in this world, our natural life. Mary has given us the life that elevates our life in this world and flowers in the next, our supernatural life.

After the sin of Adam, our souls were deprived of supernatural life. This life was restored through the Redemption of Christ and the Sacrament of Baptism. Mary made it possible for us to receive this life. She did this at Nazareth, on Calvary and at our Baptism.

At Nazareth the angel Gabriel brought to Mary the most wonderful news that has even been given to any human being. He told her that she had been chosen to be the Mother of God. Mary's consent was needed, however, before the Incarnation could take place. She thought of us at that moment. By answering "No" she could have left us in death. By answering "Yes" she could give us life. She gave her consent and the Word was made Flesh. Our Redemption had been made possible.

About 34 years later Mary stood on the hill of Calvary beneath the cross on which her divine Son was giving His life for us. He was dying that we might be delivered from sin and death. Mary united her sacrifice with His. She thought of us, her children, at that moment. She bravely and generously offered her Son to the Father for our salvation. Never did any creature make such a sacrifice. And she did it for us. Mary, ever Virgin, experienced only joy when she brought Jesus into the world. When she gave us our spiritual birth, she underwent the most agonizing sorrow.

Again at Baptism Mary gave us spiritual life. It was by her intercession that we had the opportunity to receive the sacrament of Baptism fruitfully.

Because of Mary, then, we can hope to enjoy the eternal happiness of heaven. She has given us our life in the next world. This "is not a passing life like your terrestrial one, but a life without end," says Father Emil Neubert, S.M., in *My Ideal—Jesus, Son of Mary*. "Not a life full of imperfections and anguish like your present existence, but a life incomparably happy; not a created life, human or angelical, but—and understand it well—a participation in uncreated life, in the very life of God, in the life of the Most Blessed Trinity. And that is why this life will be endless and incomparably happy, because it is a sharing in the eternity and in the beatitude of God."

So the life that Mary has given us is much greater than the life we are now living. She is truly our spiritual mother.

St. Stanislas Kostka used to repeat with great happiness, "Mater Dei, Mater mei"— "God's Mother is my Mother." Each of us can repeat this tremendous truth.

Mary's Immaculate Heart was fashioned by her Creator

so that God made Man could receive the perfect love of the perfect mother. Mary loves us with this same Immaculate Heart.

Because she loves us so much, she watches over us always. She guards the supernatural life which she has given us. If we should lose our supernatural life by falling into mortal sin, she can obtain for us the grace to recover it.

We see examples of Mary's motherly love for us in her frequent apparitions of recent years. She keeps returning to beg us to repent and to save ourselves from the effects of our sins.

"How long a time do I suffer for you!" said the weeping Lady of La Salette. "If I would not have my Son abandon you, I am compelled to pray to Him without ceasing. And, as to you, you take no heed of it.

"However much you pray, however much you do, you will never recompense the pains I have taken for you."

Those are the words of a true Mother, whose love for us passes all comprehension.

"God's Mother is my Mother." What a world of meaning in those words! What a depth of consolation and hope!

If we but heed her pleas, if we but join our prayers with hers, we need have no fears.

28

All Graces Come Through Mary

IN RECENT TIMES, special attention has been given to Mary's title of Mediatrix of all Graces. This means that Mary is our mediator with her divine Son. All our prayers and petitions go to Him through her; He distributes through her all the graces we receive.

It has not yet been declared an article of faith that Mary is the Mediatrix of All Graces. The belief, however, has gained almost universal acceptance.

In writing of Mary's Universal Mediation in *The Mother of Jesus*, Father James, O.F.M.Cap., says: "No one can attentively watch the mind of the Church, as it finds expression in the Church teaching and the Church taught, without entertaining the hope that the day is not far distant when this prerogative of Our Lady will receive solemn affirmation on the part of the Church. . . . The fact that a special Mass and Office for May 31 in honor of Mary Mediatrix was granted, at the request of the Belgian Hierarchy, to the dioceses of Belgium and to all other dioceses which should ask for it, is significant."

There are many quotations in this book which seem to bear out the fact that Mary is the Mediatrix of All Graces.

"Tell everyone that Our Lord grants us all graces through the Immaculate Heart of Mary; that all must make their petitions to her," Jacinta of Fatima said to Lucia.

Catherine Labouré saw rays of light streaming from gems in our Lady's fingers. The Blessed Virgin explained: "The rays are graces which I give to those who ask for them. But there are no rays from some of the stones, for many people do not receive graces, because they do not ask for them."

At Pellevoisin our Lady said to Estelle Faguette that the Heart of her Son bears so much love for her "that He cannot refuse me any requests."

In another apparition Estelle saw drops of rain falling from our Lady's hands. She understood these to be graces. "These graces," said the Blessed Virgin, "are from my Divine Son; I take them from His heart. He can refuse me nothing."

Pope Benedict XV clearly believed Mary to be the Mediatrix of All Graces. In May, 1917, when World War I seemed to be going on interminably, he said: "Because all graces . . . are dispensed by the hands of the most Holy Virgin, we wish the petitions of her most afflicted children to be directed with lively confidence, more than ever in this awful hour, to the Great Mother of God." As we read in Chapter XV, it was eight days after this that Mary appeared at Fatima, as if in direct response to the Pope's pleas.

Mary shared in the work of the Redemption to such an extent that she is call the Co-redemptrix. It is only fitting that she should share in distributing the graces of that Redemption.

Just as God did not *have* to come into the world through Mary, so He does not *have* to distribute His graces through her. But the fact is that He wishes to distribute them in that way.

St. Alphonsus Liguori tells us: "Jesus Christ is the unique Mediator so far as strict justice is concerned, the only One who obtains grace and salvation for us by His merits; but we say that Mary is Mediatrix by the favor of her Son. While recognizing that she obtains nothing except by the merits of Jesus Christ and by prayers made in the name of Jesus Christ, we yet maintain that all the graces we ask for are given to us at her intercession."

Mary's role as our mediator is an appropriate one to be

emphasized in our day. The people, sinking beneath the weight of their sins, can be saved only by a return to God. But God, in His august majesty, seems very far away to people who have never known Him. And the thought of an all-just God is a frightening one. Today we need mercy rather than justice.

It is most consoling, therefore, to know that we can turn to Mary, our all-merciful Mother, and ask her to intercede for us. She who is our Mother is also the Mother of God, and He can refuse her nothing. She takes the graces from His Heart and distributes them to all who ask for them.

"We cannot have peace without the cause of peace," says Father Edward Leen, C.S.Sp., in *Our Blessed Mother*. "Until the world assents to depend on its Mother Mary ... there can be no peace.... Only when Mary's rightful place, as Mother of Men, is fully accepted will the world be able to rise. The recent apparitions of Our Lady at Fatima show us the truth of this.... Mary is the Mediatrix of All Graces, and it is through Mary alone, the grace of true peace among nations can come to the world. Justly then, in these days of turmoil ... does the Church salute Our Blessed Mother with the glorious title *Mediatrix Potentissima*, Most Powerful Mediatrix."

29

Mary Is Our Queen

WHEN POPE PIUS XII defined the dogma of the Assumption he declared that Mary is in heaven, body and soul. He thus indirectly reminded the world that in heaven she reigns as Queen. It was a reminder very much needed today. Through

Mary, the Queen, people may be led back to Christ, the King.

Christ always prefers to work in co-operation with His Mother. He is the Redeemer; she is the Co-redemptrix. He is the new Adam; she is the new Eve. We honor His Sacred Heart; we honor her Immaculate Heart. He is our King; she is our Queen.

"As the glorious Virgin Mary," says St. Alphonsus Liguori, "has been raised to the dignity of Mother of the King of kings, it is not without reason that the Church honors her, and wishes her to be honored by all, with the glorious title of Queen."

Mary became our Queen, just as she became our Mother, the moment she consented to become the Mother of God. After her death and Assumption into heaven, our Lord crowned her as Queen. She did not become Queen as a result of this crowning; she was crowned because she was Queen.

"In vain," says St. Bernard, "would a person ask other saints for a favor if Mary did not interpose to obtain it."

Father Juarez says that "we beg the saints to be our intercessors with Mary, because she is the Queen and sovereign Lady."

When Mary prays for a soul, we are told, the whole heavenly court prays with her. "Nay, more," says St. Bonaventure, "whenever the most sacred Virgin goes to God to intercede for us, she, as Queen, commands all the angels and saints to accompany her and unite their prayers with hers."

Father Emil Neubert, S.M., has written a book in which he calls Mary the *Queen of Militants*. It is a very appropriate title for her in this day when all Catholics are required to be apostles.

For a time the idea that we should all be apostles was largely forgotten. A lay person tried to lead a good life and to save his own soul. That was all. Helping others to get closer to God was the work of priests, Brothers, and Sisters, not of lay people.

The idea was false and extremely harmful. "Countries that

Mary Is Our Queen

sent out no missionaries to heathen lands saw their own faith decline," says Rev. Michael O'Carroll in *This Age and Mary*. "Catholic communities which made no attempt to convert their Protestant and Jewish minorities were puzzled to see defections from their own body. With individuals it is strangely similar." Father O'Carroll goes on to say that the man who shrinks from his duty as a member of an organic body, and who does nothing to help others to be better, ends up in a state of dissatisfaction, diffidence, and frustration.

Pope Pius XI did much to revive the apostolic tradition. "The apostolate is one of the duties inherent in Christian life," he said. In other words, lay people must not hug the faith to themselves. They must do all they can to share it with others.

Since the urgent appeals of Popes Pius XI and XII, the number of persons taking part in the lay apostolate has increased greatly. Sodalists, members of the Confraternity of Christian Doctrine, the Legion of Mary, the Holy Name Society, the St. Vincent de Paul Society, the Catholic Youth Organization and many others are doing very effective work.

Only yesterday the Church grieved over the loss of the working classes. Today there is reason to hope that many of these workers will return because of the diligence of the modern lay apostles. All such lay apostles are doing the work of Mary. She is their Queen.

"The Immaculate Virgin is the Woman who must crush the head of the serpent," Father Neubert tells us. "To her God has entrusted the war against Satan and his seed. She is the commander-in-chief empowered with the strategy of the war. In this war, you are only a soldier. . . . When you have succeeded in revealing Christ to a soul, you have simply helped Mary in her mission of giving Christ to the world."

Mary has been most militant in our times. She has made numerous appearances. She has given us such aids as the Miraculous Medal, the Green Scapular, the Scapular of the Sacred Heart. At Fatima she performed the spectacular Miracle of the Sun to emphasize her message.

If we remember that Mary is our Queen, if we work under

her and follow her directives, our apostolic work will be crowned with success. There will be temporary defeats and disappointments, but there can be no permanent defeat for Mary.

Working under Mary, our Queen, our Commander in Chief, we can bring Christ back to the world!

How We Can Hasten Mary's Coming Victory

30

Total Consecration to Mary

ST. LOUIS MARIE DE MONTFORT tells us that "the devil, knowing he has but little time, and now less than ever to destroy souls, will every day redouble his efforts and his combats." The saint also tells us that "Mary must be terrible to the devil and his crew, as an army ranged in battle, principally in these latter times."

We are not bound to believe the words of even a canonized saint, but as we look at the world about us, who would deny that the devil is every day redoubling his efforts? And when we consider the many apparitions of the Blessed Virgin in our day and the other manifestations of her power and glory, who would deny that the Blessed Virgin is intensifying her campaign against Satan?

"God has formed but one enmity," St. Louis Marie says, "but it is an irreconcilable one, which shall grow and endure even to the end. It is between Mary, His worthy Mother, and the devil—between the children and servants of the Blessed Virgin, and the children and tools of Lucifer."

In this total war, we must be totally on one side or totally on the other. We cannot be neutral, and we cannot be lukewarm. We must be sure that we are "children and servants of the Blessed Virgin," not "children and tools of Lucifer."

How are we to do this?

St. Louis Marie advocates Total Consecration to the Blessed Virgin. This consecration will be discussed in this chapter.

The Blessed Mother herself, in one apparition after another, has requested three practices:

1. Prayer, especially the Rosary
2. Sacrifice
3. Devotion to Mary's Immaculate Heart

These practices will be discussed in the next three chapters. They can be called Mary's Peace Plan. By practicing them we will not only be helping to save our own souls and the souls of others, but we will also be helping to bring peace to the world.

So far as we know, our Lady has not specifically requested the Total Consecration advocated by St. Louis Marie de Montfort. There is nothing in her program, however, that contradicts De Montfort's True Devotion. Indeed, prayer, sacrifice, and devotion to the Immaculate Heart take on added value when practiced in the spirit of Total Consecration.

In order to be completely on Mary's side in her battle against Satan, we should put ourselves unreservedly at her disposal. The best way to do this is by consecrating ourselves entirely to her.

This is the True Devotion to the Blessed Virgin Mary taught by St. Louis Marie de Montfort in his book of that title. The manuscript of this book, we recall, was found in 1842.

The devotion was also taught by Father William Joseph Chaminade, founder of the Society of Mary, who lived in France in the latter part of the eighteenth century. Both men seem to have been inspired separately from above.

St. Louis Marie did not say that Total Consecration to Mary was the only means to salvation. On the contrary, he said, "It is true that we can obtain divine union by other roads. . . ." And again, ". . . the rest of the saints who are the greater number, although they have all had devotion to Our Blessed Lady, nevertheless have either not at all or at least very little entered upon this way" (the De Montfort way).

Still, De Montfort tells us that Total Consecration is the straightest and shortest way to God, the perfect way.

De Montfort called his devotion slavery to our Lady. The

Total Consecration to Mary

day we make the Act of Consecration we become Mary's slaves.

The word "slave" has an unpleasant sound to many people today. This fact alone has probably caused many people to delay making the Act of Consecration.

As Baroness de Hueck Doherty points out, however, "we take our sins lightly these days. We *are* often slaves of the Devil. Yes, the world is enslaved to Satan and seems to like it. But mention slavery, voluntary slavery, to the Mother of God whose fiat brought the Incarnation and the Redemption, and opened the doors of Paradise to us children of men! Then everyone squirms, looks the other way, shakes his head, and speaks of emotionalism and religious mania! Isn't it passably strange!"

From St. Bernard and St. Bonaventure, St. Louis Marie borrows some of his most striking arguments for putting our reliance in Mary: "Following her, thou shalt not go out of thy way; imploring her, thou shalt not despair; thinking of her, thou shalt not err; protected by her, thou shalt not fear; held by her, thou shalt not fall; guided by her, thou shalt not weary; under her auspices thou shalt gain heaven. Her hand is strong; she prevents Christ from punishing, the devil from harming, virtue from taking flight, merit from perishing, grace from escaping."

To those who think that giving great honor to Mary detracts from the honor due to God, St. Louis Marie says: "You never think of Mary without Mary in your place thinking of God. You never praise or honor Mary but she praises and honors God. Mary only lives in relation to God of Whom she is the echo, which only says and repeats God. If you say 'Mary' she says 'God.' St. Elizabeth praised Mary and called her Blessed. . . . Mary's answer was to sing the *Magnificat anima mea Dominum* (My soul doth magnify the Lord)."

De Montfort based his True Devotion on Mary's triple role as Mother, Mediatrix, and Queen.

If Mary is our Mother in the fullest sense, then we must be her children in the true sense of the word. She has a right to mother our souls.

If she is our Mediatrix, we receive all graces through her. We depend upon her for our spiritual life. She has a right to receive our prayers.

If she is our Queen, then we must be absolutely subject to her. We must be her soldiers, her servants. She has a right to reign over our hearts.

According to St. Louis Marie the perfect way to acknowledge Mary's triple role in respect to our souls is to put ourselves completely under her domination. This means a Total Consecration of oneself to Jesus through the hands of Mary, as an acknowledgment of our complete dependence upon them both.

St. Louis Marie calls this consecration "a perfect renewal of the vows of Holy Baptism." At Baptism we renounced Satan and all his works and gave ourselves to Christ. By our consecration to Jesus through Mary we renew this pledge through the "most perfect of all means, namely, the Blessed Virgin."

1. We give Mary our body. Our eyes, our tongue—all parts of the body—must serve to glorify the heavenly Mistress. This is done by offering her all our ordinary actions as well as heroic acts.

2. We give her our soul with all its faculties, such as intelligence and free will. We promise to employ these faculties in her service.

3. We give her our worldly goods. This means that we look upon these goods as belonging to her rather than to us. We simply act as "administrators" of her goods.

4. We give Mary our interior and spiritual goods. These are our merits, our virtues and our good works, past, present, and future.

This last part of the consecration means that we sacrifice to Jesus, through Mary, the right to dispose of our prayers and alms, of our mortifications and atonements. We leave everything to be disposed of by Mary. She may apply them as she sees fit, to the greater glory of God, which she alone knows perfectly. We are no longer masters of the good works we do. Mary may apply them for the relief of a soul in purga-

Total Consecration to Mary

tory, the conversion of a sinner, or for whatever purpose she chooses.

This is a sacrifice which not even a religious community requires of its members. Religious take vows of poverty, chastity and obedience. They do not, however, promise to renounce the value of their own prayers and good works.

A person who makes this Act of Consecration may still offer prayers for whatever purpose he wishes. In doing so, however, he realizes that Mary has the right to use the prayers for some other purpose. It is safe to say that the person offering the prayers loses nothing. Mary is never outdone in generosity.

In the end, this absolute stripping of ourselves will be our gain. Mary will make the least of our sacrifices agreeable to God. De Montfort tells us that this is like the old story of the peasant whose poor gift was presented to the king by the queen in a dish of gold.

"This devotion," says St. Louis Marie, "makes us give to Jesus and Mary, without reserve, all our thoughts, words, actions and sufferings all the times of our life, in such sort that whether we wake or sleep, whether we eat or drink, whether we do great actions or little ones, it is always true to say that whatever we do, even without thinking of it, is, by virtue of our offering at least, if it has not been expressly retracted, done for Jesus and Mary."

The consecration places a soul in a state of complete dependence upon Mary. We no longer think, "I shall do this." Instead we think, "If Mary wills it so, I shall do this." We acquire the habit of speaking, acting, and thinking as one who belongs to and depends on Mary, his Queen and Mother.

"We must do all our actions," St. Louis Marie tell us, "by Mary, with Mary, in Mary, and for Mary." These are the echo of the words of St. Paul which the priest recites at Mass every day, "Through Him, with Him and in Him." This is the very essence of Christian life.

After making the Act of Total Consecration it is important to live that consecration. Father Neubert in *Queen of Militants* tells us: "To live it is to act at each moment of your life as one belonging no longer to yourself but to Our Blessed Mother; to employ all that you are, all that you have, and all that you do, no longer for yourself, but for her.

"It means using all that you possess, not according to your own inclinations, but according to what you think to be the designs of Mary.

"It means employing your body and its activities, not to procure . . . the satisfaction of gluttony or laziness, but . . . in the mission of a militant of the Immaculate Virgin. . . .

"It means employing your will to wish only what Mary wishes and all she wishes. This includes constant fidelity to monotonous duties . . . and generous acceptance of all sacrifices. . . .

"And all of this you must do even when sentiment no longer upholds you, when you feel tired, when you are a prey to temptation, when you see others about you abandoning everything to think only of their own selfish interests."

This sounds difficult, and indeed it is difficult. We have the strength and the support of Mary, however. If we are sincere about working in her cause, she will give us the strength to persevere.

In order to succeed in living our consecration, we should form the habit of renewing it. We should renew it when we rise in the morning, when we begin our work, after lunch, before we go to bed. We should renew it especially in time of temptation.

St. Louis Marie tells us that an Age of Mary is coming, an age in which men will lose themselves in Mary, will become living copies of Mary in loving and glorifying Jesus.

"When will that happy time, that Age of Mary, come . . . ? That will not come until men shall know and practice this devotion which I am teaching."

31

"Say the Rosary Every Day"

"SAY THE ROSARY every day," our Lady said to the three children of Fatima.

One of her most frequent requests at Fatima was for the Rosary. She mentioned it in each of her six apparitions. When she identified herself at the end of the sixth and final apparition, she said, "I am the Lady of the Rosary." Of all the titles by which she called herself, that was the one she chose.

At Lourdes, in 1858, our Lady carried the Rosary. She looked on approvingly and allowed the beads to slip through her fingers as Bernadette said the prayers.

The devotion to Our Lady of Pompeii, instituted in 1875, is primarily a devotion to the Queen of the Rosary. In 1884 our Lady told Fortuna Agrelli of Naples that the title "Queen of the Holy Rosary" was most precious and dear to her. The Devotion at Cape de la Madeleine is also to the Queen of the Rosary.

It is evident that the Rosary plays a big part in Mary's plans for the world. It has already played a big part in the history of the world.

Near the close of the twelfth century, the Albigensian heresy was disrupting the Christian world. By force of arms, by massacre and devastation, the Albigenses spread their errors not only through France but through many other parts of the Latin world.

It seemed that the Albigenses could not be checked either

by force or by preaching. Then St. Dominic, the founder of the Dominican Order, began preaching the devotion of the Rosary. Tradition says that the Blessed Virgin appeared to him and asked him to do this. The Rosary succeeded where all other means had failed. France and the Church were saved from the Albigenses.

In the sixteenth century the Turks threatened Christian civilization, just as the Russians do today. Turkish fleets roamed the Mediterranean Sea. Cities on the coast were plundered; churches desecrated and destroyed. Men were tortured, and women were dragged off to slave marts and harems. Not even the children escaped. Those who were not killed were brought up in the Mohammedan religion and taught to hate the race from which they had sprung.

The Turks planned to capture Italy and Spain. If they had gained these footholds on the continent, all Europe would have been in great danger. Pope Pius V recognized the threat and called upon the countries of Europe to unite into one great coalition and crush the aggressors. By this time, the Protestant Revolt had taken place, and the Pope did not have the influence that had been his in the Middle Ages. Only Venice and Spain answered the Pope's plea.

The Christian fleet that was assembled was placed under the command of Don Juan of Austria. The Pope sent his blessing to Don Juan and asked him to include in his force only men who were leading moral lives. He promised the commander that he would be victorious if he did this. On September 30, 1571, after the men had received the sacraments, the fleet put to sea.

During all the time that the armada was at sea, the Pope waited anxiously for news. He asked Christians everywhere to say the Rosary for victory. He instructed the cardinals to fast and give alms in order to obtain by penance the mercy of God. Devotions were held in all the churches of Rome. The Pope himself fasted three days and spent many hours on his knees. The Confraternities of the Rosary were holding their devotions in Rome, and they added their prayers to millions of others throughout Christendom.

"Say the Rosary Every Day"

On the morning of October 7, 1571, the two fleets met near Lepanto in the Gulf of Corinth. Just before the battle began, the wind, which had been favoring the Turks, changed suddenly. The battle raged all day. It ended in a resounding victory for the Christians. Christian Europe was saved.

On the afternoon of the battle, Pope Pius V was conducting some important business with one of his officials. Suddenly, he broke off the conversation, rose to his feet, opened a window and stood looking up to heaven. Turning around, his face radiant with happiness, he said: "This is no time for business. Go and thank God. Our fleet has just won a victory over the Turks."

Two weeks later a messenger arrived, with the news of the victory.

Pius V, who has been canonized, was firmly convinced that the victory of Lepanto was due to our Lady. He ordered that every year the anniversary of the battle, October 7, should be celebrated as the feast of Our Lady of Victory. This was later changed to the feast of the Most Holy Rosary. October, the month containing the feast, has been made the Month of the Most Holy Rosary.

The Turks renewed their attacks twice in the eighteenth century. Each time they were defeated on a feast of Mary, after people had prayed the Rosary with great confidence.

Thus, the intervention of God has obviously had more to do with some of the important victories of the past than has human might. This could happen again in our own time.

The last encyclical of Pope Pius XI, issued in 1937, was on the Rosary. "The Holy Virgin," he wrote, "who once victoriously drove the terrible sects of the Albigenses from Christian countries, now suppliantly invoked by us, will turn aside the new errors, especially those of Communism. . . ." He said that if all invoke the Blessed Mother "with due disposition, with great faith and with fervent piety, it is right to hope that as in the past, so in our day, the Blessed Virgin will obtain from her Divine Son that the waves of the present tempests be calmed and that a brilliant victory crown this rivalry of Christians in prayer."

Father Patrick Peyton, C.S.C., is widely known as the Apostle of the Family Rosary. This is an idea that is as old as the Rosary itself but which had been largely abandoned in recent times. Father Peyton has done much to revive the beautiful custom.

Many Popes have urged the Family Rosary. Pope Pius IX said: "If you desire peace in your hearts, in your homes, in your country, assemble every evening to recite the Rosary."

Pope Pius XI called the Family Rosary "a beautiful and salutary custom."

Pope Pius XII, in speaking to newly married couples about reciting the Rosary, said: "You may be sure that in so doing you are insuring the success of your family life." Each evening the Pope kneels with members of the papal household for a group recitation of the Rosary.

"If families will but listen to my message," says Father Peyton, "and give our Lady ten minutes of their twenty-four hours by reciting the daily Family Rosary, I assure them that their homes will become, by God's grace, peaceful, prayerful places—little heavens, which God the Author of home life has intended they should be!"

32

"Sacrifice Yourself for Sinners"

"Do you wish to know the secret?" Pope Pius IX asked, in referring to La Salette. "This is it: Unless you do penance, you shall all perish."

At Lourdes, Bernadette repeated our Lady's plea for "Penitence! Penitence!"

"Sacrifice Yourself for Sinners"

At Fatima, our Lady asked the children: "Do you wish to offer yourselves to God to endure all the sufferings that He may choose to send you, as an act of reparation for the sins by which He is offended, and to ask for the conversion of sinners?" When Lucia answered that they did, our Lady said: "Then you will have much to suffer, but the grace of God will assist you always and bear you up."

"Sacrifice yourself for sinners," our Lady said on another occasion at Fatima, "and say many times, especially when you make sacrifices: 'O Jesus it is for Your love, for the conversion of sinners, and in reparation for sins committed against the Immaculate Heart of Mary.'"

The following words of Our Lady of Fatima put a great responsibility upon all of us: "Pray, pray a great deal and make sacrifices for sinners, for many souls go to hell because they have no one to pray for them."

In 1925 the Child Jesus and our Lady both appeared to Lucia in the convent and asked for acts of reparation to Mary's Immaculate Heart.

At Beauraing, Belgium, in 1932, our Lady said, "Sacrifice yourself for me."

How are we to make sacrifices? The three children of Fatima asked this very question of the angel who appeared to them the year before they were favored by the apparitions of our Lady. The angel had just asked the children to "offer prayers and sacrifices constantly to the Most High."

"How are we to make sacrifices?" asked nine-year-old Lucia.

"You can make sacrifices of all things," the angel replied. "Offer them in reparation for the sins that offend God, and beg of Him the conversion of sinners. In this way, try to draw down peace on your country.... Above all, accept and bear humbly the sufferings which the Lord will send you."

"You can make sacrifices of all things...."

The words were meant as much for us as for the children of Fatima.

The three children heeded the request of the angel and

made sacrifices of all things. They offered all their everyday actions to God through the Immaculate Heart of Mary.

In the spring of 1942 Lucia wrote: "This is the penance which the good Lord now asks: the sacrifice that every person has to impose upon himself to lead a life of justice in the observances of His Law. He requires that the way be made known to souls. For many, thinking that the word penance means great austerities and not feeling in themselves the strength or generosity for these, lose heart and rest in a life of lukewarmness and sin.

"Last Thursday, at midnight, while I was in chapel with my superiors' permission, Our Lord said to me: 'The sacrifice required of every person is the fulfillment of his duties in life and the observance of My Law. This is the penance I now seek and require.'"

This is the very most that is asked of us: the sacrifice required of every person is the fulfillment of his duties in life and the observance of God's law. This is heartening when we tend to become discouraged, and when we think we are not doing enough.

The most effective way to make sacrifices of all things is to make the Morning Offering: "O Jesus, through the Immaculate Heart of Mary, I offer Thee all my prayers, works and sufferings of this day for all the intentions of Thy Sacred Heart, in union with the holy sacrifice of the Mass throughout the world, in reparation for my sins, for the intentions of all our associates and in particular for the intention of the Holy Father." If we are in the state of grace, the Morning Offering turns all our actions for the day into meritorious acts.

The Act of Total Consecration has this same effect. To a person who has consecrated himself completely to Jesus through Mary, the Morning Offering is simply a daily renewal of that consecration.

"Above all, accept and bear humbly the sufferings which the Lord will send you."

When the civil administrator put the children of Fatima

in jail with the hardened criminals, they offered their suffering in reparation for the sins of the world. When Jacinta was undergoing great agony on her deathbed, she murmured through her pain: "It is for love of You, my Jesus. Now You can convert many sinners, for I suffer much."

All of us have our sufferings, small ones and big ones; the extra tasks we have to perform, the slights we receive, the plans that go wrong, the severity of the weather, the loss of a loved one, a severe illness, a financial reverse. Like Jacinta, we can offer these in reparation for sins and for the conversion of sinners.

Offering their everyday actions and their sufferings to Jesus through Mary was not enough for Lucia, Francisco and Jacinta. They were constantly thinking up *voluntary* sacrifices. When they went out to tend the sheep, they gave their lunches to children poorer than themselves, and they ate unripe olives. Under their clothes they wore shaggy ropes which chafed their skin.

All of us can make voluntary sacrifices in addition to the minimum penance which our Lord says He requires, although our sacrifices are not likely to take such extreme forms.

St. John Mary Vianney, the Curé of Ars, lived a life of heroic self-denial, penance and reparation. Because of these virtues he was able to convert an entire parish, the members of which had given up their practice of religion.

One day a neighboring pastor said to Father Vianney: "I have a hardened old sinner in my parish. Years ago he fell away from the faith. I've tried everything to convert him. I've pleaded with him: I've prayed for him: I've asked others to pray for him. But it's no use. He seems determined to die in his sins. What can I do?"

"You say, Father," replied the saint, "that you have pleaded with him and have prayed for him. But have you tried fasting for him? It is only by sacrifice and suffering—offered as penance—that you will be able, by the grace of God, to convert him."

Similarly, with the grace of God, we can accomplish stupendous things by our sacrifices. The stakes are high. We can win peace on earth. We can win a Catholic Russia. We can win peace of mind and peace of soul. We can achieve the unity of the Mystical Body all over the world. We can bring about a rebirth of the moral values so long deadened by the forces of materialism.

What sacrifices shall we make? We can make them in all categories: everyday actions, sufferings and voluntary acts of self-denial. Here are a few suggestions. We can:

1. Get up an hour earlier every morning and go to Mass.
2. Do that unpleasant task we have been shirking.
3. Be kind to someone who has slighted us.
4. Be pleasant at home and at work, even when we have severe provocation to be otherwise.
5. Bear our aches and pains in quiet patience.
6. Go out of our way to help others.
7. Live up to the duties of our religion, even when doing so is very inconvenient.
8. Give up something we want very much in order to give the money to the missions.

These are only a few ways in which we can answer Mary's call for sacrifices. With good will we should be able to think of many more ways of carrying out the wishes of the Mother of God. If made in the proper spirit, such sacrifices will help restore the world to Christ, and will help put the world on the road to true peace.

33

Mary's Immaculate Heart

"Jesus wishes to use you to make me known and loved," our Lady said to Lucia in 1917. "He wants to establish the devotion to my Immaculate Heart in the world."

When we practice devotion to the Immaculate Heart, we venerate not only the physical heart of Mary but everything the heart symbolizes. In short, veneration of the Immaculate Heart is veneration for the whole person of Mary.

We know that Mary is Our Lady of the Seven Sorrows, the Immaculate Conception, Mother of God, Spouse of the Holy Ghost, Mother of All Men, Mediatrix of All Graces. In the devotion to the Immaculate Heart, all these titles and many others are combined.

This all-embracing devotion has been saved for widespread attention in our own day. The origin of the devotion, however, can be traced back several centuries.

The devotion to the Immaculate Heart of Mary closely parallels the devotion to the Sacred Heart of Jesus. In some ways, devotion to the Immaculate Heart prepared the way for devotion to the Sacred Heart, just as Mary prepares the way for Jesus.

Until the middle of the seventeenth century, devotion to the Immaculate Heart of Mary was unknown, except to a few privileged souls.

In 1641, St. John Eudes began preaching devotion to the Hearts of Jesus and Mary. In 1638, he published his *Devotion to the Most Pure Heart and Holy Name of Mary*. Shortly before his death in 1680 he completed his *Amiable Heart of the Mother of God*. When Pope Pius XI canonized St. John Eudes in 1925, he called him the apostle of the Sacred Hearts of Jesus and Mary.

The feast of the Heart of Mary was celebrated for the first time in 1648. A special Mass and Office for the occasion were composed by St. John. The Mass was celebrated in Autun, France. In this town at that time there was a one-year-old baby, Margaret Mary Alacoque, later to be a canonized saint.

About thirty years later, our Lord appeared to St. Margaret Mary and asked for devotion to His Sacred Heart. He requested a feast of the Sacred Heart, the devotion of the First Fridays and the Holy Hour of Reparation. In one vision Margaret Mary beheld the Sacred Hearts of Jesus and Mary and between them her own. The voice of our Lord said: "It is thus that My Divine Love unites these three hearts."

St. John Eudes worked in France. Devotion to the Immaculate Heart was widely known in that country by the time he died in 1680. The French Revolution, however, almost wiped out the devotion. It was kept alive by the Eudists, an order which St. John had founded.

In 1830, our Lady gave a great impetus to the devotion when she appeared to St. Catherine Labouré and instructed her to introduce the Miraculous Medal. As we know, one side of the medal represents the Heart of Jesus and the Heart of Mary, side by side. St. Catherine was ordered by her director to ask what words should be inscribed on the Hearts. Mary replied that no words were needed. The union of the two Hearts told the whole story.

Thus, in her first message to the modern world, the heart of Mary was given great emphasis.

Six years later, Father Charles des Gennettes, of Our Lady of Victories Church in Paris, heard the words, "Consecrate your church and parish to the Most Holy and Immaculate Heart of Mary." From that moment the church underwent a great transformation. Today it is the famous Shrine of Our Lady of Victory.

Mary's Immaculate Heart

At Blangy, in 1840, our Lady gave Sister Bisqueyburu the Green Scapular, which is called the badge of the Immaculate Heart.

At Fatima, in 1917, our Lady told Lucia that she was to remain on earth to help establish devotion to the Immaculate Heart. A few moments later, the children saw in front of our Lady a heart surrounded by thorns. They understood this to be the heart of Mary pierced by sins and desiring reparation. After Lucia was in the convent, our Lady appeared to her and asked for the devotion of the five First Saturdays in reparation to her Immaculate Heart. Those who practice the devotion are promised Mary's assistance "at the hour of death with the graces necessary for salvation."

When she asked for the devotion, our Lady used words strikingly similar to those used by our Lord to St. Margaret Mary when He asked for the devotion of the nine First Fridays in reparation to His Sacred Heart.

Our Lady appeared to Lucia again in the convent and asked that Russia be consecrated to the Immaculate Heart.

In 1932, our Lady showed the five children of Beauraing her heart as a heart of gold.

In 1942, Pope Pius XII dedicated the world to the Immaculate Heart of Mary and made a special mention of Russia. The following year he fixed the feast of the Immaculate Heart of Mary for the Universal Church on August 22.

The Holy Father has set the example. If we are to carry out Mary's wishes, we must consecrate all things to her Immaculate Heart. We must consecrate our dear ones so that we will all be united more closely in the Mystical Body of Christ. We must consecrate our parish, our diocese and our country. And we must unite in the Holy Father's consecration of the whole world, because Mary is our Queen.

Today, when the world needs Mary as never before, it is well to ponder Jacinta's words to Lucia:

"Tell everyone that our Lord grants us all graces through the Immaculate Heart of Mary; that all must make their petitions to her; that the Sacred Heart of Jesus desires that the Immaculate Heart of Mary be venerated at the same time.

Tell them that they should all ask for peace from the Immaculate Heart of Mary, as God has placed it in her hands. O, if I could only put in the hearts of everyone in the world the fire that is burning in me and makes me love so much the Heart of Jesus and the Heart of Mary."

34

Mary Wants Us as Her Apostles

YOUNG FATHER PATRICK PEYTON, C.S.C., was faced by a problem that would have seemed impossible to a man of less faith. He had come to this country from Ireland while still a very young man and had entered the seminary shortly after that. While there he was stricken by a serious illness which the doctors thought would be fatal. When he was cured of this illness, he promised to dedicate his life in the priesthood to the task of persuading American families to say the Rosary together every evening.

Now Father Peyton was out of the seminary and he must fulfill his promise. Seldom has a man faced a more difficult task. He had no friends in high places. He was bashful almost to the point of being inarticulate, except when talking about Mary and the Rosary. And he had the task of selling prayer to a nation in which even the mention of the word was unfashionable.

The amazing thing is that Father Peyton succeeded. He knew nothing about Hollywood or the radio networks, but he was able to convince radio executives that they should give him time on a nationwide network, and he was able to enlist the talents of the brightest stars of the entertainment world. Now, the whole country is familiar with his slogan: "The family that prays together stays together." One television program produced by Father Peyton was seen by an audience estimated as among the largest in television history.

Impressed by Father Peyton's success, local groups, in cooperation with owners and managers of broadcasting stations, have sponsored the recitation of the Rosary over individual stations. A recent survey discloses that 26 radio stations are broadcasting *daily* recitations of the Rosary which can be heard in 5000 cities and towns. In addition, 42 stations carry weekly Rosary programs. These are not dramatizations, but actual recitations of the prayers. A short time ago, it would have been impossible to convince radio men that the "monotonous" repetition of Our Fathers and Hail Marys was "good radio."

Father Peyton's Joyful Hour, Sorrowful Hour and Glorious Hour, each broadcast once a year, are studded with Hollywood's leading actors and actresses. *Time* magazine, commenting on the effective beauty of the dramatization of the Nativity on the Joyful Hour, concluded: "One astonished cinemagnate asked how in the world he (Father Peyton) had managed to assemble such a glamour show, where the government had often tried it and sometimes failed."

"Our Lady," replied Father Peyton, "can do a lot better than the government."

Pope Pius XII said one time that mankind is facing the greatest crisis since the beginning of Christianity. The causes that have brought about this crisis are many and varied. They are at work both within and without the Church.

Outside the Church many men now deny the existence of God and ignore the hereafter. This is something new and strange and sinister in the world. In earlier heresies, and in the Protestant Revolt, men at least clung to their belief in God. They were religious, often fanatically so, even though they were in error. But today, many have rejected God completely. This is given a more perilous character because of the fact that organized atheism, in the form of Communism, is making a determined bid for the control of the whole world.

Within the Church, conditions are not so good as the statistics would indicate. We number 600 million. That is a large fraction of the human race, we tell ourselves complacently. Surely, we have nothing to fear.

But the figure is an illusion. Many Catholics are affected by the secularism that is rampant throughout the "Christian" world. A large number of Catholics keep religion away from their work, their friendships, their recreation. They blindly follow the fashions of the world. They are afraid to stand up in assemblies and councils and proclaim the eternal standards of Christ's Church.

A recent survey of eighteen million people living in the larger cities of France shows that nine million make no pretense of having any religion. The other nine million call themselves Catholics, but only a very small proportion of them practice their faith. Similar instances could be quoted from many other countries, less startling but following the same trend.

Today, a new impulse is needed within the Church to invigorate it and to spur it on to final victory. That impulse can be supplied by the Blessed Virgin Mary and, indeed, it is being supplied. Today, there is every indication that our Lady, who was rejected four hundred years ago, at the time of the Protestant Revolt, is coming back into her own.

The past century and a half have been marked by the apparitions recorded in this book: the Miraculous Medal, the Green Scapular, La Salette, Lourdes, Pellevoisin, Pontmain, Knock, Fatima, Beauraing, Banneux and others. These apparitions caused many people to think more about God and His Mother and caused them to pray more. The signs and wonders connected with the Miraculous Medal and the various shrines also helped in this respect.

The discovery of St. Louis Marie's *True Devotion to the Blessed Virgin Mary* in 1842 left a profound mark on Catholic life. The practices outlined in this book are bringing about great changes in the interior lives of many persons. These interior changes will have a great effect upon the world as a whole.

The solemn declaration of the dogma of the Immaculate Conception in 1854 brought about greatly increased devotion to our Lady, as did the definition of the Assumption in 1950.

Rev. Clem M. Henze, C.Ss.R., says: "Without doubt in our times more is done for the great Mother of God in ten years than was done formerly in a hundred years, perhaps in three hundred years. Last century more books and writings were published on Our Lady than in the other eighteen centuries of our Christian era. Never in all history have the problems of Mariology, such as the Assumption, Our Lady's Universal Mediation, Mary as co-Redeemer, found such interest as now. And how many other points could be made to show the Marian character of the Age!"

Another sign that our Lady is supplying a new impetus to Catholic life is the flowering of movements, societies, associations and religious communities devoted to her cause. Father Peyton's Family Rosary Crusade has spread throughout the world.

Other people are working as tirelessly in fostering devotion to our Lady: the Brown Scapular of Mount Carmel, the Miraculous Medal, the Green Scapular, novenas to our Lady under various titles. Groups are devoting their time and large amounts of money to mailing out literature which will make our Lady better known and better loved. They are carrying out the injunction of Our Lady of La Salette: "You will make this known to all the people." Such people work tirelessly, anonymously, neither seeking nor desiring credit. They are doing our Lady's work, they say, and they themselves count for nothing except as Mary's children and servants.

The Sodality of Our Lady, which was founded in Rome in 1563, has had a great resurgence in recent times. In 1948, Pope Pius XII, in an Apostolic Constitution, declared that the Sodality is "Catholic Action under the auspices and inspiration of the Blessed Virgin Mary." The Sodality defines itself as a "religious association, whose principal objectives are the personal sanctification of its members, the sanctification of the neighbor, and the spread and defense of the Church, under the patronage of the Blessed Mother." In 1948, there were 74,223 Sodalities throughout the world. No statistics could do justice to the great accomplishments of the Sodalists.

The Legion of Mary is worthy of particular note because its origin is so recent and because its growth has been so rapid. The Legion began very inauspiciously in Dublin on September 17, 1921. A group of pious women, factory workers for the most part, had been working as auxiliaries of the St. Vincent de Paul Society, and now they wanted an organization and a program of their own. All were familiar with De Montfort's *True Devotion* and wished to serve our Lady in that spirit. With the ladies was Frank Duff, a young St. Vincent de Paul Society man. They met in a back room of a house on a poor street of Dublin. Someone brought along a statue of Our Lady of Grace. Two candles and two vases of flowers were placed around the statue to make up a kind of informal altar. Around this altar, still the center of every Legion meeting the world over, Mr. Duff and those fifteen girls outlined a program of personal sanctification and apostolic activity. A weekly spiritual meeting was to be the center of their activity, and from it they were to get the spiritual fortification needed in their work for souls.

They began to visit jails, hospitals and slums, making themselves the servants of those who needed a spiritual stimulus. They established night shelters for the unemployed and clubs for the homeless. Catholic literature was distributed; fallen aways were brought back to Mass; children were enrolled in the instruction classes. Within a year more than 1000 lapsed Catholics were brought back to the Church in

Dublin. It was characteristic of the Legion and its concern for spiritual down-and-outers that one of its first projects was a retreat for prostitutes.

From Ireland the Legion has spread rapidly throughout the world. It has had phenomenal success in everything it has undertaken. It has a unique record in winning converts from paganism and Protestantism.

The Legion of Mary was formed a year before Pope Pius XI issued his call to every man, woman, and child to join the battle for Christ, and yet the organization meets all the requirements for Catholic Action. The Legion calls first of all for the personal sanctification of its members, and it works only with the approval of the bishops and through parish priests.

The phenomenal success of the Legion of Mary is not due to the personalities of its members. They are ordinary people from all walks of life. The success is due rather to the members' complete childlike trust in the Blessed Virgin. They are permitting our Lady to work through them.

"It is not the Legion of the Soldiers of Mary," says Cecily Hallack; "it is the Legion of Mary. . . . The Legion does not fight as a collection of people dedicated to Mary but *as Mary*. . . . Mary is a legion in herself. And those who serve in the Legion serve in Mary, merely represent her. . . ."

This brings us once more to St. Louis Marie de Montfort, the Apostle of the Age of Mary. In the early 1700's he looked into the future and saw a day when there would be an army of apostles "little and poor in the world's esteem, but rich in the grace of God which Mary shall distribute to them abundantly. They shall be great and exalted before God in their sanctity, superior to all other creatures by their lively zeal, and so well sustained with God's assistance that, with the humility of their heel, in union with Mary, they shall crush the head of the devil and cause Jesus Christ to triumph."

Continuing his prophecy of the apostles to come, De Montfort says: "We know that they shall be true disciples of Jesus Christ, walking in the footsteps of His poverty, humility, contempt of the world, charity; teaching the narrow way of God in pure truth according to the holy Gospel, and not according to the maxims of the world; troubling themselves about nothing, not accepting persons, sparing, fearing and listening to no mortal, however influential he may be. They shall have in their mouths the two-edged sword of the Word of God. They shall carry on their shoulders the bloody standard of the Cross, the Crucifix in their right hand and the Rosary in their left, the sacred Names of Jesus and Mary in their hearts and the modesty and mortification of Jesus Christ in their own behavior.

"These are the great men who are to come; but Mary is the one who, by order of the Most High, shall fashion them for the purpose of extending His empire over that of the impious, the idolaters and the Mohammedans. But when and how shall this be? God alone knows."

From these last words we see that De Montfort did not know all the circumstances of his own prophecy. It is not possible to say that today's Sodalists or members of the Legion of Mary or any of the other people working so tirelessly in Mary's cause are the apostles foretold by the saint. But they *are* apostles working in Mary, and through them Mary is transforming the world.

Today Mary is asking for the help of all of us. We must all be her apostles. As her apostles we must realize that the basic trouble of the world is not Communism or Socialism or secularism or international aggression. These things are but symptoms of the dread disease which has stricken humanity. That disease is sin. It will do no good attacking the symptoms. We must go after the germ itself. The apostolic Christian must keep himself free from sin, because he can accomplish nothing if he is a secret carrier of the germ.

At Fatima, our Lady summed up her message to the modern world: "Men must offend our Lord no more and they must ask pardon for their sins, for He is already much offended."

But while keeping free of sin ourselves, we must realize the truth of the saying, "A Christian is one to whom God has

Mary Wants Us as Her Apostles

entrusted his fellow men." We must recognize that we have a duty to help bring all souls closer to God. We can do this best through organizations set up for the purpose under the proper guidance, but we can also do much through our individual efforts. And, of course, our prayers and our sacrifices will be an essential part of our apostolic work.

Saint Pius X, who was Pontiff in the years before World War I, once asked a group of his cardinals, "What is the thing most necessary, at the present time, to save society?"

"Build Catholic schools," answered one.

"No."

"Multiply churches," replied another.

"No, again."

"Increase the recruiting of the clergy," said a third.

"No, no," the Pope said. "What is most necessary at the present time, is to have in each parish a group of laymen at the same time virtuous, well-instructed, determined and really apostolic."

While still the Patriarch of Venice, Pope Pius X said that we "will wait in vain for society to re-Christianize itself simply by the prayers of the good. Prayer is absolutely necessary because in the ordinary economy of salvation God does not concede graces except to him who prays, but India and Japan would never have been converted by the prayers alone of Xavier; the Apostles would never have conquered the world if they had not done the work of heroes and martyrs. It is necessary, therefore, to join prayer with action."

Today, Mary wants us to join prayer with action. She wants us to take part in a great crusade to make her message more widely known and more widely heeded. She wants our help in leading men from lives of sin, in bringing them back to her Son.

By joining this crusade, by being Apostles of Mary, we are hastening the coming victory of the Blessed Virgin Mary. We are bringing closer that great age which is to come, the Age of Mary.

Land of Our Lady

AMERICA IS THE LAND of our Lady. That is true whether we speak of America in the broad sense, as embracing the entire Western Hemisphere, or whether by America we mean our own United States. The Blessed Mother seems to have taken our section of the world under her special protection.

It is symbolic that the oldest historical record ever found in our country contains the prayer, "Hail Virgin Mary, save us from evil." This is the famous Kensington Stone which was found in Minnesota. The inscription is dated 1362, one hundred and thirty years before Columbus discovered America. Most authorities now believe the stone to be genuine.

About 1354, King Magnus of Norway and Sweden heard that a group of his Greenland colonists had deserted their settlement for a more favorable land and a more favorable climate farther west. More distressing to King Magnus, a fervent Christian, was the report that the colonists had left the Church and had returned to the worship of their ancient gods. The king sent an expedition, headed by Paul Knutson, to find the straying settlers and to try to bring them back to the faith. The king's instructions to Knutson are still in existence.

Knutson's expedition sailed around Newfoundland and Labrador and into Hudson Bay. The men sailed up the

Land of Our Lady

Nelson River to Lake Winnipeg and into the Red River of the North, and found themselves in the beautiful wooded lake region of Minnesota. They pitched camp on the shore of a lake. Half the party went hunting for game, which was plentiful. When the hunters came back they found their companions slain and the camp in ashes.

Sorrowfully, the survivors prepared to leave. Before doing so, they chipped an account of their visit on a stone. This is the famous Kensington Stone which a farmer found in the roots of a seventy-year-old tree in 1898. For a long time historians did not accept the stone as genuine, but today most of them do. The Harvard *Journal of Medieval Studies* said recently: "A future generation will find it hard to understand how an older generation could have been so blind."

Anyone who looks at the stone today, or at a picture of it, is struck by the letters AVM which stand out in contrast to the Old Gothic characters. These letters are the only Latin to appear on the stone. They stand for *Ave Virgo Maria,* "Hail Virgin Mary." The entire prayer reads, "Hail Virgin Mary, save us from evil."

Mary heard the prayer; the expedition returned safely many months later. A record of the expedition still exists in Norway.

The Norsemen discovered America and penetrated to the very heart of the continent, but America did not stay discovered. It was the voyage of Christopher Columbus in 1492 that really brought America to the attention of the Europeans and marked the beginning of American history. And our Lady plays an important part in this story.

Columbus had spent months in a vain attempt to get the monarchs of Spain to finance his proposed voyage. Tired and discouraged he was on his way out of the country when he stopped for a night's lodging at the Monastery of Our Lady of Rabida. The prior of our Lady's monastery listened to Columbus and then succeeded in getting the queen to help him. Before embarking on his voyage, Columbus and his men received Holy Communion in a chapel dedicated to the

Blessed Virgin. The flagship of the little expedition, the ship which bore the Discoverer himself, was the *Santa Maria*, "Saint Mary." Every evening during that memorable voyage, the crew members of the three ships sang a hymn to Mary.

The first island that Columbus discovered was named San Salvador, "Holy Saviour." Many of his other discoveries were named in honor of Mary: Our Lady of the Sea, Holy Mary of the Immaculate Conception, Star of the Sea, Port Conception and so on.

On his way back to Spain, Columbus delighted in teaching the Indians that accompanied him the *Ave Maria* and other prayers to Mary. When a great storm threatened the expedition, it sought refuge at the isle of St. Mary's in the Azores.

Columbus placed his second voyage under the protection of the Immaculate Conception. He named his ship *Gracious Mary*. He continued to name new discoveries after various titles of the Virgin. When he was preparing for a fourth voyage, he placed at the feet of our Lady all his titles and all his honors.

His funeral took place in the Church of Our Lady of Valladolid. Seven years later, his remains were moved to Seville and placed in the Church of Our Lady of the Grotto. Afterward they were moved to Santo Domingo and placed in the Church of Notre Dame. Today they are in the Cathedral of Havana—in the chapel of the Immaculate Conception.

The *Santa Maria* gave America an owner—Spain. Columbus had sailed in the service of Spain. When Pope Alexander VI drew the line which gave all the Americas except Brazil to Spain, he made a stipulation. The Spaniards and the Portuguese were to bring the Christian faith to the inhabitants of those lands or forfeit their title. Most Spaniards faithfully tried to carry out this injunction. Almost every Spanish exploring party took along a priest who was to be a missionary to the Indians. This was usually done at great inconvenience and great expense. When there was no priest, the laymen preached the word of God to the Indians, and were sometimes killed for their trouble.

Land of Our Lady

In 1521, less than thirty years after Columbus landed on San Salvador, Hernando Cortes captured the capital of the Aztec empire in Mexico. Just ten years after that, in 1531, our Lady appeared to the fifty-seven-year-old Indian, Juan Diego.

The timing of this apparition is not generally realized. Juan was eighteen years old when Columbus sighted San Salvador, and the event had not the slightest effect upon his life at the time. He continued to live as a child of the forest. He was in his middle forties when he saw his first white men, and how he must have marveled at their horses and coats of armor. He became acquainted with the priests and was attracted to the white man's religion. At the age of fifty-one he was baptized and given the Christian name Juan Diego. In 1531 he was on his way to the Saturday Mass in honor of the Virgin when our Lady appeared to him. Thus, our Lady appeared at the very beginning of the history of Christian Mexico, and to an Indian who was already a young man when Columbus made his first voyage.

Our Lady spoke to Juan in his own Aztec language, and he said later that she looked like an Indian. In the fourth apparition, she put some roses in his cloak (although it was December) and told him to take them to the bishop. When he got there, it was found that she had miraculously put her picture on his cloak. This picture can still be seen in the shrine of Our Lady of Guadalupe, near Mexico City.

Devotion to Our Lady of Guadalupe became widespread among the Indians of two continents, and it helped the priests in their missionary work. In time, almost all the Indians under Spanish rule became Christians. In Europe, the Protestant Revolt was getting under way, and millions of people were being lost to the Catholic Church. In Mexico, Central America and South America, under the loving protection of Our Lady of Guadalupe, the missionaries were adding millions of people to the rolls of the Church.

When Our Lady of Guadalupe appeared to Juan Diego in 1531, the English had not yet settled in North America. The Spaniards claimed the entire continent. Later the Spaniards settled in lands comprising about one third of the present United States. It would seem that the Catholics of the United States and Canada should have a greater devotion to Our Lady of Guadalupe. In 1910, Our Lady of Guadalupe was made Patron of Latin America. In 1945 this patronage was extended to include all North America. In that year Pope Pius XII declared her the "Empress of America."

Today we are striving for better relations with our neighbors in Latin America. Father Daniel A. Lord, S. J., says: "It is the conviction of many who know the Latin temperament of our hemisphere, that if ever the United States succeeds in winning into close union the nations of these two continents, it will be around the unifying influence of Our Lady of Guadalupe."

About the same time that the English settled the thirteen colonies, the French settled in Canada and claimed the Mississippi Valley. French priests, fur traders and explorers moved throughout what is now the central part of our country. They, too, had an intense devotion to Mary. Father Marquette was acting as an explorer for France and as a missionary of the Church when he discovered the mighty Mississippi. He named it the River of the Immaculate Conception. It is unfortunate that the name was later changed. On a map of the United States, the Mississippi appears as the very backbone of our country. It would have been fitting for a country dedicated to the Immaculate Conception to have its greatest river named in honor of Mary Immaculate.

While the Spanish and French were claiming the largest part of our country and preaching to the Indians under the banner of Mary, the English were confined to a narrow area along the eastern seaboard. But it was the English who were eventually to win the largest part of the continent and to give our country its language, its laws and its customs.

The English could not be accused of having any great devotion to the Blessed Mother. With the Protestant Revolt, England had ceased to be our Lady's Dowry. Devotion to

Mary was considered Catholic, and therefore something to be avoided. The Puritans who settled in New England and the Anglicans who settled in the southern colonies had little love for one another, but one thing they had in common: they both feared and hated Catholics.

Out of this very persecution of English Catholics came a colony founded as a refuge for Catholics, and it was named Maryland. That was a strange name to be found in a stronghold of such rock-ribbed Protestantism. It was allowed only because the colony was ostensibly named for Queen Henrietta Maria. The real intent of the colonists was shown by the fact that they named their first settlement St. Mary's.

The little strip of English colonies was the only place in the entire Western Hemisphere where an attempt was made to suppress devotion to our Lady, and even here she had already gained a foothold. Mary was not to be suppressed. She had claimed the Western Hemisphere as her own.

In England, Catholics had suffered greatly at the hands of the State-supported Church of England. In Maryland, they were determined that things would be different. In Maryland, there was no State church and there was freedom of religion. These were considered radical ideas in 1634 when Maryland was founded. Rhode Island, which for some reason is usually given credit for being the first colony to grant religious freedom, was founded two years after Maryland.

A century and a half later, Maryland citizens took a leading part in passing the First Amendment to the Constitution: "Congress shall make no laws respecting an establishment of religion, or prohibiting free exercise thereof." Charles Carroll of Carrollton, then a senator, was chairman of the committee appointed to draft the amendment. His cousin, Daniel Carroll, also from Maryland, made the most important speech in its favor in the House of Representatives. Thus grew the tiny seed that had been brought to our shores by Mary's colonists.

The Americans won their independence with the invaluable help of France and Spain. The aid of Spain is seldom acknowledged, but it was Spain who cleared the British from Pensacola and other southern strongholds and thus paved the way for the decisive American victory at Yorktown.

Father John Carroll of Maryland became the first bishop and later the first archbishop in the United States. When he was consecrated, the First Amendment guaranteed that Congress should not restrict religious liberty, but many of the states still had their anti-Catholic laws. There were only about 32,000 Catholics in the entire country. There were only about 36 priests to cover a diocese that extended from the Atlantic Ocean to the Mississippi, from Canada to Florida. The future did not look promising.

When Archbishop Carroll died in 1815, there were more than 200,000 Catholics in the country. There were an archdiocese and four dioceses. What was the secret of this remarkable growth, a growth that no one would have dared predict? An answer can be found in a statement Archbishop Carroll made shortly before he died: "Of those things that give me the most consolation at the present moment, one is that I have always been attached to the practice of devotion to the Blessed Virgin Mary; that I have established it among the people under my care, and placed my diocese under her protection."

Mother Michel Gensoul, a nun of the Ursuline Order in France, wrote to Pope Pius VII and asked whether she and a group of exiled nuns might go to the Ursuline convent in New Orleans. She felt inspired to address the Blessed Virgin in these words: "O Most Holy Virgin Mary, if you obtain a prompt and favorable answer to my letter, I promise to have you honored in New Orleans under the title Our Lady of Prompt Succor."

Pope Pius VII was a prisoner of Napoleon and was not allowed to communicate with anyone, so Mother Michel was asking quite a lot of our Lady.

Mother Michel mailed her letter on March 19, 1809. The favorable reply was dated April 28, 1809. This would have been considered prompt even in peacetime.

Mother Michel had a statue carved and blessed. On December 30, 1810, it was installed in the chapel of the convent in New Orleans under the title "Our Lady of Prompt Succor."

In 1814, the British defeated Napoleon and were ready to turn their full attention to their war against the United States. This war, which we call the War of 1812, had dragged on for two years with no decisive victories for either side.

New Orleans attracted the British as a prize worth fighting for. This city was the gateway to the Mississippi Valley. If the British could capture New Orleans they could take the entire vast territory of Louisiana which the United States had bought from France a few years before. This would forever confine the United States to the area between the Mississippi and the Atlantic. Furthermore, the Americans could be kept from using the Mississippi for their commerce any time the Britsh saw fit.

The Battle of New Orleans was fought after the treaty of peace had been signed, but the news had not reached this side of the Atlantic. The battle is often dismissed lightly as not settling anything one way or the other. The treaty of peace, however, was a strange document which was really only a cessation of hostilities. It did not mention any of the causes of the war or any territorial settlements. If the British had been able to win Louisiana in January, 1815, it seems likely that they would have kept it, regardless of any treaty of peace.

Parton, in his *Life of Jackson,* described the expedition that gathered at Jamaica to sail against New Orleans: "Here was a force of nearly 20,000 men, a fleet of fifty ships carrying a thousand guns and perfectly appointed in every way, commanded by officers, some of whom had grown gray in victory. The elite of England's army and navy were afloat in Negril Bay. . . ."

Against this huge force, General Andrew Jackson had only about 6000 poorly trained militiamen. Many of them were poorly armed. Some had no arms at all. When he assigned them their defensive positions, Jackson put the unarmed men behind the others in order to give the impression of greater strength than he actually possessed.

"Never was a city so defenseless, so exposed, so weak, so prostrate as New Orleans in the fall of 1814," says one historian.

The British were so sure of final victory that their ships carried a full staff of civil officials ready to administer the province of Louisiana.

The people of New Orleans were terrified by the might of the enemy. They filled the churches and begged heaven to help them. The Ursuline Sisters promised Our Lady of Prompt Succor that if the Americans won the battle a Solemn High Mass would be offered in her honor every year on January 8.

In just twenty-five minutes the battle was over. The British suffered tremendous casualties. "They fell like blades of grass beneath the scythe," said a British writer. Only about half of the American force came into battle and they suffered few casualties. The British withdrew and made no further attempt to capture the city.

New Orleans was saved. Louisiana still belonged to the United States, and our country was free to expand to the west in a movement that eventually took us all the way to the Pacific.

General Jackson visited the Ursuline Sisters after the battle and acknowledged that his victory was due to God's help. The Mass which the Sisters promised in honor of Our Lady of Prompt Succor is still said every year on January 8.

In November, 1895, in accordance with a decree by Pope Leo XIII, the statue of Our Lady of Prompt Succor was solemnly crowned.

It was on Christmas Eve in 1841 that the Indian boy reported to the great missionary Father de Smet that he had seen someone in a tent. This apparition was mentioned in Chapter XIV.

If the Blessed Virgin really appeared on the western plains of the United States—and Father de Smet apparently accepted the fact without question—why has not the apparition received more attention?

Sister Mary Jean Dorcy, O.P., ventures an answer: "Circumstances often dictate these things. Father de Smet did not write his accounts in English . . . and to people who called themselves Americans both he and the Flatheads were foreigners. We might expect the same reaction if some missionary in the Brazilian jungle reported an apparition to a native child. . . . It is also quite possible that Our Lady, who has definite ideas about such things, did not wish it known widely at the time but reserved it for a later date."

This may have been one of the first revelations of the Immaculate Heart. The boy said: "I could see her heart, from which rays of light burst forth and shone upon me." The manifestations at Rue du Bac in 1830, at Our Lady of Victories in 1836, and at Blangy in 1840 all had to do with the Immaculate Heart. This reputed apparition in the Bitterroot Valley in 1841 may tie in with the three manifestations in France.

It is worth noting that Father de Smet had great devotion to the Immaculate Heart. He began his work in the Bitterroot Valley by consecrating the Indians to the Immaculate Heart of Mary on August 29. This date was observed as the feast of the Immaculate Heart that year.

The Sixth Provincial Council of Baltimore convened in 1846 with one archbishop and twenty-two bishops in attendance. They met in sad and disheartening times. The country was gripped by the madness of the Native American movement. The Native Americans were against everything foreign (forgetting that the only really native Americans were the Indians), and they considered the Catholic Church to be a foreign church. Mobs had burned down convents, churches and orphanages. Bigots had burned the homes of Irish immigrants and had killed some of the inhabitants. In the midst of this movement, the United States had declared war on Mexico, a Catholic country. The Native Americans falsely accused Catholics of deserting the army and of aiding the enemy. Catholic soldiers were forced to attend services at which they heard bitter attacks upon their religion. If they did not attend these services they were flogged. There was no Catholic chaplain in the entire army.

The Nativists were talking about going into politics. (They did later, as the Know Nothings.) If they did this it seemed likely that they would gain control of many states and pass laws which would hamper the Church.

The bishops who assembled at Baltimore agreed that their problems were beyond solution by human means. Someone suggested that they declare themselves in favor of placing the United States under the protection of the Blessed Virgin Mary, conceived without sin. There was some slight hesitation on the part of a few, because the Immaculate Conception was not yet declared a dogma of the Church. It was felt, however, that the honor to Mary would be greater if we did not wait for a formal definition of the dogma. Pope Pius IX granted the requests of the American bishops. Eight years later he proclaimed the dogma of the Immaculate Conception.

Soon after the action of the bishops it was announced that Catholic soldiers would no longer have to attend services of other faiths. President Polk appointed two Catholic chaplains. The Know Nothings grew in power for a time and boasted that they would elect a president in 1856. Instead, they were soundly defeated and disappeared from American life.

Under the protection of the Immaculate Conception the Church in the United States has continued to grow. Today, Catholics are one sixth of the population and are the largest religious group in the country. And now, at last, Mary Immaculate is to have a shrine worthy of our great country. To commemorate the 100th anniversary of the promulgation of the doctrine of the Immaculate Conception, the bishops of the United States sponsored a drive for funds to complete the National Shrine of the Immaculate Conception in Washington. It ranks among the ten great basilicas of the world.

We see, then, that the influence of the Blessed Virgin has been strikingly evident in the history of the Americas and more particularly in the history of the United States. Among the most recent signs are the dates connected with American participation in World War II. Pearl Harbor was bombed on December 7, 1941, the vigil of the feast of the Immaculate Conception. Congress declared war on December 8, the feast of our national Patron. The war ended on August 14, 1945, vigil of the feast of the Assumption in our part of the world. In Japan, where the decision to surrender was made, this was August 15, the feast itself.

Such things can be called coincidences, but even as coincidences they are very striking. They remind us that our Mother and our Patron is watching over us and protecting us.

"America is our Lady's country," says John M. Haffert the editor of *SOUL* magazine. "It was founded by a ship bearing her name. It is solemnly dedicated to her. The Catholic Church in the United States is dedicated to her Immaculate Conception, and nowhere in the world is she more honored by those who know her. Where else do you have the great Family Rosary Crusade, except where it was brought by Americans? Where else did the modern Scapular crusades begin?

Mr. Haffert might also have mentioned the receptions given the Pilgrim Virgin of Fatima, which he was instrumental in bringing to the United States. The statue of Our Lady of Fatima was blessed by the Bishop of Leiria and flown to the United States. It was a case of our Lady going to the people, which is typical of Fatima. The Pilgrim Virgin toured the United States for many months, and visited a majority of the dioceses. Everywhere she went, huge throngs of people turned out to pay their respect. The vast majority of them were not curiosity seekers but were plainly motivated by a deep love for our Lady. The men who accompanied the Pilgrim Virgin were constantly amazed by the size of the crowds and by their great devotion.

Father Daniel A. Lord, S.J., says that sometimes it is possible to indicate the things of the spirit in terms of bare statistics. In *St. Joseph Magazine* (May, 1948) he offers the following as evidence of the fact that the United States is our Lady's land:

"In a predominantly non-Catholic country, the 'grand old name' of Mary, or one of its variants, is the most popular of all girls' names. More than 60 cities and towns are named for the Blessed Virgin. Thirty-eight cathedrals and 3114 parish churches are dedicated to her. Fifty-eight seminaries are named for her; this custom began with the first seminary in the country, St. Mary's in Baltimore. About 100 women's religious congregations are named for Mary. The typically American missionary society is named Maryknoll. Two universities, Notre Dame and St. Mary's in San Antonio, are named for the Blessed Mother. Six colleges for men, 39 colleges for women, 500 high schools and academies and thousands of grammar schools are named for her."

Father Lord makes these further observations:

"In no country of the world is there a more sincere and devoted affection for Mary than that which marks (the month of) May in the United States. . . .

"Societies for lay men and women dedicated to our Lady are enormously effective. . . . The Sodality of Our Lady works through 14,000 units. . . . The Legion of Mary has grown steadily. . . . The Altar and Rosary society has been established for married women in hundreds of parishes. The Confraternity of the Miraculous Medal, the Scapular Militia, the Children of Mary are among long lists of other Marian societies doing outstanding work.

"The Summer School of Catholic Action now trains close to 15,000 Catholics in the Marian Apostolate each year, as part of the program of the Sodality of Our Lady.

"Every year scores of books are published by American authors dealing with the dogma and devotion that concerns our Lady. Another score of magazines carry Mary's name in their title. The Gallery of Living Catholic Authors, established by Sister Mary Joseph, Sister of Loretto has made popular a new title, Our Lady of Letters. The University of Dayton, conducted by the Society of Mary, has assembled a library devoted exclusively to books and manuscripts concerned with Mary and her glories."

All of this, of course, is only one side of the story. We know that our country is afflicted by secularism and materialism. Among many Americans moral standards have fallen so low that the bishops of the United States warn us that we face the fate of ancient Rome. The Roman Empire collapsed more from inner weaknesses than from outside pressure, and the greatest danger to the United States in not Russian Communism but American materialism.

There is no room for complacency, but neither is there any reason for despair. If some Americans ignore God and flout His laws, the children and followers of Mary should double their sacrifices and prayers.

Our country faces great dangers, but Mary has guided us through dangers in the past, and she can do so again.

After all, America is the Land of our Lady.

Prayers, Promises and Devotions Revealed Since 1830

PROMISE OF THE MIRACULOUS MEDAL

When our Lady revealed the Miraculous Medal to Catherine Labouré, in 1830, she said:

"All those who wear it when blessed will receive many graces, especially if they wear it suspended about their necks."

PRAYER OF THE GREEN SCAPULAR

Our Lady told Sister Bisqueyburu, in 1840, that wonderful graces are attached to the scapular but they are granted in proportion to the confidence with which the scapular is given. The Green Scapular is especially efficacious in bringing about conversions.

The only prayer is the one on the scapular: "Immaculate Heart of Mary, pray for us now and at the hour of our death."

This should be said daily, if not by the one wearing it, then by the one giving it.

THE ROSARY PROMISE

In October, 1872, Bartolo Long heard a voice say:
"If you seek salvation, promulgate the Rosary. This is Mary's own promise."

SCAPULAR OF THE SACRED HEART

In 1875, our Lady showed Estelle Faguette the Scapular of the Sacred Heart and said:
"I love this devotion."

THE ROSARY NOVENAS

In 1884, Our Lady of the Rosary said to Fortuna Agrelli:
"Whosoever desires to obtain favors from me should make three novenas of the prayers of the Rosary in petition and three novenas in thanksgiving."

THE PRAYERS OF FATIMA

On July 13, 1917, our Lady taught this prayer to the children. It is to be recited after each decade of the Rosary:
"O my Jesus, have mercy on us. Save us from the fire of hell. Draw all souls to heaven, especially those in greatest need."

Our Lady also taught them the following prayer, which they were to say many times and especially when making any sacrifices:

"O Jesus, it is for Your love, for the conversion of sinners and in reparation for the sins committed against the Immaculate Heart of Mary."

This prayer was taught to the children by the angel in 1916:

"My God, I believe, I adore, I hope and I love You. I ask pardon for those who do not believe, do not adore, do not hope and do not love You."

The angel also taught the children this prayer. They recited it on their knees with their foreheads touching the ground:

"Most Holy Trinity, Father, Son and Holy Ghost, I adore You profoundly, and I offer You the most precious body, blood, soul and divinity of Jesus Christ present in all the tabernacles of the world in reparation for the outrages, sacrileges and indifferences with which He is offended, and by the infinite merits of His Most Sacred Heart and of the Immaculate Heart of Mary I ask You for the conversion of poor sinners."

THE GREAT PROMISE

In 1925, our Lady appeared to Lucia in the convent and said:

"I promise to assist at the hour of death, with the graces necessary for salvation, all those, who on the first Saturdays of five consecutive months, confess, receive Holy Communion, recite part of my Rosary and keep me company for a quarter of an hour, meditating on its mysteries with the intention of offering me reparation."

NOTE: "Part of my Rosary" is interpreted to mean five decades. Confession may be made within the eight days before or after the First Saturday Communion, according to Lucia. The fifteen minutes' meditation may be on one or several mysteries of the Rosary.

Postscript
AN EXCERPT FROM *DEAR BISHOP!*

This book by Don Sharkey should be in the hands of every Catholic, but especially in the hands of every member of the World Apostolate of Fatima (The Blue Army).

Eugene Cardinal Tisserant, while Dean of the College of Cardinals, said of the Blue Army that it was the response to the appeal of Our Lady of Fatima. And Bishop John Venancio, second Bishop of Fatima, saw in the Blue Army the instrument for the triumph of Mary. "Every Catholic," he said, "should find a place in this army of Our Lady."

When Don Sharkey wrote his effective presentation of the sequence of Our Lady's apparitions, the Blue Army was just beginning. At the time that he was writing his book about the triumph of Mary, he did not realize what special meaning this army of the Queen would have to the world apostolate of Mary.

Also at the time he did not know of the "Militia of the Immaculate," which was just emerging and which was founded by Saint Maximilian Kolbe to be a powerful voice of the Immaculate all over the world, proclaiming Her Message everywhere.

We are adding to this powerful book, which often through Our Lady's own words and miracles proclaims that She shall indeed "conquer," some excerpts from the story of the Blue Army which was written by John Haffert on orders of his

Postscript (An Excerpt from DEAR BISHOP!) 241

bishop, and on the special exhortation of the Bishop of Fatima.

This book, written under obedience, is the logical sequel to *The Woman Shall Conquer*—because it shows not only the path to victory, but the specific means indicated by Our Lady of Fatima for the very victory itself.

FROM *DEAR BISHOP!*
(A book-long "letter" from John Haffert to his bishop)

In 1946 I had been referred to the Bishop of Fatima as "a prominent American Catholic" by a Carmelite in Lisbon who knew the bishop well. As a result the bishop invited me to come to Portugal with permission to interview Sr. Lucia, sole survivor of the three children who had seen Our Lady of Fatima.

The bishop had given me a letter indicating that she was to receive me as though he himself, were also present.

The interview which followed lasted, to the best of my memory, for almost four hours. But it seemed timeless. I felt I had only just sat down when I found myself rising in farewell.

I opened the conversation by saying:

"Of course, Sister, I know that it is the Rosary which is the first and most important request of Our Lady of Fatima; but what are the other things we must do in order to obtain the conversion of Russia?"

She immediately answered: "But the Rosary is not the most important request."

And she went on to explain that the essential request of Our Lady of Fatima was conveyed to the children in the very first question Our Lady put to them when She said:

"Will you be willing to accept whatever God will send you and to offer it up for the conversion of sinners and in reparation for the offenses committed against the Immaculate Heart of Mary?"

Over and over again during those precious hours I was in her company, she emphasized that it is the fulfillment of one's daily duty, according to one's state in life (and the sanctification of this effort in reparation for our sins and for the conversion of sinners) which is the primary condition for the turning back of the tide of evil which threatens today's world, and which will also bring us the great favor of the conversion of Russia and an era of peace "for mankind."

But she also stressed that the Rosary is indeed important, because it is one of Our Lady's *principal aids* given to us *to facilitate the sanctification of our daily duty.*

In the mysteries of the Rosary, we have not only a synthesis of the principal mysteries of the life of Christ, but we have the inspiration to overcome every possible temptation. (Indeed, many years later I wrote a book called *Sex and the Mysteries,* with 450 separate and different thoughts from the mysteries of the Rosary just on the one subject of purity according to one's state in life.)

We talked about the Scapular and of the consecration to the Immaculate Heart of Mary, and of the importance of this as an additional aid to the sanctification of daily duty.

The pledge, as I wrote it down during the course of this interview, contained the following conditions: pray the Rosary daily; wear the Scapular as a sign of consecration to the Immaculate Heart; offer up the sacrifices demanded by daily duty, extending our Morning Offering through the day.

Several things about it bothered me. But before I mention them, perhaps I ought to recall—just because of their interest —at least two other events of this interview:

We had completed the pledge, and she was satisfied.

"Yes," she said, "these are the basic things which must be done in order to obtain the conversion of Russia." Yet she had not mentioned the Five First Saturdays.

When I called this to her attention, she replied that the Five First Saturdays were important because they were the occasion of *renewing our purpose,* of strengthening our resolve and our motives once a month and thus being able to do better in the month that followed in fulfilling these basic requests

Postscript (An Excerpt from DEAR BISHOP!)

of Our Lady which centered on the sanctification of daily duty.

And when one reflects upon it, this is indeed the effect of the five conditions of the First Saturdays:

We are asked *to go to confession* on the first Saturday of the month whether we have committed mortal sins or not, and thus carefully to examine what we have done in the past month, and to resolve to do better and to mend our lives. We are asked also on this particular day not only *to pray the Rosary,* as we must do every day but, in addition, *to spend fifteen minutes "with Our Lady" meditating upon the mysteries*—thus practicing that essential element of the life of Christ to sanctify our own lives. And finally, we are reminded of the importance of reparation for the offenses committed against the Immaculate Heart of Mary and of offering up our daily sacrifices in reparation. All of the First Saturday conditions *(Confession, Communion, Rosary and the fifteen minute meditation) are to be offered in the spirit of reparation* for the offenses committed against the Immaculate Heart of Mary.

And, of course, we know that in reply to a question from Lucia, Our Lord Himself explained that the reason for the *five* Saturdays was because He wants reparation made for the denial of Our Lady's Immaculate Conception, of Her divine maternity, of Her perpetual virginity, depriving children of devotion to Her, and dishonor to Her images.

Satan was there when he heard Our Lady explain the conditions for the conversion of Russia. And he was there when Lucia participated in the formulation of the pledge containing these requests, and when the Bishop of Fatima told me: *"You may promulgate this (pledge) as coming from me."*

Confronted by his implacable fury and surrounded by the great wave of evil sweeping through the world, the Blue Army might easily have foundered, but mighty forces were being raised up by Our Lady to sustain it. Your Excellency will remember the joy we experienced when Pope Pius XII endorsed Fatima so emphatically, blessed the Blue Army, gave us Cardinal Tisserant, the Dean of the College of Cardinals, as a sort of "protector," and actualy named him as his own Papal Legate for the blessing of our International Center at Fatima on October 13, 1956. Your Excellency will also remember the visit of Pope Paul VI to Fatima on May 13, 1967 and the decision taken only a few months later by the Bishop of Fatima to become the International President of the Blue Army which he then actively began to promote personally, undertaking extensive journeys around the world.

In simple terms the Blue Army is essentially an extension of the *Apostleship of Prayer* throughout the day. It is a response to those very first words of Our Lady to the children of Fatima: *"Will you be willing to accept whatever God will send you and to offer it up in reparation for sin and for the conversion of sinners?*

Even the original Morning Offering used in the Apostleship of Prayer is an almost perfect response to the requests of Our Lady of Fatima—offering all that we are, have and do through the Immaculate Heart of Mary and in union with the Sacrifice of the Mass throughout the world.

To this Morning Offering, in keeping with the Message of Fatima, the Blue Army adds two elements: A *practiced* consecration to the Immaculate Heart of Mary implemented by the Scapular devotion; meditative prayer implemented by the Rosary.

That, in a nutshell, is what the Blue Army is all about: the Morning Offering extended through the day with the help of the Scapular and Rosary devotions. However, this opens the door to a whole new life, both for the individual who practices it and for the world (because of the promise of world peace when enough persons are responding).

While the first and primary purpose of the Blue Army is this extension of the Morning Offering through the day by means of the proper use of the Scapular and the Rosary, the Blue Army has two additional goals:

Postscript (An Excerpt from DEAR BISHOP!) 245

1) To cause those fulfilling the pledge *to deepen their response in association with others* (the Blue Army Cell);

2) To encourage and to organize militant members *who will spread this messsge throughout the world* so as to hasten the fulfillment of the prophecy of Padre Pio: "Russia will be converted when there is a Blue Army member for every Communist"... and after the conversion of Russia, to aid in the triumph of Her Immaculate Heart in the entire world.

The children of Fatima practiced and lived the Message and thus became the model of the Blue Army Cell; two or three meeting at regular intervals to discuss the Message, to pray together, and to help each other to fulfill the marvelous program of sanctity given by Our Lady of Fatima to the three children, and through them to us.

The Blue Army in its basic and simplest form is really like the opening of the door of the human heart to the Heart of Mary, and through the Heart of Mary to an intimate union with the Sacred Heart of Jesus in the Eucharist.

This process, although necessarily simple, can seem complex in its explanation. But to keep it simple, imagine this picture: Our Lady, crowned as Queen, showing forth Her thorn-encircled Heart, and reaching out to you with the Rosary and the Scapular. Rays of light flowing from the Scapular and the Rosary frame the question: *"Will you be willing to accept whatever God will send you...?"* Now visualize yourself accepting the Scapular and the Rosary as signs of your "Yes!"

Completing the picture, the same rays of light carry you (through the fulfillment of daily duty) to the great light of the final vision of Fatima[1], containing mysteries of the Trinity, Calvary, Eucharist, and with the Immaculate Heart of Mary.

Historically, we can look back on the first quarter century of this Apostolate and see it from two completely different viewpoints: As an Apostolate of Holiness (which is essentially what I have describd above); and as a propaganda effort.

As this "letter" to my bishop reveals, I personally have been involved primarily in the second part, but I had years of special spiritual preparation which are described in my earlier book, *The Brother and I*. And it is to be hoped that the reader *will not think,* because of this particular "letter" to my bishop, *that the element of propaganda* ("action" of the Blue Army in making known the Message of Fatima in the world) *is by any means its primary objective.*

This is above all a silent army, an army of prayer and sacrifice, an army on its knees. The propaganda effort is merely to make known to the world the great miracle of Fatima so that more people will respond to Our Lady's appeal for prayer and penance.

The actual *organization* is based on canonical statutes, first drawn up at the direction of the first Bishop of Fatima, which were approved *ad experimentum* by the Holy See in 1956. Final approval was long delayed because of the revision of Canon Law after Vatican II, and as it was not clear as to whether the Blue Army should be considered a lay apostolate or a sort of pious union.

The statutes describe two levels of membership 1) Those who simply sign the pledge (commitment to the Morning Offering, Scapular and Rosary); 2) Those who, in addition to making the pledge, are organized into Prayer Cells and promotional groups.

Only the latter are "organized," and they are quite a small percentage of the total number who have signed the pledge... *now over twenty-five million in more than one hundred countries.*

On the parish level, the pastor has the last word. Organization or promotion *among parishes* requires permission of the bishop. And from the diocesan leaders who are recognized by their bishops a *National Council* is formed which elects its officers and its executive committee. The latter is responsible for the operation of the National Center (which in the United States is in Washington, N.J.).

On the international level, three officers from each National

Postscript (An Excerpt from DEAR BISHOP!)

Council form the International Council, and they elect their own officers and their own Executive Committee. The latter is responsible for the operation of the International Center in Fatima and the subsidiary International Secretariat in Switzerland.

Much conflict has arisen over the years, as will become evident as one reads this "letter." Some is due to the fact that Communist Russia has considered the Blue Army to be the most important deterrent in the world, at the present time, to the success of its world revolution.

We presume that millions of dollars have been spent to slur the name of the Blue Army. Such opposition, even when subtle (like the book in France which claimed that the Blue Army was financed by Archbishop Lefebvre) or blatant, like published claims in Portugal and Spain that the Blue Army is a branch of the CIA, is understandable.

We are really engaged in a battle, and the greatest and most important battle in the history of man. It is as though in the middle of the 20th century God permitted all the power of Satan to be unleashed upon the world in the wake of the promise of Our Lady, His Mother and our Queen, that She would bring about the conversion of Russia and an era of peace to mankind—that Her Immaculate Heart would triumph and that an era of peace would come to the entire world!

What more fitting title could be given to the response to this coming of Our Lady with the promise of Her triumph than the title of being "Her" army?

It is interesting that the militant atheists of Russia understood this more readily and more completely than the believers, and attributed to the Blue Army the power of being a major deterrent to the success of worldwide militant atheism (next to Hitler and the Cold War).

In this regard it is also interesting to note that at least three other Marian apostolates of modern times have a name signifying "army." Perhaps as a further aid to understanding the Blue Army, it might be helpful to distinguish it from these other apostolates: *The Army of Mary, The Militia of the Immaculate,* and *the Legion of Mary.*

The Army of Mary was founded in Canada and has one basic and essential condition of membership: Consecration to Our Lady.

The Militia of the Immaculate was founded by Saint Maximilian Kolbe without any specific conditions of membership. Its essential purpose is *to know* Our Lady, and *to make Her known* as the instrument of God for bringing about the triumph of Jesus in the world.

The Legion of Mary is an active parish apostolate which canvasses parishes to bring souls to Jesus through Mary.

The Blue Army is the fulfillment of the Message of Fatima.

All four of these apostolates represent various *degrees* of militant service to Our Lady to hasten the triumph of Her Immaculate Heart in the world, to bring about Her victory over evil, to be Her "heel" to crush the head of the serpent in today's world. Each apostolate has its own points of emphasis.

Oh, would that there were more Niepokalanows—Cities of the Immaculate—scattered over the world! I have always considered it a special gift from Saint Maximilian—in addition to the crowning of the Pilgrim Virgin in his Niepokalanow outside of Warsaw in 1917—that Brother Juventyn, who had been imprisoned with Saint Maximilian, chose to have his famous book *I Knew Saint Maximilian* published by the Blue Army, with a chapter explaining the Blue Army as something that he knew would be dear to Saint Maximilian and a movement which all the "Cities of the Immaculate" would promote in order to speed the triumph of Mary's Immaculate Heart as promised at Fatima. Indeed, some of the greatest support for the Blue Army in the United States came from America's own Niepokalanow, the publisher of *Immaculata,* and especially through that gifted and dedicated Franciscan, Br. Francis Mary, O.F.M Conv.

Perhaps the best way to look on each and all of the various apostolates of Our Lady in the Church would be as various

Postscript (An Excerpt from DEAR BISHOP!)

regiments, various "special services" in Her overall army which St. Grignion de Montfort prophesied would be raised up in the latter days to join with Our Lady and Queen in the conquest of Satan and his legions of evil.

In conclusion: The Blue Army is a response to the Message of Fatima—both in its simplest form as an extension of the Morning Offering through the day, and in its far more complex form as a complete program of being born into intimate union with the Eucharistic Heart of Jesus through living our consecration to the Immaculate Heart of Mary.

For further information, write: World Apostolate of Fatima (The Blue Army), Washington, New Jersey, 07882. (Phone: 1-201-689-1700.)

1. The vision to Lucia of June 12-13, 1929, described in her Memoirs in these words:

    I had sought and obtained permission from my superiors and confessor to make a Holy Hour from eleven o'clock until midnight, every Thursday to Friday night. Being alone one night, I knelt near the altar rails in the middle of the chapel and prostrate, I prayed the prayers of the Angel. Feeling tired, I then stood up and continued to say the prayers with my arms in the form of a cross. The only light was that of the sanctuary lamp. Suddenly the whole chapel was illuminated by a supernatural light, and above the altar appeared a cross of light, reaching to the ceiling. In a brighter light on the upper part of the cross, could be seen the face of a man and his body as far as the waist; upon his breast was a dove of light; nailed to the cross was the body of another man. A little below the waist, I could see a chalice and a large host suspended in the air, onto which drops of blood were falling from the face of Jesus Crucified and from the wound in his side. These drops ran down onto the host and fell into the chalice. Beneath the right arm of the cross was Our Lady and in Her hand was Her Immaculate Heart. (It was Our Lady of Fatima, with Her Immaculate Heart in Her left hand, without sword or roses, but with a crown of thorns and flames.) Under the left arm of the cross, large letters, as if of crystal clear water which ran down upon the altar, formed these words: "Grace and Mercy."

    I understood that it was the Mystery of the Most Holy Trinity which was shown to me, and I received lights about this mystery which I am not permitted to reveal.

    Our Lady then said to me: "The moment has come in which God asks the Holy Father, in union with all the bishops of the world, to make the consecration of Russia to my Immaculate Heart, promising to save it by this means. There are so many souls whom the Justice of God condemns for sins committed against me, that I have come to ask reparation: sacrifice yourself for this intention and pray."

Author's Sources

NEWSPAPERS AND MAGAZINES

IF YOU could see the vast pile of newspaper clippings and magazine articles that are on the shelves in front of me as I try to compile a bibliography, you would realize why it is impossible to list them all. A long list of newspaper and magazine references would have little interest anyway, and it would take up a large amount of space. Perhaps I should have used footnotes in this book, but I find footnotes a great distraction when I am trying to read, and I wished to spare my readers this distraction.

For many years I have scanned the Cincinnati *Telegraph-Register* (our archdiocesan paper), other Catholic and secular papers, and Catholic and secular magazines for anything that pertained to the Blessed Virgin in the modern world. I have also had access to all the dispatches of the N.C.W.C. News Service. People in various parts of the United States and Europe have mailed me clippings which have been a great help to me. The result has been a vast and valuable accumulation of information.

Some chapters in this book are based entirely on information from magazines and newspapers. The chapter about the Pope and the Miracle of the Sun, for example (pp. 181-182), is based entirely upon stories that appeared in Catholic newspapers. The chapter about the atom bomb (pp. 147-154) is based on two articles from *Catholic Digest* and one article from the *American Legion* magazine. The story about the Roses of Stockport (pp. 169-171) came from various sources but principally from an article in the *Messenger of the Sacred Heart*.

Because I have relied so much upon magazines and newspapers—and to some extent upon personal interviews and correspondence—I am confident that THE WOMAN SHALL CONQUER contains much information that has never before appeared in book form.

While it is impossible to name all the periodicals I have consulted, I feel that the following magazines deserve special mention:

Our Lady's Digest (monthly, published at Olivet, Ill.) has been a most valuable source of material. The editors of this magazine scan other publications for articles about the Blessed Mother and print the best of them. Thus, I found that the editors had done much of my research for me. I have a complete file of this magazine since the first issue came off the press in 1946, and I have referred to the file for almost every chapter in my book.

Immaculata (monthly, published at Libertyville, Ill. 60048) has featured many articles about apparitions of the Blessed Virgin. These articles have supplemented and brought up to date the information I found in books. For some of the apparitions, all my information came from these magazines. My account of the Red Scapular of the Passion, for example (pp. 86-87), was taken from *Immaculata*, December, 1950. The account of the reputed apparitions at Green Bay, Wisconsin (pp. 87-89), was taken from the *Scapular*, May-June, 1949.

BOOKS ABOUT SHRINES AND APPARITIONS

The first four books on the following list might be classed as general. That is, each of these four contains information about more than one shrine. After these first four, each of the other books is about just one shrine. These are listed in the order in which they are described in this book.

The Apparitions and Shrines of Heaven's Bright Queen, Volume IV (New York: Carey-Stafford Co., 1904), has as a subtitle "In Legend, Poetry, and History from the Earliest Ages to the Present Time—Compiled from Approved Catholic Sources by William J. Walsh." Some of the material in this four-volume set is reprinted directly from Catholic publications of the past century. Other material has been rewritten. Poems by masters and by amateurs are interspersed among the facts and legends. The set contains valuable raw material for anyone who is patient enough to sift it out. I was interested only in Volume IV, which deals with events between 1846 and 1900. This contains accounts of Lourdes, Pellevoisin, Pontmain and a number of little-known apparitions. Strangely, it had nothing about Knock, Pompeii or Our Lady of the Cape.

Unfortunately the set is out of print. I was able to borrow Volume IV from the Marian Library at the University of Dayton. This set was donated when the Marian Library project was first announced, in 1943. The donor was a Protestant army sergeant. My debt to this sergeant is great.

Famous Shrines of Our Lady, by H. M. Gillett (Westminster, Md.: Carroll Press, 1950), tells the stories of 31 shrines. Of special value to me were the accounts of Walsingham, Our Lady of Victories, Pompeii, the Miraculous Medal, La Salette, Lourdes, Pontmain, Pellevoisin, Fatima, Beauraing and Banneux.

Visitations of Our Lady, by Richard F. Norton (privately published by Father Norton, Dedham, Mass., 1946), contains 25 chapters, most of them short accounts of various apparitions. I consulted the chapters on the Miraculous Medal, La Salette, Lourdes, Pontmain, Pellevoisin, Cambridge (Brown Scapular), Knock, Fatima and Guadalupe.

Heroines of Christ, edited by Joseph Husslein, S.J., Ph.D. (Milwaukee: Bruce, 1939), contains accounts of 15 saintly girls and women. The stories of St. Bernadette and St. Catherine Labouré were of help to me.

The Green Scapular, by Marie Edouard Mott, C.M. (Emmitsburg, Md.: St. Joseph's College, 1942), is a small paper-bound book written by a priest who knew Sister Justine Bisqueyburu and who had access to all pertinent documents. This little book, a pamphlet or two, and a few magazine articles are all I have been able to find on a devotion which deserves to be much more widely known.

The Holy Mountain of La Salette, by the Most Rev. William Ullathorne, Archbishop of Birmingham, England (Altamont, N. Y.: La Salette Press, 1942), is a result of investigations made by the Archbishop a few years after the apparition.

Bernadette of Lourdes, by Margaret Gray Blanton (New York: Longmans, Green, 1939), is an accurate, readable biography of St. Bernadette Soubirous.

After Bernadette, by Don Sharkey (Milwaukee: Bruce, 1945), was my principal reference on Lourdes. I did a great amount of research when I wrote *After Bernadette.* I feel certain that it is accurate (any inaccuracies would have been called to my attention by this time), and I knew just where to turn in it for information. *After Bernadette,* incidentally, contains a bibliography on Lourdes. In order not to have my own works scattered throughout this list of references, I might as well say right now that I used my booklet *The Message of Fatima* (Dayton, Ohio: George A. Pflaum, 1949) as a reference on Fatima. I also used my study-club textbook, *Mary's Message* (Wichita, Kans.: Catholic Action Bookshop, 1949), as a reference on a number of occasions.

The Rosary, My Treasure (Clyde, Mo.: Benedictine Convent of Perpetual Adoration, 1948) is a 64-page booklet about the Rosary. Pages 63 and 64 tell about the apparitions to Fortuna Agrelli and the origin of the Devotion of the Rosary Novenas.

Our Lady of Knock, by William D. Coyne (New York: Catholic Book Publishing Co., 1948), contains the complete story of Knock, the apparition, the testimony, the pilgrims and the cures.

Our Land and Our Lady, by Daniel Sargent (New York:

Longmans, Green, 1939), has a brief account of the apparition to the Indian boy in Bitter Root valley. I also used this book as a reference for the appendix on the United States.

Our Lady of Fatima, by William Thomas Walsh (New York: Macmillan, 1947), is based on Dr. Walsh's personal investigations in Portugal. Readable and accurate.

The Crusade of Fatima, by John de Marchi (New York: P. J. Kenedy, 1948), is also accurate and readable. Father De Marchi lives in Portugal and has conducted extensive interviews with everyone concerned. I found his book especially valuable for the information about Lucia and Jacinta after the apparitions. The appendix contains the transcript of three interviews with Lucia.

Vision of Fatima, by Thomas McGlynn, O.P. (New York: Little, Brown, 1948), tells interesting sidelights and clears up points left in doubt by the other books. I found Father McGlynn's book to be especially valuable when used in conjunction with Walsh and De Marchi.

Five Children, by Rev. Paul Piron, S.J. (New York: Benziger, 1938), tells the story of Beauraing.

Walsingham, by H. M. Gillett (London: Burns, Oates, and Washburne, 1946), is a history of the famous English shrine.

Our Lady of Guadalupe, by Rev. George Lee, C.S.Sp. (New York: Catholic Book Publishing Co., 1947), and *Roses for Mexico,* by Ethel Cook Eliot (New York: Macmillan, 1947), tell the story of the famous shrine in Mexico.

BOOKS ABOUT MARY'S ROLE IN OUR WORLD

True Devotion to the Blessed Virgin Mary, by St. Louis Marie de Montfort (Bay Shore, N. Y.: Montfort Fathers, 1946), is the key to understanding the role of the Blessed Virgin in the modern world. The book has no literary quality and is not always easy to read. The sentences are long and involved, the phrasing awkward. Despite these handicaps, the book is still widely circulated and has had a profound effect on countless souls. *True Devotion* has provided the inspiration and also the theme for my book.

The Glories of Mary, by St. Alphonsus Liguori (published by Redemptorist Fathers, Brooklyn, made available through Scapular Press, N. Y.), is one of the finest of all books about the Blessed Virgin. I have relied upon St. Alphonsus far more than the few direct quotations would indicate.

Our Blessed Mother, by Edward Leen, C.S.Sp., and John Kearney, C.S.Sp. (New York: Kenedy, 1946), dwells upon the reality of Mary's spiritual motherhood and upon devotion to the Immaculate Heart.

This Age and Mary, by Rev. Michael O'Carroll, C.S.Sp., D.D. (Dublin: Mercier Press, 1947), tells how we can meet the problems of today by turning to Mary.

The Mother of Jesus, by Father James, O.F.M.Cap. (Westminster, Md.: Newman Bookshop, 1946), emphasizes the unique relationship of Mary to Jesus. The chapters on "Meditation" and "Queen" were of help to me.

Mariology, by Rev. M. J. Scheeben (St. Louis: Herder, 1946), is a two-volume study of Mary by a great theologian.

OTHER BOOKS

In addition to the books already listed, which might be called my basic references, I also referred to other books from time to time. These are listed below, alphabetically according to title.

Autobiography of the Blessed Virgin by Peter A. Resch, S.M. (Milwaukee: Bruce, 1946).

The Catholic Encyclopedia (New York: Universal Knowledge Foundation).

A Companion to the Summa, Vol. IV, by Walter Farrell, O.P., S.T.D., S.T.M. (New York: Sheed & Ward, 1947).

The Complete Rosary by Rev. Maurice B. Kennedy (Chicago: Ziff-Davis, 1949).

Fatima or World Suicide by Rt. Rev. William C. M. McGrath, P.A. (Scarboro Bluffs, Ontario, Canada: Scarboro Foreign Mission Society, 1950).

The Glories of Lourdes by Chanoine Justin Roussell (London: Burns, Oates, and Washburne, 1922).

Heart of the Queen by Thomas J. Moore, S.J. (New York: Apostleship of Prayer, 1949).

Legio Mariae (Official handbook of Legion of Mary, 1947).

The Legion of Mary by Cecily Hallack (New York: Longmans, Green, 1941).

Lourdes by Aileen Mary Clegg (St. Louis: Herder, 1929).

Lourdes in the High Pyrenees by Cecilia Mary Young (Belleville, Ill.: Buechler, 1932).

Lourdes, Its Inhabitants, Its Pilgrims, and Its Miracles by Richard F. Clarke, S.J. (New York: Benziger, 1888).

Mary in Her Scapular Promise by John M. Haffert (Sea Isle, N. J.: Scapular Press, 1942).

Mary of Nazareth by Igino Giordani (New York: Macmillan, 1947).

My Ideal—Jesus, Son of Mary by Emil Neubert, S.M. (Kirkwood, Mo.: Maryhurst Press, 1947).

Our Lady in the Modern World by Daniel A. Lord, S.J. (St. Louis: Queen's Work, 1940).

The Presence of Mary by Francis Charmot, S.J. (South Bend, Ind.: Fides, 1948).

Queen of Militants by Emil Neubert, S.M., S.T.D. (St. Meinrad, Ind.: Grail, 1947).

The Risen Christ by Most Rev. Tihamer Toth (St. Louis: Herder, 1938).

The Rosary and the Soul of Woman by Sister Mary Aloyi Kiener, S.N.D. (Pustet, 1941).

The Rosary, Crown of Mary (New York: Apostolate of the Rosary, 1947).

The Sacramentals by Charles J. McNeill (Wichita, Kans.: Catholic Action Bookshop, 1946).

Saint Louis De Montfort by George Rigault (Port Jefferson, N. Y.: Montfort Fathers, 1947).

The Splendor of the Rosary by Maisie Ward (New York: Sheed & Ward, 1945).

The Teaching of the Catholic Church, George D. Smith, General Editor (New York: Macmillan, 1949).

BOOKS CONSULTED FOR THE FOURTH EDITION

Our Lady of Guadalupe—The Hope of America (Pecos, N. M.: Trappist Abbey of Our Lady of Guadalupe, 1951).

The Story of La Salette by James P. O'Reilly, M.S. (Chicago: J. S. Paluch, 1953).

Light on the Mountain—The Story of La Salette by John S. Kennedy (New York: McMullen, 1953).

The Meaning of Fatima by C. C. Martindale, S.J. (New York: Kenedy, 1950).

The Immaculate Heart—The True Story of Our Lady of Fatima by John De Marchi, I.M.C. (New York: Farrar, Straus and Young, 1952).

Famous Shrines of Our Lady—Volume Two by H. M. Gillett (Westminster, Md.: Newman Press, 1952).

Index

Age of Mary, De Montfort and, 200-204, 220; foretold by mystics, 5; role of apostle in, 264-266

Agrelli, Fortuna, and Rosary Novenas, 75

Aladel, Father, and Green Scapular, 25-27; and St. Catherine Labouré, 17, 18, 20, 21, 22

Alexander VI, Pope, and Line of Demarcation, 226

Alphonsus Liguori, St., on Mary Mediatrix, 192; on Mary as Queen, 194

Altar and Rosary society, in U. S., 236

Andriveau, Sister Appoline, and apparition of Red Scapular, 86

Angel of Portugal, at Fatima, 96, 103

Apparitions, at Banneux, Belgium, 124, 131-137; at Beauraing, Belgium, 122-130; at Blangy, 25, 31; at Castelpetroso, Italy, 91-92; at Fatima, 99-113; at Green Bay, Wis., 87-89; at Knock, 77-85, 123; at La Salette, 31, 34-41, 46, 48, 57; at Lourdes, 45-51, 57; at Paris, 15-21, 31, 46, 57; at Pellevoisin, 64-72; at Pontmain, 57-63; at St. Mary's, Montana, 85-86, 232-233; at Troyes, France, 86-87

Archconfraternity of Immaculate Heart of Mary, 23

Archconfraternity of Our Mother All Merciful, 69

Arendt, Abbé, and Banneux, 136

Assumption, defined, 174-179, 182, 219

Aylesford, England, and our Lady, 169

Baltimore, Sixth Provincial Council of, 233

Banneux, Belgium, apparation at, 124, 131-137, 218; bishop's approval of, 136

Baptism, and Mary, 188; and total consecration to Mary, 202

Barbedette, Eugène, and apparitions at Pontmain, 58, 63

Barbedette, Joseph, and apparitions at Pontmain, 58, 63

Battle of New Orleans, 231-232

Beauraing, Belgium, apparitions at, 122-130, 218; approval of, 129, 130; and Immaculate Heart, 215; related to Banneux, 131, 135; and sacrifice, 123

Beco, Mariette, and apparitions at Banneux, 131-137

Beirne, Margaret and Mary, and apparition at Knock, 77

Belgium, faith in, 11, 136-137

Belloc, and faith in England, 173

Benedict XV, on Mary Mediatrix, 192; petitions Mary for peace, 99; tries to end war, 97

Bernadette, St., 46-51

Bernard, St., on total consecration to Mary, 201

Biré, Madame, cured at Lourdes, 52

Bisqueyburu, Sister Justine, and apparitions of Green Scapular, 24-26; and Immaculate Heart devotion, 215

Blangy, apparitions at, 25-27, 31

Blessed Sacrament, abuse of, 68, 69; defiled, 44; at Lourdes, 51; Pius X and, 96; and reparation, 69

Bombarral, Portugal, doves at, 156-157

Bonaventure, St., on Mary as Queen, 194; on total consecration to Mary, 201

Bourriette, Louis, cured at Lourdes, 51

258

Boyd, Charlotte, and Walsingham, 168
Bridge of Rosaries, 90
Brisse, Adele, and apparitions at Green Bay, 87-89
Byrne, Pauline, and roses of Stockport, 170-171

Canada, and Our Lady of Guadalupe, 228
Canons of St. Augustine, and Walsingham, 166
Cape de la Madeleine, Our Lady of the Cape, 90-91
Carley, Anne, and roses of Stockport, 170
Carrel, Dr. Alexis, and Lourdes, 53
Carroll, Most Rev. John, first U. S. bishop, 230
Castelpetroso, Italy, apparitions at, 91-92
Catherine, St., canonized, 21; and Immaculate Heart devotion, 214; Mary appears to, 15-21
Catholic Action, Pius XI and, 221; Sodality of Our Lady and, 180; *see also* Lay apostolate
Catholic Youth Organization, 195
Cavanagh, Archdeacon Bartholomew, and apparition at Knock, 79, 82
Chaminade, Father William Joseph, and total consecration to Mary, 200
Chastity, and Mary, 117
Chavez, James, and manifestation of Quito, Ecuador, 92
Children, and apparitions of our Lady, 124
Children of Mary, Confraternity established, 20; in U. S., 236
Church, and investigation of apparitions, 123
Coimbra, Donna Maria Emilia Martins, and doves of Bombarral, 159
Communism, in France, 38; threat of, 222
Communists, and Cardinal Mindszenty, 4; and the Church, 4; in Estonia, Latvia, and Lithuania, 4; and Fatima, 163; in Finland, China, Korea, and Indo-China, 4; forerunners of, 19; in Italy, 178; in Poland, 139; in Portugal, 160, 162; and revolution in Russia, 3; in Spain, 4, 139; sweep over Europe and Asia, 154
Confraternity of Children of Mary, 20
Confraternity of Christian Doctrine, 195
Confraternity of Rosary at Pompeii, 74
Consecration, total, to Mary, 31, 199-204, 210; De Montfort and, 31
Conversion of sinners, and Banneux, 135; and Beauraing, 128-130; and Fatima, 105, 108; and Green Scapular, 25, 26, 27, 28; and Legion of Mary, 220-221; and Lourdes, 54, 55; and our Lady at Pellevoisin, 67; and sacrifice, 209
Co-redemptrix, our Lady as, 192, 194, 219
Cova da Iria, 101, 107, 112, 114, 120, 156
Cures, at Banneux, 135; at Beauraing, 130; how investigated, 52; at Knock, 82; at Lourdes, 51-54, 56; at Pellevoisin, 65; at Pompeii, 74-75; at Pontmain, 63
Curry, John, and apparition at Knock, 80

Da Silva, Most Rev. Joseph, bishop of Leiria, approves Fatima devotion, 119
Daughters of Charity, and apparitions of our Lady, 15, 22, 24, 26, 31
Degeimbre, Andree and Gilberte, and apparitions at Beauraing, 125-130
De Marchi, Father John, I.M.C., *The Immaculate Heart*, 102

De Montfort, St. Louis Marie, 29-34, 42; canonized, 30; on consecration to Mary, 199-204; and future apostles, 221; and knowledge of Mary, 187; manuscripts found, 29, 219

De Rudder, Pierre, cured at Lourdes shrine, 52

Des Gennettes, Father Charles du Friche, and Immaculate Heart Devotion, 214; and Our Lady of Victories, 22-23

Desilets, Father Luke, and Our Lady of the Cape, 90-91

De Smet, Father Pierre, and apparition in Montana, 85-86, 232-233

Detais, Jeanette, and apparitions at Pontmain, 58-59

Dominic of Jesus and Mary, Venerable, and Immaculate Conception, 42

Dominic, St., and the Rosary, 206

Dominic Savio, Venerable, prediction on England, 171-172

Dominican Order, founded, 206

Dos Santos, Lucia, and apparitions at Fatima, 100-113, 182-183; on the consecration of the world, 140-143; and devotion to Immaculate Heart, 213, 215-216; enters Carmelites, 145; on penance, 144; on "phony war," 141; revelations after Fatima, 119-122; sees angel, 96; and Sisters of St. Dorothy, 120; and unknown light, 140; writes to Pius XII, 141

Duff, Frank, and Legion of Mary, 220

Ecuador, miraculous picture at Quito, 92-93

England, in America, 228-229; and our Lady, 165-173

Eudists, and Immaculate Heart devotion, 214

Faguette, Estelle, and apparitions at Pellevoisin, 64-71; interview with Leo XIII, 95

Fall of man, and Immaculate Conception, 49

Family Rosary Crusade, 208, 216-217, 219

Fatima, and Angel of Portugal, 96, 103; apparitions at, 29, 36, 99-113, 218; and Communist revolution, 3; and the Great Promise, 239; and Immaculate Heart devotion, 215; message of, 16, 110, 182, 195; and Moslems, 164; and penance, 209; and Portugal, 162-164; prayer at, 238-239; and Vatican (1950), 181-182

First Friday devotion, 214

First Saturday devotion, 106, 116, 118, 121, 215, 239

Fornari, Cardinal, and predictions at La Salette, 40

France, in America, 230; decadence in, 41; faith in, 214; in Franco-Prussian War, 57, 58; German occupation of, 141; and Jansenism, 30; Law of Separation in, 95; revolt against God in, 8; sufferings predicted, 16, 39, 68, 71, 95; and World War I, 95-99; and World War II, 142

Franco, General Francisco, vs. Communists, 160

Franco-Prussian War, 57

French Revolution, and the Church, 9, 22; and Immaculate Heart devotion, 214; and Lourdes, 47

Friteau, Eugène, and apparition at Pontmain, 60

Fulgens Corona, Encyclical of Pius XII, proclaiming Marian Year, 183

Gallery of Living Catholic Authors, 237

Garcia, Benito Pelegri, cured at Benneux, 135-136

Gensoul, Mother Michel, and Ursulines in America, 230

Germany invades Poland, 140; occupies Rome, 146; under Nazis, 138; withdraws from Rome, 147
Gilmartin, Archbishop, and apparition at Knock, 81
Giraud, Maximin, and apparitions at La Salette, 34-39
Giusto, Antonia and Angelo, and the "Weeping Madonna," 178
Godinho, Mother Maria da Purificacao, and Jacinta Marto, 116-119
Gordon, Delia, cured at Knock, 82
Graces, as drops of rain, 69, 192; as rays of light, 71; dispensed by Mary, 99; for all, 16, 17; from Green Scapular, 27; from Heart of Jesus, 69; from Scapular of Sacred Heart; 69, 71; future, 156; through Mary, 191-193
Great Promise, of Fatima, 239
Green Bay, Wis., apparitions at, 87-89
Green Scapular devotion, 24-29, 34, 195, 218, 219, 237
Greene, Graham, on Assumption, 176-177; and a condemned "miracle," 123-124; and faith in England, 173
Gregory XVI, Pope, and Confraternity of Immaculate Heart of Mary, 23; and Miraculous Medal, 20

Haffert, John M., on our Lady in America, 235
Happy death, Green Scapular and, 25
Hell, and lack of prayer, 209; vision of, at Fatima, 105
Henze, Father Clem H., on modern devotion to Mary, 219
Hill, Patrick, and apparition at Knock, 78-79
Hinsley, Cardinal, and Walsingham, 169
Hiroshima, bombing of, 7, 148-154
Hitler, Adolf, rise to power, 138

Holy Family, at Fatima, 110
Holy Hour of Reparation, 214
Holy Name Society, in U. S., 195
Huysmans, J. K., on Lourdes, 51

Immaculate Conception, and apparition at Lourdes, 48, 55; dogma of, 19, 23, 31, 41, 45, 46, 47, 183, 219; medal of, 19; patron of Portugal, 157; patron of U. S., 230, 235; U. S. shrine of, 235
Immaculate Heart of Mary, 23, 24, 87, 104, 105, 106, 113, 115, 190, 191, 194; badge of, 25, 28; at Beauraing, 128-30; in the Bitter Root Valley, 232-233; devotion to, 213-216; at Fatima, 104, 105, 115, 182; feast of, 84, 182; and grace, 191; Mary's request for devotion to, 200; and Miraculous Medal, 18; in our age, 28; and peace, 141; reparation to, 209; and revelations to Lucia, 120, 121; and Russia, 122, 137, 143, 156, 182-183; statue of, 24; world consecrated to, 143-145
Industrial Revolution, evils of, 10, 11, 94
Infallibility, dogma of, 40
International Union of Prayers, at Banneux, 136
Ireland, apparition at Knock, 77-85; faith preserved in, 11
Irresistible Novena, 75
Italy, under Fascists, 138

James, Father, O.F.M.Cap., on Mary's universal mediation, 191
Jamin, Abbé, and apparitions at Banneux, 132
Jansenism, 30
Japan, end of war with, significance of date, 235
Japanese, and bombing of Hiroshima, 152
Jesus, chooses Mary as Mother, 8; as Mediator, 192
Joao IV, King of Portugal, and Mary, 157

John, St., and apparition at Knock, 77-84

John Bosco, St., and Dominic Savio, 171-172

John Eudes, St., and Immaculate Heart devotion, 214

Joseph, St., and apparition at Knock, 77-84; at Fatima, 107, 110

Juan Diego, and Our Lady of Guadalupe, 227-228

Kensington Stone, 224

Kerkhofs, Bishop, and Immaculate Heart, 131

Knock, apparition at, 77-84, 123, 218; cures at, 82

Know Nothings, 234

Knutson, Paul, and Kensington Stone, 224-225

Korea, and Communists, 4; slaughter in, 154

Lambert, Abbé, and apparitions at Beauraing, Belgium, 127

La Salette, apparitions at, 31, 34-41, 46, 48, 57, 218; and Fatima, 36; message of, 110; miraculous spring at, 38; and penance, 208

Lasalle, Father, S.J., at Hiroshima, 149, 152, 153

La Voz da Fatima, 162

Lay apostolate, De Montfort's prediction for, 221; need for, 194, 195; Pius X on, 223; prayer and, 223

Lebossè, Jeanne-Marie, and apparition at Pontmain, 60, 63

Leen, Edward, C.S.Sp., on Mary Mediatrix, 193

Legion of Mary, in America, 235; history of, 220-221; spread of, 195

Lenin, Nikolai, and Communist Revolution, 3, 98

Leo XIII, and apparitions at Castelpetroso, 92; and apparitions at La Salette, 39; and apparitions at Pellevoisin, 69; and Our Lady of Prompt Succor, 232; "Pope of Workingman," 95; and Walsingham, 168

Lepanto, Battle of, 207

Lewis, Captain Robert A., and bombing of Hiroshima, 151-152

Long, Bortolo, and Our Lady of Pompeii, 72-76

Lord, Father Daniel A., on Mary in U.S., 236; on Our Lady of Guadalupe, 228

Louis XIII, King, and Our Lady of Victories, 22

Louis Marie, St., *see* De Montfort

Lourdes, apparitions at, 45-51, 57, 218; cures at, 51-54, 56; and cures of the soul, 53, 54; devotion approved, 50; faith preserved at, 11, 47; and Franz Werfel, 55-56; medical bureau at, 51; and Pellevoisin, 64; and penance, 208; perpetual miracle of, 52; purpose of, 54; and the Rosary, 55; and scientists, 52, 53; spring revealed at, 48

Lucarelli, Clarinda, cured through Our Lady of Pompeii, 74

MacHale, Archbishop John, and apparition at Knock, 80

"Madonna in Tears," 41

Magnus, King, and Kensington Stone, 224

Margaret Mary, St., and Immaculate Heart devotion, 214; and Sacred Heart devotion, 67

Marian Library, at Banneux, 136; at University of Dayton, 237

Marian Year, proclaimed by Pius XII, 183

Mariology, of Pius XII, 180

Marquette, Father, and our Lady, 228

Marriage, not of God, 116

Marto, Francisco, and Angel of Portugal, 96; and apparitions at Fatima, 101-113; last illness and death of, 113-114

262

Marto, Jacinta, and Angel of Portugal, 96; and apparitions at Fatima, 101-113; and Immaculate Heart, 256; last days of, 113,119; sayings of, 114-117; sufferings of, 114-115

Marx, Karl, contrasted with Leo XIII, 95; false prophet, 11; influence in Belgium, 129, 132, 137; influence in Paris, 19; *Manifesto*, parallels La Salette in time, 40

Mary, and America, 222-237; and apostles of future, 222; apparitions since 1830, 5; appears at Banneux, 131-137; appears at Beauraing, 131-137; appears at Fatima, 99-113; appears at Knock, 77-85; appears at La Salette, 34-41; appears at Lourdes, 45-51; appears at Pellevoisin, 64-72; appears at Pontmain, 57-63; appears to Rathisbonne, 20; appears to St. Catherine Labouré, 15-21; appears to Sister Justine, 24-27; Assumption defined, 173-179; attraction of, 4; and Battle of New Orleans, 230-232; at Calvary, 189; challenge to intellectuals, 53; and Christ's second coming, 32; and city of Rome, 145, 146; and conversion of sinners, 67; Co-redemptrix, 192, 194, 219; in England, 165-173; and France, 57; and Green Scapular, 25; Immaculate Conception proclaimed, 41-45; and Incarnation, 189; manifestations between 1841 and 1906, 85-94; Mediatrix of all Graces, 71, 83, 191-193, 202, 219; message of, 5; and Middle Ages, 6; and Miraculous Medal, 18; modern interest in, 219; Mother of God, 8, 213; Mother of Men, 193, 213; Mother of the Roman Empire, 147; Mother of the Saviour, 135; Mother of Sorrows, 91; the new Eve, 193; Our Lady of the Cape, 90-91; Our Lady of Ceylon, 146; Our Lady of Divine Love, 146, 147; Our Lady of Guadalupe, 227-228; Our Lady of Letters, 237; Our Lady of Pompeii, 72-76; Our Lady of Prompt Succor, 232; Our Lady of Victories, 22-24; Our Lady of Walsingham, 165-169; Our Mother, 187-190; Our Queen, 193-196, 201; Patron of U. S., 228, 235; and peace, 193, 200; and Pius XII, 179-183; prayers, promises, and devotions revealed since 1830, 237-239; and Protestant Revolt, 7, 8, 9; Queen of the Heavens, 88-89; Queen of the Holy Rosary, 75-76; Queen of Ireland, 83; Queen of lay apostles, 195; Queen of Peace, 99; Queen of Portugal, 157; and Redemption, 189; revelations to Lucia in convent, 120-122; role in modern world, 31; and the Rosary, 205; and Russia, 3; and Satan, 4, 33, 34, 44-45, 66, 195, 199, 200, 221; total consecration to, 31, 199-204; victory of, 5; Virgin Most Powerful, 21; and world of 1830, 11

Mary Edward, Sister, and apparitions at Pontmain, 61

Mary Joseph, Sister, and Gallery of Living Catholic Authors, 237

Maryknoll Mission Society, 236

Maryland, founding of, 229

Mary's, St., San Antonio, 236

Masson, Archbishop J. M., and our Lady in Ceylon, 146

Materialism, Jacinta Marto on, 117; spread of, 11; in U. S., 155, 237

Mathieu, Melanie, and apparitions at La Salette, 35-41

McGlynn, Father Thomas, O.P., on consecration to Immaculate Heart, 144; on doves of Bombarral, 159-160; and Fatima, 100, 111, 112

McLaughlin, Mary, and apparition at Knock, 77

Mediator Dei, Encyclical of Pius XII, and attributes of Mary, 181

Mediatrix of all Graces, 30, 71, 83, 191-193, 213, 219

Merton, Thomas, on heeding Mary's message, 5

Message, of Fatima, 110, 112, 182-195; of La Salette, 40, 110; Mary's, 36; of Pontmain, 62, 63

Mexico, persecution in, 138; war in, 233

Middle Ages, devotion to Mary in, 6

Mindszenty, Cardinal, fate of, 154; sentenced by Communists, 4

Minnesota, and Kensington Stone, 224

Miracle of the Sun, occurs, 111-113, 195; promised, 108, 109, 113; repeated in 1950, 181-182

Miracles, Church's position on, 52

Miraculous Medal, 18-21, 34, 48, 195, 218, 219; and Immaculate Heart devotion, 214; at Pontmain, 62; promise of, 237; statue of Our Lady of, 21; in U. S., 236

Missionaries of Our Lady of La Salette, 39

Mohammedans, and Fatima, 164

Montana, St. Mary's, apparition at, 85-86

Montfort Fathers, 29

Mother of Sorrow, 91-92

Mussolini, Benito, rise to power, 138

Muta, Giovannina, cured by Our Lady of Pompeii, 74

Mystics Corporis, Encyclical of Pius XII, and Mariology, 180

Nagasaki, bombing of, 150

Napoleon, Louis, and Lourdes, 50; and Pius IX, 44

Neubert, Father Emil, S.M., on "living" your consecration to Mary, 203-204; on Mary as Our Mother, 189; on Mary, Queen of Militants, 194

Newman, John Henry, and England's "Second Spring," 172

New Orleans, battle of, 231-232

Notre Dame University, 236

Novena, Irresistible, 75

Oblates of Mary Immaculate, 69

O'Carroll, Father Michael, on apostolate, 195

O'Carroll, Patrick, C.S.Sp., on message of Knock, 84

O'Reilly, James P., M.S., *The Story of La Salette*, 40

Osservatore Romano, on Miracle of the Sun (1950), 182; on "Weeping Madonna" of Sicily, 179

Ottaviana, Monsignor Alfredo, warns of unproved visions, 123

Our Lady of Banneux, 135

Our Lady of Beauraing, statue, 130

Our Lady of Fatima, statue, 156, 157

Our Lady of Good Counsel, 180

Our Lady of Grace, 91

Our Lady of Hope, 156; at Pontmain, 63

Our Lady of La Salette, 190; Missionaries of, 39

Our Lady of Mount Carmel, 91

Our Lady of Pellevoisin, in United States, 69

Our Lady of the Poor, 134

Our Lady of the Rosary at Fatima, 107, 109, 110

Our Lady of the Seven Dolors, 92

Our Lady of Sorrows, 253; at Fatima, 107

Our Lady of Victory, church of, 207

Our Lady's Memorial Shrine for World Peace, 154

Our Lord, at Fatima, 110; and later revelations to Lucia, 120, 121

Our Mother all Merciful, Archconfraternity of, 69

Paris, apparitions at, 31, 46, 57; apparitions to St. Catherine, 15-21; apparitions to Sister Justine, 25; Mary begins campaign in, 11; Our Lady of Victories, 22-24; revolt against God in, 9; revolution in, 17; War on Commune in, 18

Paul (Indian boy), and apparition at St. Mary's, Montana, 85

Peace, and Immaculate Heart of Mary, 141; Mary as cause of, 193; Mary's plan for, 200; Memorial Shrine at Hiroshima, 154; and penance, 141, 163, 164; and prayer, 164; promised at Fatima, 105, 108, 121, 156, 164

Pearl Harbor, significance of date, 235

Pellevoisin, apparitions at, 64-72, 218; cures at, 65

Penance, at Fatima, 209; and La Salette, 40, 54, 208; at Lourdes, 208; Mary's requests for, 208-212; our Lord's present requirement, 144, 209-210; and peace, 110, 116, 141, 163, 164; requested at Lourdes, 48, 54, 57

Persecution, foretold at Fatima, 106; in Germany, 138; in Mexico, 138; predicted by De Montfort, 33; in Prussia, 44; in Russia, 44; in Switzerland, 44

Peyramale, Abbé, pastor at Lourdes, 49

Peyton, Father Patrick, and Family Rosary, 208, 216-217, 219

Pilgrim Virgin, and Moslems, 164 n; in U. S., 235

Pilgrimages, to Beauraing, 129; to Fatima, 162; to Knock, 82; to Pontmain, 63

Pius V, St., and the Turks, 206-207

Pius VII, and Napoleon, 10; and Ursulines in America, 230

Pius IX, driven from Rome, 43-44; and England, 172; on Family Rosary, 208; and Immaculate Conception, 41-42, 49; and La Salette, 39-40; and Patron of U. S., 234; and Red Scapular of the Passion, 86; returns to Rome, 44

Pius X, Blessed, on apostolic laymen, 223; and frequent Communion, 51; and Our Lady of the Cape, 91; and peace, 97; "Pope of the Eucharist," 96

Pius XI, and the apostolate, 195; and call to Catholic Action, 221; and Fatima, 106, 121; on Italian fascism, 138; on Mexico, 138; and Our Lady of Pompeii, 76; and Poland, 139; on the Rosary, 208; war in his reign, 140

Pius XII, and the apostolate, 195; and Cardinal Mindszenty, 4; and centenary of La Salette, 41; consecrated bishop, 179; defines Assumption, 173-178; on Family Rosary, 208; and Fatima, 141; and Immaculate Heart of Mary, 28, 143, 215; and Mary our Queen, 193; and Miracle of the Sun, 182; and occupation of Rome, 146; and Our Lady of Beauraing, 129; and Our Lady of Ceylon, 146; and Our Lady of Guadalupe, 228; Pope of Our Lady, 179-183; on the Sodality, 220

Poland, Communist invasion of, 139; German invasion of, 140

Pompeii, cures at, 73-76; Our Lady of, 72-76

Pontmain, apparition at, 57-63, 218; cures at, 63

Pope of Our Lady, 179-183

Portugal, faith in, 106, 109, 161; Land of Our Lady, 157; Law of Separation in, 96; republic established, 96; and World War I, 98; and World War II, 162

Prayer, and apostolate, 223; International Union of, 136; and La Salette, 37; Mary's requests for, 200; a national need, 216; and peace; 164; requested at Banneux, 134; requested at Beauraing, 128; requested at Fatima, 208; and Spanish Civil War, 160; and total consecration to Mary, 202

Pro, Father Miguel, Mexican martyr, 138

Protestant Revolt, effect in England, 228; and our Lady, 7, 8, 218

Prussia, persecution in, 44

Queen of Heaven, 88-89; at Beauraing, 128, 130
Queen of Ireland, 83
Queen of Militants, 194, 203
Queen of Peace, 119, 157
Queen of Portugal, 157
Queen of the Rosary, 75, 91, 205
Quito, Ecuador, miraculous picture at, 92-93

Rathisbonne, Alphonse, and Miraculous Medal, 19-20, 34
Red Scapular of the Passion, 86, 87
Redemption, and Immaculate Conception, 49; and Mary, 189, 192, 201
Reparation, holy hour of, 214; requested at Fatima, 113
Rerum Novarum, 95
Revelations, to Lucia after Fatima, 119-122
Richeldis de Faverches, and apparition at Walsingham, 165-166
Richer, Francoise, and apparition at Pontmain, 60, 63
Rome, and dogma of Assumption, 174; and dogma of Immaculate Conception, 41-45; falls to "liberals," 43, 44; rebellion against Pius IX, 42, 43; and Republic of 1848, 43; and return of Pius IX, 44; saved from destruction, 146-147

Rosary, and Albigenses, 205; at Banneux, 132, 133, 135; at Cape de la Madelaine, 205; and Communism, 207; Confraternity of, 74; daily recitation of, 205-208; at Fatima, 76, 100, 102, 103, 104, 105, 106, 107, 108, 109, 163, 205, 238, 239; Feast of, 207; and First Saturday devotion, 121; and Great Promise, 239; at Hiroshima, 154; at Lourdes, 47, 55, 205; month of, 207; at Naples, 205; novenas of, 75, 238; and Our Lady of the Cape, 90-91; Pius XI's encyclical on, 208; at Pompeii, 73-76, 205; at Pontmain, 58; on radio and television, 217; requested by Mary, 200; and sparing of Rome, 146; and the Turks, 205

Roses of Stockport, 170-171

Royanne, Father Jarlath, O.Cist., on message of Knock, 83

Russia, Communist revolution in, 3, 98; and consecration to Immaculate Heart, 121, 137, 143, 182; conversion delayed, 143; conversion predicted at Fatima, 106, 155, 156, 182-183; and First Saturday devotion, 121; and Immaculate Heart of Mary, 215; persecution in, 44; secures atomic bomb, 155; and World War I, 98

Sacred Heart of Jesus, and apparitions at Pellevoisin, 68; graces from, 69; and Immaculate Heart of Mary, 213-216; and Miraculous Medal, 18; and Red Scapular, 87; Scapular of 67, 68, 69, 70

Sacrifices, and the apostolate, 208-212; and Beauraing, 208; Mary's request for, 200; and Morning Offering, 212; Our Lord's pres-

Sacrifices (Continued)
ent requirement, 212; pleasing to God, 117; program for making, 212; and Spanish Civil war, 160; and total consecration to Mary, 202; voluntary, 211

Salazar, Oliveira, and government of Portugal, 161

Saliege, Archbishop of Toulouse, on war in France, 141

Satan, and Mary's enmity, 33, 34, 44-45, 195, 199, 200, 221; at Pellevoisin, 66; renounced at Baptism; 202; in the Roman rebellion (1848), 43; slavery to, 201

Scapular medal, 87

Scapular Militia, in U. S., 235

Scapulars, Scapular of Mt. Carmel, 169, 219; Red Scapular of the Passion, 86, 87; Scapular of the Sacred Heart, 67, 68, 69, 70, 195, 238

Schiffer, Father Hubert, S.J., and Hiroshima, 148-154

Secret of Mary, 30

Secularism, danger of, 218; growth of, 38; and modern Catholics, 217; in U. S., 237

Sheen, Bishop Fulton J., on Fatima and Communism, 163-164; on Fatima and Moslems, 164*n*

Sicily, and the "Weeping Madonna," 178-179

Simon Stock, St., and Scapular of Mt. Carmel, 169

Sin, effects of, 36, 37; and Fatima, 104, 105, 108; as root of all evil, 222

Sisters of Christian Doctrine, at Beauraing, 125

Slipper Chapel, at Walsingham, 168-169

Snite, Fred, visit to Lourdes, 54

Society of Mary, 200; and Marian library, 237

Sodality of Our Lady, in America, 236; Pius XII on, 180; modern resurgence of, 220; spread of, 195

Song of Bernadette, 56

Soubirous, Bernadette, *see* Bernadette, St.

Spain, in America, 226-227; faith in, 160; persecution in, 139; spirit of sacrifice in, 160

Spellman, Francis Cardinal, and encyclical on Fascism, 138

Spring, miraculous, at Banneux, 133, 134, 135; at La Salette, 38; at Lourdes, 51, 56

Stanislaus Kostka, St., on Mary as our Mother, 189

Stockport, England, famous roses of, 170-171

Suffering, and Banneux, 134; of children of Fatima, 104; and Fatima, 113, 114; promised at Lourdes, 48; promised at Pellevoisin, 67, 68; as punishment for sin, 36, 37; of St. Bernadette, 50; of St. Catherine Labouré, 16, 20

Summer School of Catholic Action, 236

Switzerland, persecution in, 44

Tedeschini, Federico Cardinal, and Miracle of the Sun, 181-182

Teresa of the Child Jesus, St., and Our Lady of Victories, 24

Theophile, Mother, and apparitions at Beauraing, 126-7

Trench, Bridget, and apparition at Knock, 80

Trotsky, Leon, and Communist Revolution, 3, 98

True Devotion to the Blessed Virgin Mary, 29-34, 200, 219; and Legion of Mary, 207

Turks, and the Rosary, 207

Turner, Father James, and roses of Stockport, 170-171

United States, and Mary, 224-237; materialism in, 155; and Mexican War, 233; and World War I, 98; and World War II, 142

University of Dayton, and Marian library, 237
Unknown light, promised at Fatima, 106, 114, 140
Ursulines, in America, 230-232

Varone, Father Anthony, cured by Our Lady of Pompeii, 74
Vasterilla, Concetta, cured by Our Lady of Pompeii, 74
Vatican, and Miracle of the Sun, 182
Vianney, St. John Mary, and penance, 211
Vincent de Paul, St., 15, 16; Society of, 195; Society of, and Legion of Mary, 220
Virgin Most Powerful, statue of, 21
Virgin of the Poor, at Banneux, 134, 136
Vision of hell, at Fatima, 105
Vitaline, Sister, and apparition at Pontmain, 59-61

Voisin, Fernande, Gilberte, and Albert, and apparitions at Beauraing, Belgium, 125-130

Walloons, 124, 125, 132
Walsh, Patrick, and apparition at Knock, 78
Walsingham, England, shrine at, 165-169
Wang Commune, 18
War, Mary's power to end, 105; and penance, 164; as punishment for sin, 116
Waugh, Evelyn, and faith in England, 173
"Weeping Madonna" of Sicily, 178
Werfel, Franz and *Song of Bernadette*, 55-56
Willock, Ed, on Middle Ages, 7
Working classes, lost to religion, 195
World War I, 97-99
World War II, 140-147; foretold at Fatima, 106, 114